KV-675-434

Contents

How to use this guide

This official VisitBritain guide is packed with information from where to stay, to how to get there and what to see on arrival. In fact, this guide captures everything you need to know when exploring Britain.

Choose from a wide range of quality assessed places to stay to suit all budgets and tastes. This guide contains a comprehensive listing of touring, camping and holiday parks and holiday villages participating in the British-Graded Holiday Parks Scheme.

Each park is visited annually by professional assessors, who apply nationally agreed standards, so that you can book with confidence knowing your accommodation has been checked and rated for quality.

Check out the places to visit in each region, from towns and cities to spectacular coast and countryside, plus historic homes, castles and great family attractions! Maps show accommodation locations, selected destinations and some of the National Cycle Networks. For even more ideas go online at www.visitbritain.com.

Regional tourism contacts and tourist information centres are listed in each of the regional sections of this guide, before booking your stay why not contact them to find out what's going on in the area? You'll also find events, travel information, maps and useful indexes that will help you plan your trip, throughout this guide.

OFFICIAL TOURIST BOARD GUIDE

New 39th edition

Camping, Touring & Holiday Parks

Britain's star-rated holiday parks

2014

Welcome to Britain one of the most admired countries in the world, where there is plenty to see and do no matter what your interests!

Whether you're to enjoy some of the most beautiful countryside in the world, take a walk along our dramatic coastline or enjoy a land which is rich in culture and heritage, we're delighted you've decided that Britain should be your holiday of choice.

Holidaying here encapsulates all experiences, whether it's a glamorous stay in or near one of our vibrant cities such as Manchester and Glasgow, or a quieter break off the beaten track exploring the width and breadth of Britain. Whatever it may be, I'm sure this guide will make your decision that little bit easier.

We want you to come to Britain and enjoy your favourite spots again or explore new places you've always wanted to experience. The Wales Coast Path has recently opened and offers a coastal experience never before seen in what is one of the most striking areas of the country. Or if you plan to go further north you could enjoy the sparkling Scottish lochs, maybe relax in the capital at the Royal Botanic Gardens in Kew or enjoy the dramatic vistas of the Lake District.

If you're into your music make sure you time your visit to catch a gig or music festival in countless locations across the country. If it's sport that catches your eye, then get yourself to one of our Barclays Premier League football games or tee yourself up for the Ryder Cup at Gleneagles which promises to be just as dramatic as previous contests. Rugby fans will be delighted to hear that we are to host the Rugby World Cup across Britain in 2015. Of course if you can't make it for the World Cup then you should get tickets for a passionate Six Nations rugby game. Nothing beats hearing the national anthems in a packed stadium before a fierce contest of blood, sweat and tears - I can assure you it's an experience you'll never forget.

So whatever your destination, activity or budget, this guide is sure to inspire and inform.

Joss Croft
Marketing Director, VisitBritain

Accommodation entries explained

Each accommodation entry contains detailed information to help you decide if it is right for you. This has been provided by proprietors and our aim is to ensure that it is as objective and factual as possible.

① ② ③ ④ ⑤

Rivendale Caravan & Leisure Park

Rivendale Caravan & Leisure Park, Buxton Road, Nr Alsop En Le Dale, Ashbourne DE6 1QU
T: (01335) 310311 **F:** (01335) 310100 **E:** enquiries@rivendalecaravanpark.co.uk
W: rivendalecaravanpark.co.uk **£ BOOK ONLINE**

(65)	£14.25-£16.50
(65)	£14.25-£16.50
(15)	£10.75-£15.50
	£375.00-£899.00
(14)	£375.00-£899.00
(57)	£310.00-£550.00

80 touring pitches

SPECIAL PROMOTIONS
Discounts for senior citizen groups annd for 2dn week. Quotes arranged for block booking, rallies etc.

TOURERS & TENTS
1st March to 31st October

Surrounded by spectacular Peak District scenery, convenient for Alton Towers, Chatsworth, Dove Dale and Carsington Water. Ideal for cyclists and ramblers with the Tissington Trail 100 metres away and footpaths running directly from site into Dove Dale and Mill Dale . Choice of all-grass, hardstanding or 50/50 pitches. Yurts, Camping Pods, Fly fishing lake. Overnight holding area available.

Directions: From A515, Rivendale is situated 6.5 miles north of Ashbourne, directly off the A515 Buxton road on the right-hand side, travelling north.

Bedrooms: 2 double, 2 twin.
Open: Open all year except 3rd Jan - 28th Jan.

Site: ✿ P **Payment:** 💳 **Leisure:** 🚲 🎵 ☋ **Property:** 🖥 🗄 **Children:** 🍼 🛏 🚸 **Catering:** 🍴 🍽
Room: 🕹 🖳 📻 📺 🛗

Sample entry

⑥ ⑦ ⑧ ⑨ ⑩

① Listing sorted by town or village, including a map reference

② Rating (and/or) Award, where applicable

③ Prices per pitch per night for touring pitches; per unit per week for static holiday units

④ Establishment name, address, telephone number and email address

⑤ Website information

⑥ Walkers, cyclists, pets and families welcome accolades, where applicable

⑦ Accessible rating, where applicable

⑧ Accommodation details

⑨ Indicates when the property is open

⑩ At-a-glance facility symbols

There are hundreds of "Green" places to stay and visit in England from small bed and breakfasts to large visitor attractions and activity holiday providers. Businesses displaying this logo have undergone a rigorous verification process to ensure that they are sustainable (green) and that a qualified assessor has visited the premises.

We have indicated the accommodation which has achieved a Green award... look out for the  symbol in the entry.

Key to symbols

Information about many of the accommodation services and facilities is given in the form of symbols.

Pitches/Units

🚐 Caravans (number of pitches and rates)
🚙 Motor caravans (number of pitches and rates)
▲ Tents (number of pitches and rates)
🏠 Caravan holiday homes (number of pitches and rates)
🏡 Log cabins/lodges (number of units and rates)
🏘 Chalets/villas (number of units and rates)

Site Features

▲🅿 Parking next to pitch
🍺 Public house/Inn

Booking & Payment Details

☼ Booking recommended in summer
€ Euros accepted
💷 Visa/Mastercard/Switch accepted

Leisure Facilities

🎾 Tennis court(s)
🏊 Swimming pool – outdoor
🏊 Swimming pool – indoor
🎯 Games room
U Riding/pony-trekking nearby
⛳ Golf available (on site or nearby)
🎣 Fishing nearby
🚲 Cycles for hire

Children

⛰ Childrens outdoor play area
🧒 Children welcome

Catering

🛒 Foodshop/Mobile foodshop
✕ Restaurant on site

Park Facilities

🚿 Showers available
📞 Public telephone
🧺 Laundry facilities
💻 Wi-Fi/Internet access
🎵 Regular evening entertainment
🐕 Dogs/Pets welcome by arrangement

Camping & Touring Facilities

🚰 Water/waste hookup
🔌 Electrical hook-up points
🔥 Calor Gas/Camping Gaz purchase/ exchange service
🚽 Chemical toilet disposal point

Visitor Attraction Quality Assurance

Participating attractions are visited annually by a professional assessor. High standards in welcome, hospitality, services, presentation; standards of toilets, shop and café, where provided, must be achieved to receive these awards.

Places of Interest Quality Assurance

The Places of Interest sign indicates that the site has a biennial visit from an independent assessor and meets the standard required to be awarded the Quality Rose Marque.

Pets Come Too - Accommodation displaying this symbol offer a special welcome to pets. Please check for any restrictions when booking.

VisitScotland Thistle Award for Excellence. Award winning parks listed in this guide show the logo on their entries.

Businesses displaying this logo have undergone a rigorous verification process to ensure that they are sustainable (green). See page 16 for further information.

National Accessible Scheme

The National Accessible Scheme includes standards for hearing and visual impairment as well as mobility impairment – see pages 10-11 for further information.

Welcome Schemes

Walkers, cyclists, families and pet owners are warmly welcomed where you see these signs – see page 9 for further information.

Motorway Service Area Assessment Scheme

The star ratings cover over 300 different aspects of each operation including cleanliness, the quality and range of catering and also the quality of the physical aspects as well as the service provided.

– See page 292 for further information.

A special welcome

To help make booking your accommodation easier VisitEngland has four special Welcome schemes which accommodation in England can be assessed against. Owners participating in these schemes go the extra mile to welcome walkers, cyclists, families or pet owners to their accommodation and provide additional facilities and services to make your stay even more comfortable.

For further information go online at www.qualityintourism.com/types-of-schemes/welcome-schemes

Families Welcome

If you are searching for the perfect family holiday look out for the Families Welcome sign. The sign indicates that the proprietor offers additional facilities and services catering for a range of ages and family units. For families with young children, the accommodation will have special facilities such as cots and highchairs, storage for push-chairs and somewhere to heat baby food or milk. Where meals are provided, children's choices will be clearly indicated, with healthy options also available. They'll have information on local walks, attractions, activities or events suitable for children, as well as local child-friendly pubs and restaurants. However, not all accommodation is able to cater for all ages or combinations of family units, so do remember to check for any restrictions before confirming your booking.

Welcome Pets!

Do you want to travel with your faithful companion? To do so with ease make sure you look out for accommodation displaying the Welcome Pets! sign. Participants in this scheme go out of their way to meet the needs of guests bringing dogs, cats and/or small birds. In addition to providing water and food bowls, torches or nightlights, spare leads and pet washing facilities, they'll buy in pet food on request, and offer toys, treats and bedding. They'll also have information on pet-friendly attractions, pubs, restaurants and recreation. Of course, not everyone is able to offer suitable facilities for every pet, so do check if there are any restrictions on the type, size and number of animals before you confirm your booking.

Walkers Welcome

If walking is your passion, seek out accommodation participating in the Walkers Welcome scheme. Facilities include a place for drying clothes and boots, maps and books for reference and a first-aid kit. Packed breakfasts and lunches are available on request in hotels and guesthouses, and you have the option to pre-order basic groceries in self-catering accommodation. On top of this proprietors provide a wide range of information including public transport, weather forecasts, details of the nearest bank, all night chemists and local restaurants and nearby attractions.

Cyclists Welcome

Are you an explorer on two wheels? If so seek out accommodation displaying the Cyclists Welcome symbol. Facilities at these properties include a lockable undercover area, a place to dry outdoor clothing and footwear, an evening meal if there are no eating facilities available within one mile, and a packed breakfast or lunch on request. Information is also available on cycle hire, cycle repair shops, maps and books for reference, weather forecasts, details of the nearest bank, all night chemists and much much more.

National Accessible Scheme

Finding suitable accommodation is not always easy, especially if you have to seek out rooms with level entry or large print menus. Use the National Accessible Scheme to help you make your choice.

Proprietors of accommodation taking part in the National Accessible Scheme have gone out of their way to ensure a comfortable stay for guests with special hearing, visual or mobility needs. These exceptional places are full of extra touches to make everyone's visit trouble-free, from handrails, ramps and step-free entrances (ideal for buggies too) to level-access showers and colour contrast in the bathrooms. Members of staff may have attended a disability awareness course and will know what assistance will really be appreciated.

Appropriate National Accessible Scheme symbols are included in the guide entries (shown opposite). If you have additional needs or special requirements, we strongly recommend that you make sure these can be met by your chosen establishment before you confirm your reservation. The index at the back of the guide gives a list of accommodation that has received a National Accessible Scheme rating.

'Holiday in the British Isles' is an annual guidebook produced by Disability Rights UK. It lists NAS rated accommodation and offers extensive practical advice to help you plan your trip.

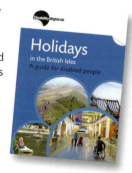

£12.99 (inc. P&P), www.disabilityrights.org

England

Mobility Impairment Symbols

Older and less mobile guests
Typically suitable for a person with sufficient mobility to climb a flight of steps but who would benefit from fixtures and fittings to aid balance.

Part-time wheelchair users
Typically suitable for a person with restricted walking ability and for those who may need to use a wheelchair some of the time and can negotiate a maximum of three steps.

Independent wheelchair users
Typically suitable for a person who depends on the use of a wheelchair and transfers unaided to and from the wheelchair in a seated position. This person may be an independent traveller.

Assisted wheelchair users
Typically suitable for a person who depends on the use of a wheelchair and needs assistance when transferring to and from the wheelchair in a seated position.

Access Exceptional is awarded to establishments that meet the requirements of independent wheelchair users or assisted wheelchair users shown above and also fulfil more demanding requirements with reference to the British Standards BS8300.

The criteria VisitEngland has adopted does not necessarily conform to British Standards or to Building Regulations. They reflect what the organisation understands to be acceptable to meet the practical needs of guests with mobility or sensory impairments and encourage the industry to increase access to all.

Visual Impairment Symbols

Typically provides key additional services and facilities to meet the needs of visually impaired guests.

Typically provides a higher level of additional services and facilities to meet the needs of visually impaired guests.

Hearing Loss Symbols

Typically provides key additional services and facilities to meet the needs of guests with hearing loss.

Typically provides a higher level of additional services and facilities to meet the needs of guests with hearing loss.

For more information on the NAS and tips and ideas on holiday travel in England go to:
www.visitengland.com/accessforall

Additional help and guidance on accessible tourism can be obtained from the national charity Tourism for All:

Tourism for All

Tourism for All UK
7A Pixel Mill
44 Appleby Road
Kendal
Cumbria LA9 6ES

Information helpline 0845 124 9971
(lines open 9-5 Mon-Fri)
E info@tourismforall.org.uk
W www.tourismforall.org.uk
    www.openbritain.net

Peace of Mind with Star Ratings

   Most camping and caravan parks in Britain have a star rating from one of the four assessing bodies – VisitEngland, VisitScotland, Visit Wales or the AA. They all assess to the same national standards so you can expect comparable services, facilities and quality standards at each star rating.

All the parks in this guide are checked annually by national tourist board assessors. So when you see the star rating sign you can be confident that we've checked it out.

The national standards are based on our research of consumer expectations. The independent assessors decide the type (classification) of park – for example if it's a 'touring park', 'holiday park', 'holiday village', etc. – and award a star rating based on over fifty separate aspects, from landscaping and layout to maintenance, customer care and, most importantly, cleanliness.

The Quality marque helps you choose with confidence knowing that the park has been thoroughly checked out before you check in.

Accommodation Types

Always look at or ask for the type of accommodation as each offers a very distinct experience. The parks you'll find in this guide are:

Camping Park – these sites only have pitches available for tents.

Touring Park – sites for your own caravan, motor home or tent.

Holiday Park – sites where you can hire a caravan holiday home for a short break or longer holiday, or even buy your own holiday home. Sites range from small, rural sites to larger parks with added extras, such as a swimming pool.

Many of the above parks will offer a combination of these classifications.

Holiday Villages – usually comprise of a variety of types of accommodation, with the majority in custom-built rooms for example, chalets. The option to book on a bed and breakfast, or dinner, bed and breakfast basis is normally available. A range of facilities, entertainment and activities are also provided, which may, or may not, be included in the tariff. Holiday Villages must meet minimum requirements for provision and quality of facilities and services, including fixtures, fittings, furnishings, décor and any other extra facilities.

Forest Holiday Village – a holiday village situated in a forest setting with conservation and sustainable tourism being a key feature. Usually offering a variety of accommodation, often purpose built and with a range of entertainment, activities and facilities on site, free of charge or at extra cost.

Star ratings are based on a combination of the range of facilities, level of service offered and quality - if a park offers the facilities required to achieve a certain star rating but does not achieve the quality score required for that rating, a lower star rating is awarded.

A random check is made of a sample of accommodation provided for hire (caravans, chalets, etc) and the quality of the accommodation itself is included in the grading assessment.

Holiday Villages in England are assessed under a separate rating scheme (for details see www.qualityintourism.com).

Also included in this guide are **Bunkhouses and Camping Barns** – safe, budget-priced, short-term accommodation for individuals and groups.

So much to see, so little time – how do you choose?

Make the most of your leisure time; look for attractions with the Quality Marque.

VisitEngland operates the Visitor Attraction Quality Assurance Scheme.

Annual assessments by trained impartial assessors test all aspects of the customer experience so you can visit with confidence.

For ideas and inspiration go to www.visitengland.com

VisitEngland Awards for Excellence

VisitEngland awards for Excellence recognise the best of the best in the tourism industry. Whether it's for a day trip, a weekend break or a fortnight's holiday.

Celebrating its Silver Jubilee in 2014, the VisitEngland Awards for Excellence celebrate the best of English tourism. They promote healthy industry competition and help drive high standards in the industry, ensuring England's place as a world-class destination.

Competition is fierce and entries are submitted to regional tourism organisations across England, before being short-listed for the national finals, culminating in an Awards ceremony in May each year.

The 15 award categories are fiercely contested and this years winners include a fantastic Holiday Park overlooking the stunning North Norfolk coastline and a park widely recognised for its commitment to excellence in tourism nestled in the delights of Devon.

Seek them out and experience them for yourself – you won't be disappointed.

The complete list of winners can be found online at **www.visitengland.com/awards**

The Caravan Holiday Park of the Year 2013 Gold winner is Kelling Heath Holiday Park, with its fantastic facilities and attention to detail it sets itself apart from the crowd.

Set amongst 250 acres of woodland and rare open heathland in an Area of Outstanding Natural Beauty, Kelling Heath is also very close to the North Norfolk coastline at Weybourne.

Its vision, to be "Passionate about people, service and environment" is simply who they are and what they do, and this has driven the continual investment and development of their staff, facilities and habitat as a result.

Welcoming, friendly, excellent facilities and all in a beautiful location, what more is there to say!

Caravan Holiday Park of the Year 2013

GOLD WINNERS
Kelling Heath Holiday Park, Norfolk ★ ★ ★ ★ ★

SILVER WINNER
Trethem Mill Touring Park, Cornwall ★ ★ ★ ★

BRONZE WINNER
Woodclose Park, Cumbria ★ ★ ★ ★

HIGHLY COMMENDED
Carr Royd Parks Ltd. t/a Sunset Park, Lancashire
Oakdown Country Holiday Park, Devon ★ ★ ★ ★

Sustainable Tourism in England

More and more operators of accommodation, attractions and events in England are becoming aware of sustainable or "green" issues and are acting more responsibly in their businesses. But how can you be sure that businesses that 'say' they're green, really are?

Who certifies green businesses?

There are a number of green certification schemes that assess businesses for their green credentials. VisitEngland only promotes those that have been checked out to ensure they reach the high standards expected. The members of those schemes VisitEngland have validated are truly sustainable (green) businesses and appear amongst the pages of this guide with the heart-flower logo on their entry.

 Businesses displaying this logo have undergone a rigorous verification process to ensure that they are sustainable (green) and that a qualified assessor has visited the premises.

The number of participating green certification scheme organisations applying to be recognised by VisitEngland is growing all the time. At the moment, VisitEngland promotes the largest green scheme in the world - Green Tourism Business Scheme (GTBS) - and the Peak District Environmental Quality Mark.

Peak District Environmental Quality Mark

This certification mark can only be achieved by businesses that actively support good environmental practices in the Peak District National Park. When you buy a product or service that has been awarded the Environmental Quality Mark, you can be confident that your purchase directly supports the high-quality management of the special environment of the Peak District National Park.

Green Tourism Business Scheme

 GTBS recognises places to stay and attractions that are taking action to support the local area and the wider environment. With over 2000 members in the UK, it's the largest sustainable (green) scheme to operate globally and assesses hundreds of fantastic places to stay and visit in Britain, from small bed and breakfasts to large visitor attractions and activity holiday providers.

Businesses that meet the standard for a GTBS award receive a Bronze, Silver, or Gold award based on their level of achievement. Businesses are assessed in areas that include management and marketing, social involvement and communication, energy, water, purchasing, waste, transport, natural and cultural heritage and innovation.

How are these businesses being green?

Any business that has been certified 'green' will have implemented initiatives that contribute to reducing their negative environmental and social impacts, whilst trying to enhance the economic and community benefits to their local area.

Many of these things may be behind the scenes, such as energy efficient boilers, insulated lofts or grey water recycling, but there are many fun activities that you can expect to find too. For example, your green business should be able to advise you about traditional activities nearby, the best places to sample local food and buy craft products, or even help you to enjoy a 'car-free' day out.

David Bellamy Conservation Award

'These well-deserved awards are a signpost to parks which are making real achievements in protecting our environment. Go there and experience wrap-around nature ... you could be amazed at what you find!' says Professor David Bellamy.

591 gold, silver and bronze parks were named in the 2012/13 David Bellamy Conservation Awards, organised in conjunction with the British Holiday and Home Parks Association.

These parks are recognised for their commitment to conservation and the environment through their management of landscaping, recycling policies, waste management, the cultivation of flora and fauna and the creation of habitats designed to encourage a variety of wildlife onto the park. Links with the local community and the use of local materials are also important considerations.

Parks wishing to enter for a David Bellamy Conservation Award must complete a detailed questionnaire covering different aspects of their environmental policies, and describe what positive conservation steps they have taken. The park must also undergo an independent audit from a local wildlife or conservation body which is familiar with the area. Final assessments and the appropriate level of any award are then made personally by Professor Bellamy.

An index of award-winning parks featured in the regional pages of this guide can be found on page 310.

VisitEngland™
Awards for
Excellence 2013
SILVER WINNER

Trethem Mill

Trethem Mill Touring Park in Cornwall is a family-run business with three generations working together to ensure the site retains the highest of standards.

The Akeroyds bought the park at St Just in Roseland in July 1992 and have spent every winter since working through a programme of development, and transforming the site from open fields with basic facilities into a multi award-winning business.

Trethem Mill is owned and run by four family members – Ian Akeroyd, his wife Jane, and parents Derek and Lorna. Ian and Jane's son Jake is now employed full-time after completing his apprenticeship in customer service.

The family manages all aspects of the business, including the day-to-day running of the park and general site maintenance.

"All our pitches are individually hedged which provides privacy, shelter and clear pitch markers,"

Ian

launderette and ice-pack freezer room. There is also excellent access for disabled visitors.

A play-park and separate recreation field will keep children occupied throughout their stay, while the whole family can experience a three-acre dog and nature walk, which has numerous wildlife habitats, bird boxes and interpretation boards.

The park is situated in an area of outstanding natural beauty, nestling in a valley surrounded by farmland, and less than 1.5 miles to the sea.

"Trethem Mill is dedicated towards providing our guests with that special experience and to leave us with a feeling of well-being. Our attention to detail is evident throughout and we offer a range and quality of facilities rarely seen on touring parks" says Ian.

Trethem Mill Touring Park won Silver in the VisitEngland awards for excellence 2013, Caravan Holiday Park/Holiday Village of the Year category.

A typical day starts at around 5am with cleaning the facilities, followed by a team meeting at 9am to discuss the forthcoming day. The mornings are usually busy with departures and preparing the pitches for new arrivals as well as cutting the grass. Facilities are cleaned again at lunchtime, and the afternoon is usually busy with arrivals and general maintenance.

Contact details: Trethem Mill Touring Park, St Just-In-Roseland, nr St Mawes, Cornwall TR2 5JF. Tel: 01872 580504, email reception@trethem.com, website ww.trethem.com

The shop, which sells essential groceries and camping accessories as well as a variety of local produce, is open until 7pm and the reception usually closes around 8pm with someone on duty to 9.30pm for any problems that may arise. On top of this, there is always an array of things to deal with, such as broken toilets, gardening, sorting rubbish, ordering stock, and moving caravans. The telephone and website remain busy all day with requests and bookings.

There are 84 pitches at Trethem Mill, including premium, all weather and grass suitable for caravans, motorhomes and tents. The park has everything holidaymakers need in a touring park, including toilets and showers, an indoor dishwashing room,

South West

Cornwall & Isles of Scilly, Devon, Dorset, Gloucestershire, Somerset, Wiltshire

This is the home of Stonehenge, magnificent Bath Spa and quaint honey-coloured Cotswolds villages. Beautiful Cornish beaches, gently rolling Devon hills and miles of lush English countryside make this landscape heaven for anyone who loves the great outdoors. Exciting cities mix fascinating history with vibrant culture and you'll find superb festivals, and events all year round. The South West can rightly claim to be one of the most beautiful areas of the UK.

Highlights

Bodmin Moor

Bodmin Moor is of one the last great unspoilt areas in the South West and much of its prehistoric and medieval past remains untouched by the passing of the centuries. The Moor is dominated by dramatic granite tors which tower over the sweeping expanses of open moorland.

City of Bath

Founded by the Romans as a thermal spa, Bath became an important centre of the wool industry in the Middle Ages. In the 18th century it developed into an elegant town with neo-classical Palladian buildings.

Cornwall and West Devon Mining Landscape

Tin and copper mining in Devon and Cornwall boomed in the 18th and 19th centuries, and at its peak the area produced two-thirds of the world's copper.

Dartmoor

Purple, heather clad moorland, wide open landscapes, rushing rivers and obscure stone tors shape the landscape of Dartmoor.

Dorset and East Devon Coast

The cliffs that make up the Dorset and Devon coast are an important site for fossils and provide a continuous record of life on land and in the sea since 185 million years ago.

Dorset

Dorset's countryside is almost entirely designated as an Area of Outstanding Natural Beauty. It includes iconic landmarks such as the Gold Hill in Shaftesbury (famous for the 1973 Hovis Advert).

English Riviera

Incorporating Torquay, Paignton and Brixham, this area is one of the UK's most popular holiday destinations. Famous for its award winning beaches and exotic palm trees, it is also a Global Geopark.

Exmoor

Exmoor National Park contains a variety of landscapes within its 267 square miles, including moorland, woodland, valleys and farmland.

Land's End

The most westerly point of mainland Cornwall and England. The headland has been designated as an Important Plant Area, by the organisation Plantlife, for rare species of flora.

Stonehenge

The Neolithic sites of Avebury and Stonehenge in Wiltshire are two of the most famous megalithic monuments in the world, and relate to man's interaction with his environment.

Editor's Picks

Defy gravity in a canal boat

At Caen Hill, near Devizes, canal boats defy gravity and take to hill climbing in one of the most spectacular stretches of waterway thanks to 29 locks in just two miles.

Walk the South West Coast Path

Trek all 630 stunning miles of unbroken coastline or maybe just a section. The path takes you from Minehead, round Devon and Cornwall, to Poole Harbour in Dorset.

Travel through time

Take a boat trip from Poole and witness the dramatic geology of the Jurassic Coast. Switch to the Swanage Steam Railway and be transported on a magical journey to Corfe castle.

Beat the tides

The tidal causeway linking the Devon coast with Burgh Island can catch out the casual visitor. But fear not as the unique Sea Tractor – an amphibious 'bus-on-stilts' – will carry you safely to shore.

See Land's End from the sky

Take off from a Cornish cliff and fly past the spectacular Longships Lighthouse before getting a spectacular bird's eye view of the Isles of Scilly archipelago.

Things to do

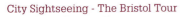

Entertainment & Culture

Castle Combe Museum
Castle Combe,
Wiltshire SN14 7HU
(01249) 782250
www.castle-combe.com
*Displays of life in Castle Combe
over the years.*

City Sightseeing - The Bristol Tour
Central Bristol, BS1 4AH
(03333) 210101
www.citysightseeingbristol.co.uk
*Open-top bus tours, with guides and headphones,
around the city of Bristol, a service that runs daily
throughout the summer months.*

Corinium Museum
Cirencester, Gloucestershire GL7 2BX
(01285) 655611
www.cotswold.gov.uk/go/museum
*Discover the treasures of the Cotswolds as you explore
its history at this award winning museum.*

Dean Heritage Centre
Cinderford, Gloucestershire GL14 2UB
(01594) 822170
www.deanheritagemuseum.com
*The Centre is open again after the fire. On display is an
exhibition showing the damage caused by the fire so
that visitors can come along and see what plans the
Museum has in place to clean and refurbish.*

Gloucester Waterways Museum
Gloucester GL1 2EH
(01452) 318200
www.nwm.org.uk
*Three floors of a Victorian warehouse house, interactive
displays and galleries, which chart the story of Britain's
waterways.*

Haynes International Motor Museum
Yeovil, Somerset BA22 7LH
(01963) 440804
www.haynesmotormuseum.co.uk
*An excellent day out for everyone. With more than 400
vehicles displayed in stunning style, dating from 1886
to the present day, it is the largest international motor
museum in Britain.*

National Maritime Museum Cornwall

Falmouth, Cornwall TR11 3QY
(01326) 313388
www.nmmc.co.uk
Voted SW Attraction of the Year, this Museum delivers something for everyone.

Plymouth City Museum and Art Gallery
Devon PL4 8AJ
(01752) 304774
www.plymouth.gov.uk/museumpcmag.htm
The museum presents a diverse range of contemporary exhibitions, from photography to textiles, modern art to natural history.

Roman Baths
Bath, Somerset BA1 1LZ
(01225) 477785
www.romanbaths.co.uk
The Romans built a magnificent temple and bathing complex that still flows with natural hot water.

Tate St Ives
St. Ives, Cornwall TR26 1TG
(01736) 796226
www.tate.org.uk/stives
Tate St Ives offers an introduction to international Modern and contemporary art, including works from the Tate Collection.

The Jane Austen Centre
Bath, Somerset BA1 2NT
(01225) 443000
www.janeausten.co.uk
Celebrating Bath's most famous resident.

Family Fun

At-Bristol

Bristol BS1 5DB
0845 345 1235
www.at-bristol.org.uk
21st century science and technology centre, with hands-on activities, interactive exhibits.

Corfe Castle Model Village and Gardens

Corfe Castle, Dorset BH20 5EZ
(01929) 481234
www.corfecastlemodelvillage.co.uk
Detailed 1/20th scale model of Corfe Castle and village before its destruction by Cromwell.

Cornwall's Crealy Great Adventure Park
Wadebridge, Cornwall PL27 7RA
(01841) 540276
www.crealy.co.uk/cornwall/index.aspx.
Enter the magical land of Cornwall's Crealy and hold on tight for Morgawr, the exciting NEW roller coaster.

Flambards
Helston, Cornwall TR13 0QA
(01326) 573404
www.flambards.co.uk
"Do not forget to visit the award-winning and unique exhibitions including the Victorian Village and the Britain in the Blitz."

Food & Drink

Wadworth Visitor Centre

Devizes, Wiltshire SN10 1JW
(01380) 732277
www.wadworthvisitorcentre.co.uk
Sample the delights and discover the history & heritage of Wadworth brewing. Featuring an exhibition of Wadworth brewing memorabilia, and products created by our Master Cooper.

Heritage

Avon Valley Railway
Bristol, Gloucestershire BS30 6HD
(0117) 932 5538
www.avonvalleyrailway.org *Railway that's much more than your average steam train ride, offering a whole new experience for some or a nostalgic memory for others.*

Brunel's SS Great Britain

Bristol BS1 6TY
(0117) 926 0680
www.ssgreatbritain.org
Award-winning attraction showing the world's first great ocean liner and National Brunel Archive.

Dartmouth Castle
Dartmouth, Devon TQ6 0JN
(01803) 833588
www.english-heritage.org.uk/dartmouthcastle
For over six hundred years Dartmouth Castle has guarded the narrow entrance to the Dart Estuary and the busy, vibrant port of Dartmouth.

Forde Abbey & Gardens
Chard, Dorset TA20 4LU
(01460) 221290
www.fordeabbey.co.uk
Founded 850 years ago, Forde Abbey was converted into a private house in c.1649.

Glastonbury Abbey

Somerset BA6 9EL
(01458) 832267
www.glastonburyabbey.com
Glastonbury Abbey – Somewhere for all seasons ! From snowdrops and daffodils in the Spring, to family trails and quizzes during the school holidays and Autumn colour on hundreds of trees.

Gloucester Cathedral
Gloucestershire GL1 2LR
(01452) 528095
www.gloucestercathedral.org.uk
A place of worship and an architectural gem with crypt, cloisters and Chapter House set in its precincts.

Lulworth Castle & Park
Wareham, Dorset BH20 5QS
0845 450 1054
www.lulworth.com
Walk in the footsteps of Kings & Queens as you enjoy wide open spaces, historic buildings & stunning landscapes. Enjoy the tranquillity of the nearby 18th century Chapel, wander through the park & woodland & bring a picnic.

Number One Royal Crescent
Bath, Somerset BA1 2LR
(01225) 428126
www.bath-preservation-trust.org.uk
The magnificently restored and authentically furnished town house creates a wonderful picture of fashionable life in 18th century Bath.

Old Sarum
Salisbury, Wiltshire SP1 3SD
(01722) 335398
www.english-heritage.org.uk/oldsarum
Discover the story of the original Salisbury and take the family for a day out to Old Sarum, two miles north of where the city stands now. The mighty Iron Age hill fort was where the first cathedral once stood and the Romans, Normans and Saxons have all left their mark.

Quay House Visitor Centre
Exeter, Devon EX2 4AN
(01392) 271611
www.exeter.gov.uk/quayhouse
Discover the history of Exeter in 15 minutes at the Quay House Visitor Centre on Exeter's Historic Quayside.

Portland Castle
Portland, Dorset DT5 1AZ
(01305) 820539
www.english-heritage.org.uk/portland
A well preserved coastal fort built by Henry VIII to defend Weymouth harbour against possible French and Spanish attack.

Salisbury Cathedral
Salisbury, Wiltshire SP1 2EJ
(01722) 555120
www.salisburycathedral.org.uk
Britain's finest 13th century cathedral with the tallest spire in Britain. Discover nearly 800 years of history, the world's best preserved Magna Carta (AD 1215) and Europe's oldest working clock (AD 1386).

Stonehenge
Amesbury, Wiltshire SP4 7DE
0870 333 1181
www.english-heritage.org.uk/stonehenge
Stonehenge stands impressively as a prehistoric monument of unique importance, a World Heritage Site, surrounded by remains of ceremonial and domestic structures - some older than the monument itself.

Sudeley Castle Gardens and Exhibition
Winchcombe, Gloucestershire GL54 5JD
(01242) 602308
www.sudeleycastle.co.uk
Award-winning gardens surrounding Castle and medieval ruins.

Swanage Railway
Swanage, Dorset BH19 1HB
(01929) 425800
www.swanagerailway.co.uk
Enjoy a nostalgic steam-train ride, running from Swanage to Norden on the Purbeck line.

West Somerset Railway
Minehead, Somerset TA24 5BG
(01643) 704996
www.west-somerset-railway.co.uk
Longest independent steam railway in Britain at 20 miles in length.

Nature & Wildlife

Blue Reef Aquarium
Newquay, Cornwall TR7 1DU
(01637) 878134
www.bluereefaquarium.co.uk
A dazzling undersea safari through the oceans of the world.

Bristol Zoo Gardens

Bristol BS8 3HA
(0117) 974 7300
www.bristolzoo.org.uk
A visit to this city zoo is your passport for a day trip into an amazing world of animals, exhibits and other attractions.

Eden Project
St. Austell, Cornwall PL24 2SG
(01726) 811911
www.edenproject.com
With a worldwide reputation this epic destination definitely deserves a day of your undivided attention.

Escot Gardens, Maze & Forest Adventure

Ottery St. Mary, Devon EX11 1LU
(01404) 822188
www.escot-devon.co.uk
Historical gardens and fantasy woodland surrounding the ancestral home of the Kennaway family.

Fistral Beach
Newquay, Cornwall TR7 1HY
(01637) 850584
www.fistralbeach.co.uk
Excellent surfing conditions, a large beach, west facing with fine golden sand. International surfing events regularly take place here.

Hidcote Manor Garden

Chipping Campden,
Gloucestershire GL55 6LR
(01386) 438333
www.nationaltrust.org.uk/hidcote
Famous for its rare trees and shrubs, outstanding herbaceous borders and unusual plants from all over the world.

HorseWorld

Bristol, Somerset BS14 0QJ
(01275) 540173
www.horseworld.org.uk
Meet and help feed the rescued horses, ponies, donkeys in order to support this charity's animal welfare work.

Ilfracombe Aquarium
Ilfracombe, Devon EX34 9EQ
(01271) 864533
www.ilfracombeaquarium.co.uk
A fascinating journey of discovery into the aquatic life of North Devon.

Longleat

Warminster, Wiltshire BA12 7NW
(01985) 844400
www.longleat.co.uk
Widely regarded as one of the best loved tourist destinations in the UK, Longleat has a wealth of exciting attractions and events to tantalise your palate.

Lost Gardens of Heligan
St. Austell, Cornwall PL26 6EN
(01726) 845100
www.heligan.com
An exploration through Victorian Productive Gardens & Pleasure Grounds, a sub-tropical Jungle, pioneering Wildlife Project and beyond.

National Seal Sanctuary
Helston, Cornwall TR12 6UG
(01326) 221361
www.sealsanctuary.co.uk
The National Seal Sanctuary rescues, rehabilitates and releases over 40 seal pups a year, providing a home for those that can't be released back to the wild.

Newquay Zoo

Newquay, Cornwall TR7 2LZ
(01637) 873342
www.newquayzoo.org.uk
Multi-award winning Newquay Zoo set in sub-tropical lakeside gardens and home to over 130 species of animals.

Painswick Rococo Garden

Painswick, Gloucestershire GL6 6TH
(01452) 813204
www.rococogarden.org.uk
A unique Garden restoration, situated in a hidden valley.

Stourhead House and Garden
Warminster, Wiltshire BA12 6QD
(01747) 841152
www.nationaltrust.org.uk/stourhead
A breathtaking 18th century landscape garden with lakeside walks, grottoes and classical temples is only the beginning.

Westonbirt, The National Arboretum

Tetbury, Gloucestershire GL8 8QS
(01666) 880220
www.forestry.gov.uk/westonbirt
600 acres with one of the finest collections of trees in the world.

Events 2014

Swanage and Purbeck Walking Festival
April-May, Swanage
An exciting blend of special and general interest walks in this stunning area of Dorset.
www.walkswanage.com

Sherborne Abbey Music Festival
May, Sherborne
Five days of music performed by both nationally acclaimed artists and gifted young musicians.
www.sherborneabbey.org

Lyme Regis Fossil Festival
May 2-4, Lyme Regis
A natural science and arts cultural extravaganza on the UNESCO World Heritage Jurassic Coast.
www.fossilfestival.com

BMAD Bike Festival
May 2-5, Paignton
A festival of motorbikes on Paignton seafront, including live music and acrobatic displays.
www.bmad.co.uk/festival

Brixham Pirate Festival
May 4-5, Brixham
Brixham turns pirate with live music, games, re-enactments, skirmishes on the Golden Hind.
www.brixhampiratefestival.co.uk

Dorset Knob Throwing Festival
May, Cattistock, nr Dorchester
World famous quirky festival.
www.dorsetknobthrowing.com

Baby swans hatching at Abbotsbury Swannery
Mid May-late June, Abbotsbury, nr Dorchester
Hundreds of fluffy cygnets hatch from eggs in nests on or near the pathways.
www.abbotsbury-tourism.co.uk

Christchurch Food and Wine Festival
May 10-11, Christchurch
Celebrity chefs, over 100 trade stands, culinary treats, cookery theatres and some eminent food critics.
www.christchurchfoodfest.co.uk

The Super Weekend
June, Torquay
A celebration of all things super on England's Riviera coast – super cars, super bikes and super yachts.
www.thesuperweekend.co.uk

Glastonbury Festival
June 25-29, Shepton Mallet
Best known for its contemporary music, but also features dance, comedy, theatre, circus, cabaret and other arts.
www.glastonburyfestivals.co.uk

Spirit of the Sea Festival
June-July, Weymouth
Celebrating the area's close relationship with the sea, the festival brings together a range of sporting activities, cultural events and entertainment.
www.spiritofthesea.org.uk

Larmer Tree Festival
July 16-20, Cranborne Chase, North Dorset
Boutique festival featuring over 70 diverse artists across six stages, a comedy club, 150 free workshops, street theatre, carnival procession, all in front of an intimate crowd of 4,000.
www.larmertreefestival.co.uk

Tolpuddle Martyrs Festival
July 18-20, Tolpuddle, nr Dorchester
An annual festival to commemorate the bravery of the martyrs' struggle featuring music, speakers and family entertainment.
www.tolpuddlemartyrs.org.uk

Camp Bestival
July 31- August 3, Lulworth Castle, nr Wareham
Camp Bestival is a fairytale jamboree with a great mix of music, comedy and performing arts, suitable for all ages.
www.campbestival.net

Swanage Regatta
July 26-August 2, Swanage
The South's premier carnival.
www.swanagecarnival.com

Boardmasters
August 6-10, Newquay
Europe's largest surf and music festival on Fistral Beach and Watergate Bay.
www.boardmasters .co.uk

Buckham Fair
August 17, Beaminster
Martin Clunes' country show with funfair, dog show, dressage, entertainment, beer tent and food stalls.
www.buckhamfair.co.uk

Great Dorset Steam Fair
August 27-31, Tarrant Hinton, nr Blandford Forum
Dorset's biggest festival – five days of nostalgia and steam, widely recognised as the leading event of its kind in the world with over 2,000 exhibits and 500 trade stands, and traditional working demonstrations.
www.gdsf.co.uk

Dorset County Show
TBC, Dorchester
The South West's biggest two-day show featuring over 450 trade stands and a fantastic array of attractions.
www.dorsetcountyshow.co.uk

Bournemouth Air Festival
August 28-31, Bournemouth
Free four-day seafront air show.
www.bournemouthair.co.uk

Sturminster Newton Cheese Festival
September 13-14, Sturminster
A celebration of the region's dairy heritage with quality local food and crafts.
www.cheesefestival.co.uk

The Agatha Christie Festival
September, Torquay
Celebrate the life and works of the world's most famous crime writer, Dame Agatha Christie, who was born in Torquay in 1890. A literary festival with a murder mystery twist!
www.agathachristiefestival.co.uk

Bridport Hat Festival
September, Bridport
A three-day celebration of hats with live music, stalls and competitions.
www.bridporthatfest.org

Fishstock
September, Brixham
A one-day festival of seafood and entertainment held in Brixham.
www.fishstockbrixham.co.uk

Newquay Fish Festival
September, Newquay
Three days celebrating Newquay harbour and delightful fresh local produce.
www.newquayfishfestival.co.uk

Crantock Bale Push
September, Crantock, nr Newquay
Over 100 teams pushing giant hay bale around the village September 2013.
www.balepush.co.uk

Forest Food Showcase
October, Forest of Dean
A celebration of the foods and fruits of the forest. Held annually at Speech House on the first Sunday in October. With many food stalls and demonstrations it's a great opportunity to try what the area has to offer.
www.forestshowcase.org

Cornwall Film Festival
November, Newquay
3 days of iconic films in the Lighthouse Cinema -
www.cornwallfilmfestival.com

Tourist Information Centres

When you arrive at your destination, visit an Official Partner Tourist Information Centre for quality assured help with accommodation and information about local attractions and events, or email your request before you go. To find a Tourist Information Centre visit www.visitengland.com

Bath	Abbey Chambers	0906 711 2000	tourism@bathtourism.co.uk
Bodmin	Shire Hall	01208 76616	bodmintic@visit.org.uk
Bourton-on-the-Water	Victoria Street	01451 820211	bourtonvic@btconnect.com
Bridport	Bridport Town Hall	01308 424901	bridport.tic@westdorset-weymouth.gov.uk
Bristol : Harbourside	E Shed	0906 711 2191	ticharbourside@destinationbristol.co.uk
Brixham	18-20 The Quay	01803 211 211	holiday@englishriviera.co.uk
Bude	Bude Visitor Centre	01288 354240	budetic@visitbude.info
Cartgate	South Somerset TIC	01935 829333	cartgate.tic@southsomerset.gov.uk
Chard	The Guildhall	01460 260051	chard.tic@chard.gov.uk
Cheltenham	Municipal Offices	01242 522878	info@cheltenham.gov.uk
Chippenham	High Street	01249 665970	info@chippenham.gov.uk
Chipping Campden	The Old Police Station	01386 841206	info@campdenonline.org
Christchurch	49 High Street	01202 471780	enquiries@christchurchtourism.info
Cirencester	Corinium Museum	01285 654180	cirencestervic@cotswold.gov.uk
Corsham	31 High Street	01249 714660	enquiries@corshamheritage.org.uk
Dorchester	11 Antelope Walk	01305 267992	dorchester.tic@westdorset-weymouth.gov.uk
Fowey	5 South Street	01726 833616	info@fowey.co.uk
Frome	The Library	01373 465757	touristinfo@frome-tc.gov.uk
Glastonbury	The Tribunal	01458 832954	info@glastonburytic.co.uk
Gloucester	28 Southgate Street	01452 396572	tourism@gloucester.gov.uk

Looe	The Guildhall	01503 262072	looetic@btconnect.com
Lyme Regis	Guildhall Cottage	01297 442138	lymeregis.tic@westdorset-weymouth.gov.uk
Malmesbury	Town Hall	01666 823748	tic@malmesbury.gov.uk
Moreton-in-Marsh	High Street	01608 650881	moreton@cotswold.gov.uk
Padstow	Red Brick Building	01841 533449	padstowtic@btconnect.com
Penzance	Station Approach	01736 335530	beth.rose@nationaltrust.org.uk
Plymouth: Mayflower	Plymouth Mayflower Centre	01752 306330	barbicantic@plymouth.gov.uk
Salisbury	Fish Row	01722 342860	visitorinfo@salisburycitycouncil.gov.uk
Shepton Mallet	70 High Street	01749 345258	enquiries@visitsheptonmallet.co.uk
Sherborne	3 Tilton Court	01935 815341	sherborne.tic@westdorset-weymouth.gov.uk
Somerset Visitor Centre	Sedgemoor Services	01934 750833	somersetvisitorcentre@somerset.gov.uk
St Austell	Southbourne Road	01726 879 500	staustelltic@gmail.com
St Ives	The Guildhall	01736 796297	ivtic@stivestic.co.uk
Street	Clarks Village	01458 447384	info@streettic.co.uk
Stroud	Subscription Rooms	01453 760960	tic@stroud.gov.uk
Swanage	The White House	01929 422885	mail@swanage.gov.uk
Swindon	Central Library	01793 466454	infocentre@swindon.gov.uk
Taunton	The Library	01823 336344	tauntontic@tauntondeane.gov.uk
Tetbury	33 Church Street	01666 503552	tourism@tetbury.org
Tewkesbury	100 Church Street	01684 855040	tewkesburytic@tewkesbury.gov.uk
Torquay	The Tourist Centre	01803 211 211	holiday@englishriviera.co.uk
Truro	Municipal Building	01872 274555	tic@truro.gov.uk
Wareham	Discover Purbeck	01929 552740	tic@purbeck-dc.gov.uk
Warminster	Central Car Park	01985 218548	visitwarminster@btconnect.com
Wells	Wells Museum	01749 671770	visitwellsinfo@gmail.com
Weston-Super-Mare	The Winter Gardens	01934 417117	westontic@parkwood-leisure.co.uk
Weymouth	The Pavilion	01305 785747	tic@weymouth.gov.uk
Winchcombe	Town Hall	01242 602925	winchcombetic@tewkesbury.gov.uk
Yeovil	Petters House	01935 462781	yeoviltic@southsomerset.gov.uk

Regional Contacts and Information

For more information on accommodation, attractions, activities, events and holidays in South West England, contact one of the following regional or local tourism organisations. Their websites have a wealth of information and many produce free publications to help you get the most out of your visit.

Visit the following websites for further information on South West England:

• visitsouthwest.co.uk
• swcp.org.uk
• accessiblesouthwest.co.uk

Or call 01392 360050
Email: post@swtourism.co.uk

Publications available from South West Tourism:
• The Trencherman's Guide to Top Restaurants in South West England
• Adventure South West
  Your ultimate activity and adventure guide.
• World Heritage Map
  Discover our World Heritage.

Entries appear alphabetically by town name in each county. A key to symbols appears on page 7

BLACKWATER, Cornwall   Map ref 1B3
SatNav TR4 8HR

Trevarth Holiday Park
Blackwater, Truro TR4 8HR
T: (01872) 560266 **E:** trevarth@btconnect.com
W: www.trevarth.co.uk

🚗	(30)	£12.50-£20.00
🚐	(30)	£12.50-£20.00
⛺	(30)	£12.50-£20.00
🏠	(20)	£175.00-£655.00

30 touring pitches

Luxury caravan holiday homes, touring and camping. A small, quiet park conveniently situated for north and south-coast resorts. Level touring and tent pitches with electric hook-up. Overnight holding area available. Laundry room, games room and play area.

Directions: Leave A30 at Chiverton roundabout (signed St Agnes). At the next roundabout take the road to Blackwater. Park on right after 200m.

Open: April to October.

Payment: 💷 ☼ **Leisure:** ♪ ∪ 🔍 **Children:** 🐎 ⚠ **Park:** 🖥 📖 🛎 **Touring:** 🚿 🛁 🍴

BUDE, Cornwall   Map ref 1C2
SatNav EX23 0NA

Budemeadows Touring Park
Widemouth Bay, Bude, Cornwall EX23 0NA
T: (01288) 361646 **F:** 0870 7064825 **E:** holiday@budemeadows.com
W: www.budemeadows.com

🚗	(145)	£16.00-£28.50
🚐	(40)	£16.00-£28.50
⛺	(105)	£16.00-£28.50

145 touring pitches

SPECIAL PROMOTIONS
Over 60's £14/night until 22nd May and from 31st August. £17.50/night 2nd June - 18th July. Includes 2 adults, 2 dogs with electric hook-up on hard standing or grass. Premier Pitches also available £17/£20.50.

Great family run site providing a superb base for surfing, scenery and sightseeing. All usual facilities, heated pool, licensed bar, shop, launderette, large children's playground, games room with TV and pool table. Well maintained grounds. 4 miles from Bude and a mile from the surf and sand at Widemouth Bay. Quoted prices are for a grass pitch, 2 adults and include electric hook-up and awnings etc.

Directions: Signposted from A39, 3 miles south of Bude. Look for signs after signpost to Widemouth Bay. Full directions available on our website.

Open: All year (Pool, bar & shop late May - end August).

Site: 🏠 **Payment:** 💷 ☼ **Leisure:** ♪ ▶ ∪ 🔍 ⚓ **Children:** 🐎 ⚠ **Catering:** 🛒 **Park:** 🐕 🖥 📖 🛎 **Touring:** 🚿 🛁 🍴 ♪

Wooda Farm Holiday Park
Poughill, Bude, Cornwall EX23 9HJ
T: (01288) 352069 **F:** (01288) 355258 **E:** enquiries@wooda.co.uk
W: www.wooda.co.uk **£ BOOK ONLINE**

🚐 (80)	£18.00-£32.00
🚏 (60)	£14.00-£32.00
⛺ (60)	£14.00-£27.00
🚐 (55)	£273.00-£889.00

200 touring pitches

SPECIAL PROMOTIONS
See our website for
special offers.

Stunning views over Bude Bay and countryside; 1.5 miles from safe, sandy beaches. Family-owned and run with excellent facilities for touring and camping and luxury holiday homes for hire. Activities include fishing, sports barn, tennis court, woodland walks and golf. An ideal base for touring the delights of Devon and Cornwall. Overnight holding area available.

Directions: 1.5 miles from Bude, just outside the village of Poughill.   **Open:** April to October.

Payment: 💷 **Leisure:** 🏊 🎣 ▶ ♒ 🎯 **Property:** 🐕 🚐 📺 🛒 **Children:** 🐎 🎠 **Catering:** ✗ 🍴

Juliots Well Holiday Park
Juliots Well, Camelford, Cornwall PL32 9RF
T: (01840) 213302 **F:** (01840) 212700 **E:** holidays@juliotswell.com
W: www.juliotswell.com

🚐	£12.00-£24.00
🚏	£12.00-£24.00
⛺	£9.00-£24.00
🏠 (35)	£125.00-£1075.00
🚐 (26)	£125.00-£795.00

39 touring pitches

SPECIAL PROMOTIONS
Seasonal Tourers are
welcome. For further
information please
contact the office on
01840 213302.

Set in 33 acres of woodlands with extensive views across some of the finest Cornish Countryside. Excellent facilities including an outdoor heated swimming pool open mid May to Mid September, children's play area, games room and launderette.

Directions: From Exeter follow A30. Turn right onto A395, left onto A39 to Camelford. Beyond Camelford town turn right onto B3266, left on sharp bend.   **Open:** 5th April - 1st Nov.

Site: 🏪 ⛺ **Payment:** 💷 ☀ **Leisure:** 🏊 🎣 ▶ ♒ 🎯 **Children:** 🐎 🎠 **Catering:** ✗ 🍴
Park: 🐕 🎵 🚐 📺 **Touring:** 🚐

FOWEY, Cornwall Map ref 1B3
SatNav PL23 1JU

Penhale Caravan & Camping Park

Penhale Caravan & Camping Park, Penhale Farm, Fowey, Cornwall PL23 1JU
T: (01726) 833425 **F:** (01726) 833425 **E:** info@penhale-fowey.co.uk
W: www.penhale-fowey.co.uk **£ BOOK ONLINE**

🚐 (35)	£15.00-£30.00
🚎 (16)	£15.00-£25.00
⛺ (56)	£8.00-£18.00
🚏 (10)	£195.00-£535.00

56 touring pitches

Friendly, uncrowded family run park that overlooks un-spoilt farmland and lovely views of the sea. In Area of Outstanding Natural Beauty close to sandy beaches, many scenic walks and the Eden Project. David Bellamy Award. Choice of caravans. Touring pitches, electric hook-ups, free showers. Overnight holding area available.

Directions: From A30 west from Lostwithiel, on A390 turn left after 1 mile onto B3269, after 3 miles turn right onto A3082.

Open: Easter or 1st April to End October.

Site: 🅰️🅿️ **Payment:** 💷 ☀ **Leisure:** 🎣 ▶ ∪ 🔍 **Children:** 🎠 **Catering:** 🍴 **Park:** 🐾 🚃 📖 📷 **Touring:** 🚽 🔌 💧

HAYLE, Cornwall Map ref 1B3
SatNav TR27 5BL

Atlantic Coast Holiday Park

53 Upton Towans, Hayle, Cornwall TR27 5BL
T: (01736) 752071 **E:** enquiries@atlanticcoastpark.co.uk
W: www.atlanticcoastpark.co.uk

🚐 (15)	
🚎 (15)	
⛺ (15)	
🚏 (19)	

15 touring pitches

The park is situated alongside the sand dunes of St Ives bay, bordering Gwithian beach, a fantastic quiet beach ideal for families and surfers. The park is also pet friendly. Please contact us for prices. **Directions:** Leave the A30 at the Hayle exit, turn right onto the B3301, approx 1 mile on left is where we are situated. **Open:** 1st March - January.

Payment: 💷 ☀ **Leisure:** 🎱 🎣 ▶ ∪ 🔍 **Children:** 🎠 🎢 **Catering:** 🍴 **Park:** 🐾 🚃 📖 📷 **Touring:** 🚽 🔌 🎣

HAYLE, Cornwall Map ref 1B3
SatNav TR27 5AW

Beachside Holiday Park

Phillack, Hayle TR27 5AW
T: (01736) 753080 **F:** (01736) 757252 **E:** reception@beachside.co.uk
W: www.beachside.co.uk **£ BOOK ONLINE**

🚐 (80)	£10.00-£37.00
🚎 (80)	£10.00-£37.00
⛺ (80)	£10.00-£37.00
🏠 (29)	£280.00-£1135.00
🏚 (80)	£220.00-£655.00

80 touring pitches

Beachside is a family holiday park, set amidst sand dunes right on the beach in the famous St Ives Bay. With a range of accommodation and touring pitches, our location is ideally situated in West Cornwall for a touring and beach holiday. **Directions:** Travel west on A30 and turn off into Hayle. Turn right, following the sign to Phillack & Beachside. Our entrance is approximately 400m on right. **Open:** Easter to End October.

Site: 🏠 🅰️🅿️ **Payment:** 💷 ☀ **Leisure:** 🎣 ∪ 🔍 🎣 **Children:** 🎠 🎢 **Catering:** 🍴 **Park:** 🎵 🚃 📖 📷 **Touring:** 🚽 💧

The Official Tourist Board Guide to **Camping, Touring & Holiday Parks 2014**

HAYLE, Cornwall Map ref 1B3 — SatNav TR27 5BH

St Ives Bay Holiday Park

73 Loggans Road, Upton Towans, Hayle TR27 5BH
T: (01736) 752274 **F:** (01736) 754523 **E:** enquiries@stivesbay.co.uk
W: www.stivesbay.co.uk **£ BOOK ONLINE**

🚐	(250)	£10.00-£35.00
🚍	(250)	£10.00-£35.00
⛺	(250)	£10.00-£35.00
🏠	(4)	£524.00-£1542.00
🏕	(150)	£159.00-£722.00
🚐	(250)	£145.00-£1017.00

250 touring pitches

Magnificent location in dunes overlooking huge sandy beach. Caravans, chalets and camping. Many units and pitches with sea views. Overnight holding area available. **Directions:** Take first Hayle exit from A30 going West. Turn immediately right at Lidl. Park entrance 500 metres on left. **Open:** Easter to 2nd November.

Site: Payment: Leisure: Children: Catering: Park: Touring:

HELSTON, Cornwall Map ref 1B3 — SatNav TR13 9NN

Poldown Camping & Caravan Park

Carleen, Breage, Helston, Cornwall TR13 9NN
T: (01326) 574560 **E:** info@poldown.co.uk
W: www.poldown.co.uk **£ BOOK ONLINE**

🚐	(10)	£15.00-£21.00
🚍	(4)	£11.50-£17.00
⛺	(13)	£11.50-£17.50
🏠	(2)	£125.00-£345.00
🚐	(7)	£195.00-£595.00

13 touring pitches

Small, peaceful and friendly site near the Lizard coast. Nestled in a suntrap hollow in wooded land away from the road. Provides unrivaled freedom for children and tranquillity for adults. Fully equipped luxury holiday caravans. **Directions:** From A30 wait for Camborne exit then follow Helston. 2 miles before Helston, turn right in direction of Godolphin, we are 1/2 mile further on. **Open:** April - September.

Site: Payment: Leisure: Children: Park: Touring:

HELSTON, Cornwall Map ref 1B3 — SatNav TR12 7LZ

Silver Sands Holiday Park

Gwendreath, Kennack Sands, The Lizard, Helston TR12 7LZ
T: (01326) 290631 **F:** (01326) 290631 **E:** stay@silversandsholidaypark.co.uk
W: www.silversandsholidaypark.co.uk **£ BOOK ONLINE**

🚐	(15)	£14.50-£22.00
🚍	(15)	£14.50-£22.00
⛺	(20)	£12.50-£22.00
🚐	(15)	£179.00-£579.00

15 touring pitches

Unwind & relax in our beautifully landscaped family park on the Lizard. Caravan homes, touring & camping pitches are spacious, screened & numbered for privacy. A 1km downhill walk to sandy beaches. Easy access to coast path. Dogs welcome. **Directions:** A3083 from Helston past RNAS Culdrose, L onto B3293 (St Keverne). Passing Goonhilly Satellite Station, 1st Xroad R (Kuggar), 1.5m 1st L (Gwendreath). **Open:** Late March to Early November.

Payment: Leisure: Children: Park: Touring:

LANIVET, Cornwall Map ref 1B2 — SatNav PL30 5HD

Kernow Caravan Park

Clann Farm, Clann Lane, Lanivet, Bodmin PL30 5HD
T: (01208) 831343
W: www.kernowcaravanpark.co.uk

🚐	(6)	£160.00-£490.00

Kernow Caravan Park is quiet and peaceful, in a tranquil setting run by a Cornish family. An ideal touring location to visit The Eden Project, The Lost Gardens of Heligan, Lanhydrock, Camel Trail, Saints Way or Wenford Steam Railway. A few minutes walk from Lanivet village shop, pub and fish & chip restaurant. **Directions:** Leave A30 Innis Downs roundabout. Follow sign to Lanivet 0.75 miles. Left in village centre, opposite shop. Along Clann Lane 300m left into concrete drive. **Open:** March to October.

Leisure: Property: Children:

LOOE, Cornwall Map ref 1C2 *SatNav PL13 2JR*

Tencreek Holiday Park

Polperro Road, Looe PL13 2JR
T: (01503) 262447 **F:** (01503) 262760 **E:** reception@tencreek.co.uk
W: www.dolphinholidays.co.uk **£ BOOK ONLINE**

🚐 (100)　£11.00-£20.50
🚏 (40)　£11.00-£20.50
⛺ (100)　£11.00-£20.50
🏠 (100)　£125.00-£530.00

240 touring pitches

The nearest holiday park to Looe-panoramic countryside and coastal views. Selection of fully equipped modern caravans. Marked grass and hardstanding pitches. Newly built heated toilet and shower facilities. Overnight holding area available. **Directions:** A38 from Tamar bridge. Left at roundabout. Follow Looe signs. Right onto A387, becomes B3253. Through Looe towards Polperro. Tencreek 1.25 miles from Looe bridge. **Open:** All year.

Payment: 🏧 € **Leisure:** 🎵 ⚑ 🎯 ⤢ 🎱 **Property:** 🐕 🎵 📺 🖥 🎮 **Children:** 🛝 🎪 **Catering:** ✕ 🍴

MEVAGISSEY, Cornwall Map ref 1B3 *SatNav PL26 6LL*

Seaview International Holiday Park

Boswinger, Gorran, St. Austell PL26 6LL
T: (01726) 843425 **F:** (01726) 843358 **E:** holidays@seaviewinternational.com
W: www.seaviewinternational.com

🚐 (189)　£11.00-£20.00
🚏 (189)　£11.00-£50.00
⛺ (166)　£11.00-£50.00
🏠 (4)　£315.00-£1150.00
🏠 (26)　£235.00-£875.00

189 touring pitches

SPECIAL PROMOTIONS
Please visit our website
for special offers.

A 5 star park with everything from camping pitches to lodges with incredible sea views. Set in beautiful grounds with far reaching views. With an outdoor heated pool, play area with equipment and ball games, licensed cafe and shop, plus park wide Wi-Fi. Come and experience why so many families return time and time again.

Directions: From St Austell roundabout take B3273 to Mevagissy, at brow of hill before village, turn right and follow signs for Gorran and then brown Seaview signs.

Open: April to October.

Site: ⛺🅿 **Payment:** 🏧 ☀ **Leisure:** ♿ 🎵 ⚑ ↻ ⤢ 🎱 **Children:** 🛝 🎪 **Catering:** ✕ 🍴 **Park:** 🐕 📺 🖥 🎮
Touring: 🚰 ⚡ 💧 🎵

NEWQUAY, Cornwall Map ref 1B2 *SatNav TR8 5HH*

Treworgans Holiday Park

Cubert, Nr Newquay, Cornwall TR8 5HH
T: (01637) 830200 **E:** enquiry@treworgansholidaypark.co.uk
W: www.treworgansholidaypark.co.uk **£ BOOK ONLINE**

🏠 (22)　£280.00-£745.00

Small and quiet, picturesque static caravan park for families and couples. Located on the beautiful North Cornwall coast in a secluded hamlet. No clubhouse or road noise to disturb you. The golden sands of Holywell and Crantock within 1.5 miles. **Directions:** A30 to Newquay, A39, A3075 to Redruth. Turn right to Cubert. At mini-roundabout turn right, follow road for 0.75 miles. Treworgans is on the left. **Open:** April to October.

Payment: 🏧 **Leisure:** ♿ 🎵 ⚑ ↻ **Property:** 🐕 📺 🖥 🎮 **Children:** 🛝 🎪 **Catering:** 🍴

PENZANCE, Cornwall Map ref 1A3   SatNav TR20 9AU

🚐 (20)   £17.00-£26.00
🚏 (20)   £17.00-£26.00
⛺ (40)   £12.00-£26.00
🏠 (7)   £275.00-£555.00
40 touring pitches

Kenneggy Cove Holiday Park

Higher Kenneggy, Rosudgeon, Penzance, Cornwall TR20 9AU
T: (01736) 763453 **E:** enquiries@kenneggycove.co.uk
W: www.kenneggycove.co.uk

A tranquil park (no noise after 10pm), surrounded by glorious countryside in an Area of Outstanding Natural Beauty. Panoramic sea views. 12 min walk to SW coastpath and secluded coves. Short footpath walks to Prussia Cove and a gastro-pub. Immaculate facilities. Lashings of free hot water. Renowned standards of cleanliness and friendliness (resident owners). Quality homemade breakfasts and evening meals.

Directions: We are equidistant from Penzance and Helston off the A394 coast road (3m east of Marazion). At our blue sign, turn down the lane towards to sea. We are near the end of the lane on the left.

Open: Mid May - End of September.

Site: ⛺🅿 **Payment:** € ☀ **Leisure:** ♿ ⚓ ▶ ∪ **Children:** 🛝 ⛰ **Catering:** ✕ 🛒 **Park:** 🐕 🚽 🗄 🖋
Touring: 🚰 🔌 🚿

PENZANCE, Cornwall Map ref 1B3   SatNav TR20 9SH

🏠 (136) £149.00-£1119.00

SPECIAL PROMOTIONS
Please contact us for
special offers.

Praa Sands Holiday Village

Praa Sands, Penzance, Cornwall TR20 9SH
T: (01736) 762201 **E:** info@praa-sands.co.uk
W: www.praa-sands.co.uk **£ BOOK ONLINE**

Within walking distance of one of Cornwall's finest sandy beaches, Praa Sands is the perfect retreat for families and couples looking for something extra special. Facilities include an indoor swimming pool, bar with terrace, sea views and restaurant, plus the superb 9-hole golf course.

Directions: Please contact us for directions.

Open: All year except 9th Jan - 11th Feb.

Site: 🏠 ⛺🅿 **Payment:** 💳 **Leisure:** ⚓ ▶ 🏊 **Children:** 🛝 ⛰ **Catering:** ✕ 🛒 **Park:** 🐕 🎵 🚽 🗄 🖋

QUINTRELL DOWNS, Cornwall   Map ref 1B2 — SatNav TR8 4QR

Trethiggey Touring Park
Quintrell Downs, Newquay TR8 4QR
T: (01637) 877672 **F:** (01637) 879706 **E:** enquiries@trethiggey.co.uk
W: www.trethiggey.co.uk **£ BOOK ONLINE**

🚐 (70)	£14.00-£21.00
🚏 (30)	£14.00-£21.00
⛺ (86)	£9.00-£21.00
🏠 (14)	£200.00-£785.00

186 touring pitches

SPECIAL PROMOTIONS
Holiday home short breaks available in spring and autumn and other offers featured on the park website.

Two miles from Newquay and surf beaches and 15 miles from The Eden Project. A sheltered well landscaped park with beautiful panoramic views. Restaurant and bar, shop, off-licence, childrens' play area and two games rooms. Two modern shower/toilet blocks with disabled facilities. 7 acre recreation field with a small fishing lake and dog walking area. A David Bellamy Gold Award park.

Directions: Leave the A30 at the Newquay exit, follow the A392 to Quintrell Downs. Turn left at roundabout. The park is half a mile on the right.

Open: March 2nd to January 2nd.

Site: Payment: **Leisure:** **Children:** **Catering:** **Park:** **Touring:**

REDRUTH, Cornwall   Map ref 1B3 — SatNav TR16 4JQ

Tehidy Holiday Park
Harris Mill, Illogan, Nr Portreath, Redruth TR16 4JQ
T: (01209) 216489 **F:** (01209) 213555 **E:** holiday@tehidy.co.uk
W: www.tehidy.co.uk

🚐 (10)	£14.00-£23.00
🚏 (8)	£14.00-£23.00
⛺ (20)	£14.00-£23.00
🏠 (4)	£350.00-£700.00
🏠 (20)	£240.00-£760.00

30 touring pitches

SPECIAL PROMOTIONS
To celebrate being voted BEST FAMILY SITE in UK 2013, Book a week in the summer and get a 1/2 price (similar type) out of season break. Special offers on our website.

Cottages, holiday caravans, touring/camping and wigwam cabins, on our multi award winning holiday park, including voted Best Small Site in Europe 2012 - Alan Rogers - Top 3 and Best Small Site in UK 2012 - Practical Motorhome. David Bellamy Gold Award 2013. Nestled in a wooded valley, woodland walks, play area and excellent facilities close to beautiful sandy beaches, gardens and cycling.

Directions: Exit A30 to Redruth/Porthtowan. Rigth to Porthtowan. 300m left at corssroads. Straight on over B3300 (Portreath) crossroads. Past Cornish Arms. Site 500m on left.

Open: March to November.

Payment: **Leisure:** **Property:** **Children:** **Catering:**

ST. JUST IN ROSELAND, Cornwall   Map ref 1B3   SatNav TR2 5JF

Trethem Mill Touring Park
St. Just in Roseland, Nr St Mawes, Truro, Cornwall TR2 5JF
T: (01872) 580504 **F:** (01872) 580968 **E:** reception@trethem.com
W: www.trethem.com

Offering peace and tranquillity with an exceptional standard of facilities. Caravan Park of the Year EnjoyEngland Excellence Awards 2010 'Consistent winners offering consistent quality.' Say hello to a new experience. **Directions:** A3078 towards Tregony/St Mawes, over Tregony bridge. After 5 miles follow brown caravan and camping signs from Trewithian. Site 2 miles beyond on right-hand side. **Open:** April to mid-October.

(84)	£18.00-£27.00
(55)	£18.00-£27.00
(30)	£18.00-£27.00
84 touring pitches	

Payment: **Leisure:** **Children:** **Catering:** **Park:** **Touring:**

ST. MERRYN, Cornwall   Map ref 1B2   SatNav PL28 8PR

Trevean Farm Caravan & Camping park
St. Merryn, Padstow PL28 8PR
T: (01841) 520772 **F:** (01841) 520772 **E:** trevean.info@virgin.net
W: www.treveancaravanandcamping.net

Small, pleasant farm site, 1 mile from the sea. Ideally situated for beaches, walking and many visitor attractions. **Directions:** From St. Merryn crossroads take B3276 towards Newquay. Take first left after approximately ¾ mile. We are along this road on the right. **Open:** 1st April to end of October.

	£10.00-£14.00
	£10.00-£14.00
	£10.00-£14.00
(3)	£200.00-£500.00
70 touring pitches	

Payment: **Leisure:** **Children:** **Catering:** **Park:** **Touring:**

WATERGATE BAY NEWQUAY, Cornwall   Map ref 1B2   SatNav TR8 4AD

Watergate Bay Touring Park
Tregurrian, Newquay, Cornwall TR8 4AD
T: (01637) 860387 **F:** 0871 661 7549 **E:** email@watergatebaytouringpark.co.uk
W: www.watergatebaytouringpark.co.uk

(200)	£11.00-£22.00
(200)	£11.00-£22.00
(220)	£11.00-£22.00
(2)	£250.00-£695.00
200 touring pitches	

SPECIAL PROMOTIONS
Outside of the dates 18th July - 25th August, book 7 nights or more and receive a 10% discount.

Half mile from Watergate Bays sand, surf and cliff walks. Rural Location in an Area of Outstanding Natural Beauty. Personally run & supervised by resident owners. Heated indoor/outdoor pool, tennis courts, skate park, games room, shop/cafe, licensed clubroom, free entertainment including kids club and kids play area. Overnight holding area available.

Directions: From A30 follow signs for Newquay then airport. After passing the airport, turn left onto the B3276. Park 0.5 miles on the right. **Open:** 1st March to the 1st November.

Site: **Payment:** **Leisure:** **Children:** **Catering:** **Park:** **Touring:**

AXMINSTER, Devon Map ref 1D2

SatNav EX13 7DY

Andrewshayes Caravan Park
Dalwood, Axminster, Devon EX13 7DY
T: (01404) 808309 **F:** 01404 831893 **E:** info@andrewshayes.co.uk
W: www.andrewshayes.co.uk **£ BOOK ONLINE**

(15)	£15.00-£32.00	
(10)	£15.00-£32.00	
(8)	£15.00-£32.00	
(19)	£255.00-£695.00	

33 touring pitches

Peaceful, clean park with excellent facilities for touring, camping & motorhomes on a family run site. Covered heated swimming pool, play areas and quiet bar (open in peak weeks). Close to the Jurassic Coast & Blackdown Hills. **Directions:** Between Axminster and Honiton on A35 at Taunton Cross. Follow signpost for Dalwood and Stockland, park is on your right. Entrance 150 yds. **Open:** Last week in March to end of October.

Site: ℗ A🅿 **Payment:** 💳 ☼ **Leisure:** ♣ ♒ **Children:** ⚠ **Catering:** ✕ **Park:** 🐾 🚊 🗓 🏧 ☆ **Touring:** 🚰 ① 🛒 🔧

BRAUNTON, Devon Map ref 1C1

SatNav EX33 1HG

Lobb Fields Caravan and Camping Park
Saunton Road, Braunton EX33 1HG
T: (01271) 812090 **E:** info@lobbfields.com
W: www.lobbfields.com

(181)	£11.00-£29.00	
(25)	£11.00-£29.00	
(181)	£10.00-£14.00	

181 touring pitches

South facing park with panoramic views over the sea. On edge of Braunton, with Saunton beach only 1.5 miles down the road. Excellent bus service. Ideal for families, surfers and other activities. Surf board hire and snack bar on site. **Directions:** From Barnstaple to Braunton on A361. Then follow B3231 for 1 mile towards Saunton. Lobb Fields is marked on the right of the road. **Open:** 28th March to 2nd November.

Payment: 💳 ☼ **Leisure:** ♿ ♪ ♭ ∪ **Children:** 🐾 ⚠ **Park:** 🐾 🚊 🗓 🏧 ☆ **Touring:** 🚰 ① 🛒 🔧

BRIXHAM, Devon Map ref 1D2

SatNav TQ5 0EP

Galmpton Touring Park
Greenway Road, Galmpton, Nr. Brixham TQ5 0EP
T: (01803) 842066 **E:** enquiries@galmptontouringpark.co.uk
W: www.galmptontouringpark.co.uk

(60)	£17.50-£27.50	
(60)	£17.50-£27.50	
(50)	£14.50-£20.50	

120 touring pitches

Quiet family park in a stunning location with spectacular views over the River Dart. The perfect base to explore the nearby delights of the South Hams, with ferries, steam railway, beautiful gardens, local pub & shop all a short walk away. **Directions:** South on Ring Road (A380) then straight onto A3022 towards Churston. At lights turn right, then 2nd right, through village 600yds past school. **Open:** 4th April - 31st October.

Site: A🅿 **Payment:** 💳 ☼ **Leisure:** ♭ **Children:** 🐾 ⚠ **Catering:** 🛒 **Park:** 🐾 🗓 🏧 ☆ **Touring:** 🚰 ① 🛒 🔧

COMBE MARTIN, Devon Map ref 1C1

SatNav EX34 0NS

Manleigh Holiday Park
Rectory Road, Combe Martin, Combe Martin, Devon EX34 0NS
T: (08453) 453426 **E:** enquiries@csmaclubretreats.co.uk
W: www.manleighpark.co.uk **£ BOOK ONLINE**

(3)	£390.00-£812.00	
(9)	£390.00-£749.00	
(14)	£280.00-£651.00	

For a great value getaway and an ideal base to explore the beautiful North Devon coast, Manleigh Park is just perfect. Take your pick from Deluxe Static Caravans, Log Cabins and Chalets. **Directions:** From the M5, take exit 27 to Tiverton/Barnstaple (A361) then head for the A399 for Combe Martin. **Open:** From 7th February.

Payment: 💳 € **Leisure:** ⚲ **Property:** 🐾 🗓 🏧

The Official Tourist Board Guide to *Camping, Touring & Holiday Parks 2014*

CREDITON, Devon   Map ref 1D2   SatNav EX17 4TN

259 touring pitches

Yeatheridge Farm Caravan Park

East Worlington, Crediton, Devon EX17 4TN
T: (01884) 860330 **F:** (01884) 860330 **E:** yeatheridge@talk21.com
W: www.yeatheridge.co.uk

Paint a country picture of lush green fields, butterflies, wild flowers, shady trees, lakes calm and still, disturbed only by the plop of rising fish. In the distance, are rolling hills, misty against a blue sky. Placid farm animals nearby, content in the sun. Please contact us for prices. **Directions:** By Road: From From B3137 take B3042 before Witheridge. Site 3.5 miles on left. Alternatively, turn off A377 at Eggesford Station onto B3042. By Public Transport: From Eggesford - 6 miles. **Open:** All Year.

Site: Payment: Leisure: Catering: Park: Touring:

DAWLISH, Devon   Map ref 1D2   SatNav EX6 8RP

	(450)	£13.50-£38.50
	(450)	£13.50-£38.50
	(450)	£13.50-£31.00
	(17)	£555.00-£1010.00
	(70)	£225.00-£910.00

450 touring pitches

SPECIAL PROMOTIONS
Save 25% on touring/ camping in winter, low, mid and high season for advance bookings of 5 or more nights.

Cofton Country Holidays

Starcross, Nr Dawlish, Devon EX6 8RP
T: (01626) 890111 **F:** (01626) 890160 **E:** info@coftonholidays.co.uk
W: www.coftonholidays.co.uk **£ BOOK ONLINE**

A stunning setting surrounded by rolling meadows, mature woods, fishing lakes and just minutes from Dawlish Warren's Blue Flag beach. Superb countryside views. Hardstanding and super pitches available. Fantastic facilities in clean, tidy surroundings with indoor and outdoor swimming pools, play areas, restaurant, bars, park shop, take-away, woodland walks and games room complete with Bowling.

Directions: Leave M5 at junction 30, take A379 towards Dawlish. After passing through harbour village of Cockwood, park is on the left after half a mile.   **Open:** All year.

Site: Payment: Leisure: Children: Catering: Park: Touring:

Book your accommodation online

Visit our new 2014 guide websites for detailed information, up-to-date availability and to book your accommodation online. Includes over 20,000 places to stay, all of them star rated.

www.visitor-guides.co.uk

DAWLISH, Devon   Map ref 1D2

SatNav EX7 0LX

🏕 (400)   £7.50
🚐 (120) £170.00-£1115.00

Lady's Mile Touring and Camping Park

Exeter Road, Dawlish, Devon EX7 0LX
T: (01626) 863411 **F:** 01626 888689 **E:** info@ladysmile.co.uk
W: www.ladysmile.co.uk **£ BOOK ONLINE**

Lady's Mile is an award winning, family run park designed to please everyone! With a fabulous range of indoor and outdoor sports and leisure facilities, you won't have to leave the site to enjoy a holiday full of family fun, come rain or shine!

Directions: Leave the M5 at Junction 30, take A379 to Dawlish, pass the Cockwood harbour for 2 miles over the Sainsburys roundabout, then take 2nd left.

Open: Park - All Year, Facilities - mid March till end Oct.

Site: 🏠 ♿🅿 **Payment:** 💷 ☀ **Leisure:** ▶ 🏸 🎣 🏊 **Children:** 🎠 ⛰ **Catering:** ✕ 🛒 **Park:** 🎵 📺 🖥 📶
Touring: 🚿 🚽 🚐

DAWLISH, Devon   Map ref 1D2

SatNav EX7 0ND

🚐 (100)   £140.00-£970.00

Oakcliff Holiday Park

Mount Pleasant Road, Dawlish Warren, Dawlish, Devon EX7 0ND
T: (01626) 863347 **F:** 01626 888689 **E:** info@ladysmile.co.uk
W: www.oakcliff.co.uk **£ BOOK ONLINE**

Oakcliff is an 8 acre park laid out in lawns and parkland around an elegant Georgian house, complete with a heated outdoor swimming pool and children's playground. Set in a prime location in Devon's premier holiday resort of Dawlish Warren, 600 yards from a Blue Flag beach and nature reserve. Away from the hustle and bustle, Oakcliff offers more peaceful surroundings with views across the estuary.

Directions: Leave M5 at junction 30, take A379 to Dawlish, continue past Cockwood harbour, pass Sainsburys roundabout, then take the 3rd left to Dawlish Warren for 3/4 mile.

Open: Accommodation - All Year . Pool - May to September.

Site: ♿🅿 **Payment:** 💷 **Leisure:** ▶ 🏊 **Children:** 🎠 ⛰ **Park:** 🐕 🖥

ILFRACOMBE, Devon   Map ref 1C1

(15)	£16.00-£33.00
(15)	£16.00-£33.00
(40)	£16.00-£33.00
(9)	£455.00-£1010.00
(16)	£310.00-£875.00

Hele Valley Holiday Park

Hele Bay, Ilfracombe, North Devon EX34 9RD
T: (01271) 862460 **F:** 01271 867926 **E:** holidays@helevalley.co.uk
W: www.helevalley.co.uk **£ BOOK ONLINE**

Family run holiday park, offering peace and tranquility at the heart of North Devon. Hele Valley offers the perfect holiday choice in beautiful cottages, stunning lodges, luxury caravans and sheltered camping & touring (including cedar pods). The only camping park in Ilfracombe, we are only a stroll away from local inns and Hele beach; and walking distance to Ilfracombe center. Pets are welcome.

Directions: From J27 of the M5 take the A361 to Barnstaple. A39 & then A3230 to Ilfracombe. After 12 miles turn right at traffic lights for Combe Martin (A399). Follow tourist signs for Hele Valley Holiday Park.

Open: 1st April or Easter (if earlier) to 15th January.

Site: **Payment:** **Leisure:** **Children:** **Park:** **Touring:**

IPPLEPEN, Devon   Map ref 1D2

(110)	£15.50-£28.50
(87)	£15.50-£28.50
(8)	£14.50-£28.50
110 touring pitches	

SPECIAL PROMOTIONS
Weekly rates available except Easter, Whitsun and July, August.

Ross Park

Park Hill Farm, Moor Road, Ipplepen, Newton Abbot, Devon TQ12 5TT
T: (01803) 812983 **F:** (01803) 812983 **E:** enquiries@rossparkcaravanpark.co.uk
W: www.rossparkcaravanpark.co.uk

Ross Park is an award winning, family-run park providing excellent facilities in beautiful rural surroundings. Magnificent floral displays, high standards throughout the park with a tranquil atmosphere and friendly service.

Directions: 3 miles from Newton Abbot, 6 miles from Totnes on A381 at Park Hill Cross, follow tourist sign to Ross Park and sign to Woodland.

Open: March - 2nd January.

Site: **Payment:** **Leisure:** **Children:** **Catering:** **Park:** **Touring:**

MORTEHOE, Devon   Map ref 1C1

SatNav EX34 7EG

North Morte Farm Caravan & Camping Park

North Morte Road, Mortehoe, Woolacombe EX34 7EG
T: (01271) 870381 **E:** info@northmortefarm.co.uk
W: www.northmortefarm.co.uk

🚐 (25)	£15.50-£21.00
🚏	£12.00-£21.00
🅰 (150)	£12.00-£18.50
🏕 (21)	£275.00-£670.00

Set in beautiful countryside overlooking Rockham Bay, close to village of Mortehoe and Woolacombe. **Directions:** Take A361 from Barnstaple, turn left at Mullacott roundabout signed Mortehoe and Woolacombe, head for Mortehoe, turn right at Post Office, park 500m on left. **Open:** April to October.

Payment: 💷 ☼ **Leisure:** 🎵 ∪ **Children:** 🛝 ⚠ **Catering:** 🍴 **Park:** 🐕 🖥 🗄 📮 🐾 **Touring:** 🚻 🚽 🚐 🔧

NEWTON ABBOT, Devon   Map ref 1D2

SatNav TQ12 6QT

Twelve Oaks Farm Caravan Park

Teigngrace, Newton Abbot TQ12 6QT
T: (01626) 335015 **E:** info@twelveoaksfarm.co.uk
W: www.twelveoaksfarm.co.uk

🚐 (50)	£10.00-£17.50
🚏 (50)	£10.00-£17.50
🅰 (30)	£10.00-£17.50
🏕 (6)	£300.00-£1350.00
50 touring pitches	

A working farm specialising in Charolais beef cattle. Friendly, personal service. Luxury showers and toilets, heated outdoor swimming pool. Coarse fishing. Good dog walks nearby. Children's play park, Overnight holding area available. Wi-Fi Available. **Directions:** Please come via the A38 south bound exit for Teigngrace straight through the village for two miles Twelve Oaks Farm on left. **Open:** All year.

Payment: 💷 ☼ **Leisure:** ♿ 🎵 ∪ ⚹ **Children:** 🛝 ⚠ **Catering:** 🍴 **Park:** 🐕 🖥 🗄 📮 🐾 **Touring:** 🚻 🚽 🚐 🔧

NORTH MOLTON, Devon   Map ref 1C1

SatNav EX36 3HQ

Riverside Caravan and Camping Park

Marsh Lane, North Molton Road, South Molton, North Devon EX36 3HQ
T: (01769) 579269 **E:** relax@exmoorriverside.co.uk
W: www.exmoorriverside.co.uk

🚐 (42)	£15.00-£25.00
🚏 (42)	£15.00-£25.00
🅰 (40)	£10.00-£24.00
🏕 (2)	£210.00-£485.00
42 touring pitches	

SPECIAL PROMOTIONS
For special offers, please visit our website for full details.

70 acres of parkland with lakes and rivers for fishing, woods and meadowland for walking. We are a 4 star park with 5 star facilities. Overnight holding area available.

Directions: M5 turn off on junction 27 onto the A361 turn right when you see North Molton and riverside sign.   **Open:** All year.

Site: 🏢 **Payment:** 💷 ☼ **Leisure:** 🎵 ∪ **Children:** 🛝 ⚠ **Catering:** ✗ 🍴 **Park:** 🐕 🎵 🖥 🗄 📮 🐾 **Touring:** 🚻 🚽 🚐 🔧

OTTERTON, Devon   Map ref 1D2   SatNav EX9 7BX

Ladram Bay Holiday Park

Otterton, Budleigh Salterton, Devon EX9 7BX
T: (01395) 568398 **F:** (01395) 568338 **E:** info@ladrambay.co.uk
W: www.ladrambay.co.uk **£ BOOK ONLINE**

🚐 (65)	£16.00-£36.00
🚍 (65)	£16.00-£36.00
⛺ (35)	£16.00-£36.00
🏠 (500)	£189.00-£1745.00

160 touring pitches

SPECIAL PROMOTIONS
Short Breaks Available.
Over 55s / Under 5s
Discounts, Up to £20
Off. Early Booking
Discounts.

Nestled in the rolling Devon Hills overlooking the unspoilt Jurassic Coast, Ladram Bay is the Holiday Park in Devon that has something to offer everyone. Previously voted as Best in Britain, you can be assured that your holiday is better than ever before! Whether you choose to stay in one of our luxury holiday homes or your own touring caravan or tent, our extensive range of facilities will suit all.

Directions: M5 Junct 30, follow A376 to Clyst St Mary then A3052 to Newton Poppleford, then B3178 and follow signposts to Ladram Bay.

Open: 14th March - 2nd November.

Site: 🏪 🅰🅿 **Payment:** 💷 ☼ **Leisure:** 🎵 ▶ ♻ ♜ 🎣 **Children:** 🛝 ⛰ **Catering:** ✕ 🍴
Park: 🐾 🎵 🚻 📺 🏧 🌳 **Touring:** 🚰 🔌 🚿 🎵

SALCOMBE, Devon   Map ref 1C3   SatNav TQ7 3DY

Bolberry House Farm Caravan & Camping

Bolberry, Malborough, Kingsbridge TQ7 3DY
T: (01548) 561251 **E:** enquiries@bolberryparks.co.uk
W: www.bolberryparks.co.uk

🚐 (20)	
🚍 (20)	
⛺ (50)	
🏠 (10)	

70 touring pitches

Friendly family-run park between sailing paradise of Salcombe and Hope Cove (old fishing village). Peaceful, mostly level and good facilities. Children's play area. Good access to coastal footpaths. Sandy beaches nearby. Overnight holding area available. Please contact us for prices. **Directions:** A381 from Totnes, ringroad Kingsbridge to Salcombe. At Malborough sharp right through village, signs to Bolberry approx 1m. Do not follow Sat Nav from Totnes. **Open:** Easter to October.

Site: 🅰🅿 **Payment:** ☼ **Leisure:** 🎿 🎵 ▶ ♻ **Children:** 🛝 ⛰ **Catering:** 🍴 **Park:** 🐾 🚻 📺 🏧 🌳
Touring: 🚰 🔌

Need more information?

Visit our new 2014 guide websites for detailed information, up-to-date availability and to book your accommodation online. Includes over 20,000 places to stay, all of them star rated.

www.visitor-guides.co.uk

2014 Official Tourist Board Guides

SHALDON, Devon   Map ref 1D2

SatNav TQ14 0BG

(20)	£16.00-£40.00
(20)	£16.00-£40.00
(200)	£16.00-£26.00
(29)	£127.00-£869.00
(22)	£249.00-£795.00

SPECIAL PROMOTIONS
Please contact us for
special offers.

Coast View Holiday Park

Torquay Road, Shaldon, Teignmouth TQ14 0BG
T: (01626) 818350 **E:** holidays@coastview.co.uk
W: www.coastview.co.uk **£ BOOK ONLINE**

Coast View is situated just a stroll away from the pretty village and beaches of Shaldon and a stones throw away from the traditional seaside town, Teignmouth. Offering self catering chalets and caravans along with camping and top class facilities, you have all you need for a great holiday.

Directions: A38 from Exeter, A380 towards Torquay, A381 Teignmouth turnoff, right at the lights over Shaldon bridge, proceed up hill, we are on the right.

Open: April to October.

Site: 🏠 **Payment:** 💳 € ☼ **Leisure:** ♪ ⚲ ☂ **Children:** 🛝 ⚮ **Catering:** ✗ 🍴 **Park:** 🐕 🎵 ▦ ▣ 🛢 🚿 **Touring:** 🚻 🚽 🚐

TAVISTOCK, Devon   Map ref 1C2

SatNav PL19 9LS

(40)	£14.20-£23.40
(40)	£14.20-£23.40
(40)	£14.20-£23.40
(1)	£345.00-£570.00
(13)	£280.00-£510.00

125 touring pitches

Harford Bridge Holiday Park

Peter Tavy, Tavistock, Devon PL19 9LS
T: (01822) 810349 **F:** (01822) 810028 **E:** stay@harfordbridge.co.uk
W: www.harfordbridge.co.uk **£ BOOK ONLINE**

Beautiful park set in Dartmoor beside the River Tavy offering riverside and other spacious pitches. A little over two miles from the historic market town of Tavistock beside the River Tavy. The park offers 120 level, spacious camping and caravan pitches. For motor homes and large touring caravans, there are fully serviced, all-weather hardstand pitches and a motor home service point.

Directions: M5 onto A30 to Sourton Cross; take A386 Tavistock Road. 2 miles north of Tavistock take Peter Tavy turn off, entrance 200 yards on left.

Open: 15th March - 14th November.

Site: ⛺🅿 **Payment:** 💳 ☼ **Leisure:** ♪ ▸ ∪ ⚲ ⚲ **Children:** 🛝 ⚮ **Park:** 🐕 ▦ ▣ 🛢 🚿 **Touring:** 🚻 🚽 🚐 ♪

TAVISTOCK, Devon Map ref 1C2

SatNav PL19 9JZ

HOLIDAY, TOURING & CAMPING PARK

🚐	(15)	£14.00-£19.00
🚎	(15)	£14.00-£19.00
⛺	(15)	£14.00-£19.00
🏠	(12)	£195.00-£511.00

45 touring pitches

SPECIAL PROMOTIONS
Off peak weekly camping rate for over 55's camping. A small party discount on self-catering weekly bookings available.

Langstone Manor Holiday Park

Moortown, Tavistock, Devon PL19 9JZ
T: (01822) 613371 **F:** (01822) 613371 **E:** jane@langstonemanor.co.uk
W: www.langstonemanor.co.uk

Fantastic location with direct access onto moor, offering great walks straight from the park. Peaceful site with beautiful views of the surrounding moorland. Level pitches, some hardstanding with brand new four star facilities. Camping pods also available. The Langstone Bar provides evening meals. A warm welcome awaits!

Directions: Take the B3357 Princetown road from Tavistock. After approx 1.5 miles, turn right at x-roads, go over cattle grid, up hill, left following signs.

Open: March 15th to November 15th.

Site: 🏕 **Payment:** 💳 ☀ **Leisure:** ♿ ♪ ▶ ∪ 🎣 **Children:** 🎠 🎪 **Catering:** ✕ **Park:** 🐕 🚐 🛢 🗄 🛍 📷
Touring: 🚽 🚿 🔌 ♫

TOTNES, Devon Map ref 1D2

SatNav TQ9 6PU

TOURING & CAMPING PARK

🚐	£12.00-£20.50
🚎	£12.00-£20.50
⛺	£12.00-£20.50

85 touring pitches

Broadleigh Farm Park

Coombe House Lane, Stoke Gabriel, Totnes TQ9 6PU
T: (01803) 782110 **E:** enquiries@broadleighfarm.co.uk
W: www.broadleighfarm.co.uk

Situated in beautiful South Hams village of Stoke Gabriel, close to River Dart and Torbay's wonderful beaches. Local walks. Bus stop at end of lane. Dartmoor within easy reach. Overnight holding area available. **Directions:** Please visit our website for directions. **Open:** Early March - November 15th for non-caravan club members. All year for caravan club members.

Site: 🏕🅿 **Payment:** 💳 ☀ **Leisure:** ♪ ▶ ∪ **Children:** 🎠 **Park:** 🐕 🚐 🛢 🛍 📷 **Touring:** 🚽 🔌 ♫

Win amazing prizes, every month...

Visit our new 2014 guide websites for detailed information, up-to-date availability and to book your accommodation online. Includes over 20,000 places to stay, all of them star rated.

Enter our monthly competition at www.visitor-guides.co.uk/prizes

WOODBURY, Devon   *Map ref 1D2*   *SatNav EX5 1HA*

HOLIDAY, TOURING & CAMPING PARK

🚐	£12.00-£25.00
🚍	£12.00-£25.00
⛺	£12.00-£25.00
🏠 (15)	£250.00-£700.00

46 touring pitches

Castle Brake Holiday Park

Castle Lane, Woodbury, Exeter EX5 1HA
T: (01395) 232431 **E:** reception@castlebrake.co.uk
W: www.castlebrake.co.uk

Castle Brake is situated 1.5 miles from the village of Woodbury in the idyllic setting of Woodbury Common. It is a short drive to the Jurassic Coast beaches at Exmouth, Budleigh Salterton & Sidmouth or the city of Exeter.

Directions: From M5 Jct 30 follow A3052 to Halfway Inn. Turn right onto B3180. Turn right for Woodbury at the sign for Caravan Sites, 500 yards to Castle Brake.

Open: 1st March - 30th November.

Site: 🏕 **Payment:** 💷 ☀ **Leisure:** 🎣 ⚓ ∪ **Children:** 🐎 ⛰ **Catering:** ✕ 🛒 **Park:** 🐕 🚮 🗎 🛁 🛎 **Touring:** 🚰 🚽 🔌

ALDERHOLT, Dorset   *Map ref 2B3*   *SatNav SP6 3EG*

TOURING & CAMPING PARK

🚐 (35)	£18.00-£27.00
🚍 (35)	£18.00-£27.00
⛺ (50)	£14.00-£29.00
🛖 (1)	£36.00-£39.00

100 touring pitches

Hill Cottage Farm Camping and Caravan Park

Sandleheath Road, Alderholt, Fordingbridge, Hants SP6 3EG
T: (01425) 650513 **F:** (01425) 652339 **E:** hillcottagefarmcaravansite@supanet.com
W: www.hillcottagefarmcampingandcaravanpark.co.uk

Regional winners for South East England 2012 Top 100 Sites (Practical Caravan). Fully serviced pitches. Edge of New Forest, Dorset/Hants border. Large camping field. Rallies welcome. 5 star AA pennant. Overnight holding area available. **Directions:** From Fordingbridge take B3078 to Alderholt for 2 miles. On sharp left hand bend, take a right. We are 0.5 miles on left. **Open:** March to November.

Payment: 💷 ☀ **Leisure:** ♿ 🎣 ∪ 🎯 **Children:** 🐎 ⛰ **Catering:** 🛒 **Park:** 🐕 🚮 🗎 🛁 🛎 **Touring:** 🚰 🚽 🔌 🎏

Book your accommodation online

Visit our new 2014 guide websites for detailed information, up-to-date availability and to book your accommodation online. Includes over 20,000 places to stay, all of them star rated.

www.visitor-guides.co.uk

BLANDFORD FORUM, Dorset   *Map ref 2B3*   SatNav DT11 9AD

🚐	(90)	£14.00-£22.00
🚏	(10)	£14.00-£22.00
⛺	(25)	£14.00-£22.00

125 touring pitches

Inside Park

Fairmile Road, Blandford Forum DT11 9AD
T: (01258) 453719   **E:** mail@theinsidepark.co.uk
W: www.theinsidepark.co.uk   **£ BOOK ONLINE**

Secluded park and woodland with facilities, built into 18th century stable and coach house. Ideal location for touring the county. 1.5 miles south west of Blandford on road to Winterborne Stickland. Country walks, cycling and wildlife. **Directions:** Take Blandford St Mary exit at junction of A350/A354, proceed 1.5 miles SW of Blandford Forum on Fairmile Road. OS Ref: ST 864 052. **Open:** April to October.

Payment: 💷 ☼ **Leisure:** 🎣 🏊 ⛳ ✎ **Children:** 🎠 ⚠ **Catering:** 🍴 **Park:** 🐕 📶 🏪 🛒 **Touring:** 🔌 🚰 🚮

BOURNEMOUTH, Dorset   *Map ref 2B3*   SatNav BH23 2PQ

🚐	(41)
🚏	(41)
🏠	(75)

41 touring pitches

Meadowbank Holidays

Stour Way, Christchurch BH23 2PQ
T: (01202) 483597   **F:** (01202) 483878   **E:** enquiries@meadowbank-holidays.co.uk
W: www.meadowbank-holidays.co.uk

Meadowbank Holidays operate Bournemouth's closest holiday caravan and touring park. We are superbly located on the beautiful River Stour and provide a wonderful relaxing environment for a peaceful, carefree holiday or break. Visit the superb local beaches, New Forest, the famous Jurassic Coast, the Isle of Wight and the lovely town of Christchurch. Please contact us for prices. **Directions:** Please see website or contact us for directions. **Open:** March to October.

Site: ⛺🅿 **Payment:** 💷 ☼ **Leisure:** 🎣 🏊 ⛳ ✎ **Children:** 🎠 ⚠ **Catering:** 🍴 **Park:** 🐕 📶 🏪 🛒 **Touring:** 🔌 🚰 🚮 🎵

BRIDPORT, Dorset   *Map ref 2A3*   SatNav DT6 6AR

🚐		£15.90-£30.50
🚏		£15.90-£30.50
⛺	(80)	£13.70-£25.40
🏠	(21)	£315.00-£680.00

120 touring pitches

Highlands End Holiday Park

Eype, Bridport, Dorset DT6 6AR
T: (01308) 422139   **F:** (01308) 425672   **E:** holidays@wdlh.co.uk
W: www.wdlh.co.uk   **£ BOOK ONLINE**

This family run, 5 star park has all you will need for your relaxing break away. Being just 500 metres from the lovely unspoiled Eype Beach; Highlands End is at cliff top height with outstanding panoramic views over Lyme Bay and surroundings. **Directions:** On approaching Bridport follow the A35 and take the turning signposted Eype. Pass a service area and continue until you see the park entrance. **Open:** March to November.

Site: 📶 ⛺🅿 **Payment:** 💷 ☼ **Leisure:** 🏊 ♥ ✎ 🎣 ♦ **Children:** 🎠 ⚠ **Catering:** ✕ 🍴 **Park:** 🐕 📶 🏪 **Touring:** 🔌 🚰 🚮 🎵

BRIDPORT, Dorset   *Map ref 2A3*   SatNav DT6 6QL

🚐	(300)	£14.00-£31.00
🚏	(300)	£14.00-£31.00
⛺	(300)	£14.00-£28.00

300 touring pitches

Manor Farm Holiday Centre

The Street, Charmouth, Bridport, Dorset DT6 6QL
T: (01297) 560226   **F:** 01297 560429   **E:** enquiries@manorfarmholidaycentre.co.uk
W: www.manorfarmholidaycentre.co.uk

Large, open site in an Area of Outstanding Natural Beauty, Manor Farm is located within 10 minutes level walk from the beach. We accept tents, caravans, motor caravans, and have electric, hard standing and all weather pitches, toilets, showers, laundrette, swimming pool, bar and children's play area. **Directions:** Come into Charmouth, site 0.75 miles on right. **Open:** All Year.

Site: 📶 ⛺🅿 **Payment:** 💷 **Leisure:** ♥ ✎ 🎣 ♦ **Children:** 🎠 ⚠ **Catering:** ✕ 🍴 **Park:** 🐕 🎵 🏪 📶 🛒 **Touring:** 🔌 🚰 🚮 🎵

CHARMOUTH, Dorset Map ref 1D2 — SatNav DT6 6QS

Seadown Holiday Park
Bridge Road, Charmouth, Bridport DT6 6QS
T: (01297) 560154 **F:** (01297) 561130 **E:** bookings@seadownholidaypark.co.uk
W: www.seadowncaravanpark.co.uk

🚐	(40)	£16.00-£22.00
🚎	(10)	£16.00-£22.00
⛺	(10)	£16.00-£22.00
🏠		£455.00-£935.00
🚃	(68)	£175.00-£635.00

60 touring pitches

SPECIAL PROMOTIONS
Please see website for details.

Quiet, family-run park which runs alongside the River Char. It has it's own direct access to Charmouth's famous fossil beach, which is situated on the World Heritage Coastline. Overnight holding area available.

Directions: Please see website for directions.   **Open:** Mid-March to end of October.

Payment: 💷 ☀ **Leisure:** 🎣 ♪ ▶ ∪ ⚲ **Children:** 🛝 ⛏ **Catering:** 🍴 **Park:** 🐕 🔲 ⬛ 🎪 **Touring:** 🚰 🗑 🔌 🎣

DORCHESTER, Dorset Map ref 2B3 — SatNav DT2 7TR

Giants Head Caravan & Camping Park
Old Sherborne Road, Cerne Abbas, Dorchester, Dorset DT2 7TR
T: (01300) 341242 **E:** holidays@giantshead.co.uk
W: www.giantshead.co.uk **£ BOOK ONLINE**

🚐	(50)	£8.00-£18.00
🚎	(50)	£8.00-£18.00
⛺	(50)	£8.00-£18.00
🚃	(3)	£165.00-£275.00

50 touring pitches

A quiet site with wonderful views of Dorset Downs and the Blackmoor Vale. 2 miles north-east of Cerne Abbas, 3 miles south of Middlemarsh, 8 miles from Dorchester. Overnight holding area available. **Directions:** On the Old Sherborne Road between Dorchester and Sherborne, 2 miles north of Cerne Abbas. **Open:** All year.

Payment: ☀ **Leisure:** 🎣 ♪ ▶ ∪ **Children:** 🛝 **Park:** 🐕 🔲 🎪 **Touring:** 🚰 🗑 🔌

EYPE, Dorset Map ref 1D2 — SatNav DT6 6AL

Eype House Caravan Park Ltd
Eype, Bridport, Dorset DT6 6AL
T: (01308) 424903 **F:** (01308) 424903 **E:** enquiries@eypehouse.co.uk
W: www.eypehouse.co.uk

🚎	(20)	£15.00-£23.00
⛺	(20)	£15.00-£23.00
🏠	(1)	£33.00-£43.00
🚃	(35)	£235.00-£550.00

20 touring pitches

Small, quiet site, 200 yards from the beach on the Jurassic Coast in Area of Outstanding Natural Beauty. **Directions:** From A35 turn to Eype Take 3rd turn, sign Lower Eype and to the sea, follow lane past pub and Hotel, Caravan Park on right. **Open:** Easter to October.

Site: ⛺🅿 **Payment:** ☀ **Leisure:** ♪ **Children:** 🛝 **Catering:** 🍴 **Park:** 🐕 🔲 ⬛ 🎪 **Touring:** 🚰 🗑

LYME REGIS, *Dorset*   Map ref 1D2

SatNav TA20 4NL

Crafty Camping

Woodland Workshop, Yonder Hill, Holditch, Dorset TA20 4NL
T: (01460) 221102 **E:** enquiries@mallinson.co.uk
W: www.mallinson.co.uk **£ BOOK ONLINE**

SPECIAL PROMOTIONS
Yurts, Tipi, Shepherds hut & Bell tents Start from £70/night low season. 'Have a go' woodworking courses start at £30 per person. Please see website for all courses, pricing and availability.

Luxury 'glamping' in an adults-only, hand-crafted environment. Stay with us and our cosy bell tents and beautiful yurts, tipi and shepherds hut can be your home-from-home. Our Wonderful 'glamping' facilities include a Woodland Workshop, where Woodworking Courses can be booked, woodland showers, a sauna yurt and a communal yurt with games and craft library, while the 'Out of Africa' kitchen and pizza oven further help ensure a restful holiday with a difference. We offer a peaceful woodland setting in Dorset, near to the Jurassic Coast 'World Heritage Site' and perfect for a short break or longer holiday. We're close to Devon and Somerset too - so we make a great base for exploring all three counties. Please see website for more details. Please Contact for prices.

Directions: Google maps link and pdf directions on the information page of our website.   **Open:** All year.

Payment: 💷 **Leisure:** 🚴 🎣 🔍 **Property:** 🖥 **Catering:** 🍖

WAREHAM, *Dorset*   Map ref 2B3

SatNav BH20 5PU

Durdle Door Holiday Park

West Lulworth, Wareham BH20 5PU
T: (01929) 400200 **F:** (01929) 400260 **E:** durdle.door@lulworth.com
W: www.lulworth.com **£ BOOK ONLINE**

🚐 (58)	£18.00-£46.00
🚏 (16)	£18.00-£46.00
⛺ (50)	£15.00-£40.00
🛖 (19)	£295.00-£800.00
108 touring pitches

SPECIAL PROMOTIONS
Please see website for further details.

Situated between Weymouth & Swanage on the Jurassic Coast. The park has direct access to the South West Coast Path, beaches and is surrounded by stunning countryside. Open & woodland camping areas; camping pods; electric & fully serviced pitches; seafront pitches available for tourers & motorhomes. Holiday homes available. Close to the picturesque Lulworth Cove & many other family attractions.

Directions: Please see website for details.   **Open:** 1st March to 31st October.

Site: 🏢 🅰🅿 **Payment:** 💷 ☀ **Leisure:** ♻ **Children:** 🛝 **Catering:** ✕ 🍖 **Park:** 🐴 🎵 📺 📻 🛎 **Touring:** 🚰 🔌 🚿 🎵

WAREHAM, Dorset Map ref 2B3   SatNav BH20 5AZ

The Lookout Holiday Park

Corfe Road, Stoborough, Wareham BH20 5AZ
T: (01929) 552546 **F:** (01929) 556662 **E:** lookout@caravan-sites.co.uk
W: www.thelookoutholidaypark.co.uk

⊟ (126)	£16.00-£28.00
⊞	£15.00-£29.50
⚠ (24)	£11.00-£25.00
⊡ (37)	£199.00-£657.00
140 touring pitches	

This small holiday park is situated 1 mile south of Wareham in the village of Stoborough on A351. At the gateway to the beautiful Purbeck Hills. New Camping Pods. Check out our new website for details.

Directions: Take the A351 from Poole to Wareham, go through Wareham town, crossing the river Frome, pass through Stoborough village and we are on the left.

Open: Touring park 23rd March. Static caravan site - All year.

Payment: ⊞ ☀ **Leisure:** ♿ ♪ ∪ ♦ **Children:** ⛱ ⚠ **Catering:** ⛽ **Park:** ▱ ▤ ▦ ⸙ **Touring:** ⚑ ⟳ ⌨

WOOL, Dorset Map ref 2B3   SatNav BH20 6HG

Whitemead Caravan Park

East Burton Road, Wool, Wareham BH20 6HG
T: (01929) 462241 **F:** (01929) 462241 **E:** whitemeadcp@aol.com
W: www.whitemeadcaravanpark.co.uk

⊟ (95)	£15.00-£22.50
⊞ (95)	£15.00-£22.50
⚠ (95)	£12.00-£19.50
95 touring pitches	

Within easy reach of beaches and beautiful countryside, this friendly site is maintained to a high standard of cleanliness. Turn west off the A352 near Wool level crossing. Overnight holding area available. **Directions:** Turn west off A352, Wareham-Dorchester Road, along East Burton Road, by Wool level crossing. We are along this road on the right. **Open:** 15th March to 31st October.

Payment: ⊞ ☀ **Leisure:** ♪ ♦ **Children:** ⚠ **Catering:** ⛽ **Park:** 🐕 ▤ ▦ ⸙ **Touring:** ⚑ ⟳ ⌨

LYDNEY, Gloucestershire Map ref 2A1   SatNav GL15 4LA

Whitemead Forest Park

Whitemead Forest Park, Parkend, Lydney, Gloucestershire GL15 4LA
T: (0845) 345 3425 **F:** 01594 564174 **E:** enquiries@csmaclubretreats.co.uk
W: www.whitemead.co.uk **£ BOOK ONLINE**

⊟ (110)	£26.00-£53.00
⚠ (110)	£25.00-£35.00
⌂ (29)	£476.00-£1260.00

With a range of woodland lodges, log cabins, and apartments, as well as camping and caravanning pitches in the heart of the forest, you can enjoy the free indoor pool, gym, sauna and Jacuzzis; join in with some great activities and entertainment; explore the acres of ancient woodland right on your doorstep, or simply curl up in your cabin and relax. **Directions:** (M5 headling South) Leave at J11 (signposted Gloucester). Take the A40 and then the A48 towards Lydney. **Open:** 20th January, throughout 2014.

Site: ⚠🅿 **Payment:** ⊞ **Leisure:** ♪ ▸ ♦ ☁ **Children:** ⛱ ⚠ **Catering:** ✕ ⛽ **Park:** ♬ ▱ ▤ ▦ ⸙ **Touring:** ⚑ ⟳ ⌨

BREAN, Somerset   Map ref 1D1 · SatNav TA8 2SE

Northam Farm Holiday Park

South Road, Brean TA8 2SE
T: (01278) 751244 **E:** stay@northamfarm.co.uk
W: www.northamfarm.co.uk

(350)	£9.20-£27.00
(350)	£11.60-£27.00
(150)	£9.20-£23.00

450 touring pitches

An attractive touring park, situated 200m from a sandy beach. 30-acre park offering children's outdoor play areas, fishing lake, diner, take-away, mini-supermarket, launderette, dog walks, hardstanding and grass pitches. Please contact us for updated prices. **Directions:** M5 jct 22. Follow signs to Burnham-on-Sea. Continue through Brean and Northam Farm is on the right, 0.5 miles past Brean Leisure Park. **Open:** March to October.

Site: ▲🏕 **Payment:** 💷 ☼ **Leisure:** ♿ ♪ ► ♆ **Children:** 🎠 ⚒ **Catering:** ✕ ⛽ **Park:** 🐕 🔲 📖 🌿 **Touring:** 🚰 ♻ 🚿 🎵

CROWCOMBE, Somerset   Map ref 1D1 · SatNav TA4 4AW

Quantock Orchard Caravan Park

Flaxpool, Crowcombe, Taunton, Somerset TA4 4AW
T: (01984) 618618 **F:** (01984) 618618 **E:** member@flaxpool.freeserve.co.uk
W: www.quantock-orchard.co.uk

(31)	£14.00-£29.00
(19)	£14.00-£29.00
(19)	£14.00-£29.00
(9)	£35.00-£85.00

68 touring pitches

Award-winning campsite with superb panoramic views of the Quantock Hills; open all year, fully heated toilet and shower block; tastefully landscaped with several stunning holiday homes for hire. **Directions:** On the A358 between Williton and Taunton. Behind Flaxpool Garage. **Open:** All year.

Payment: 💷 ☼ **Leisure:** ♿ ♪ ► ♆ ⚲ ⚵ **Children:** 🎠 ⚒ **Catering:** ⛽ **Park:** 🐕 🔲 📖 🌿 **Touring:** 🚰 ♻ 🚿 🎵

PORLOCK, Somerset   Map ref 1D1 · SatNav TA24 8HT

Burrowhayes Farm Caravan & Camping Site & Riding Stables

West Luccombe, Porlock, Minehead TA24 8HT
T: (01643) 862463 **E:** info@burrowhayes.co.uk
W: www.burrowhayes.co.uk

(54)	£16.00-£23.00
(54)	£16.00-£23.00
(66)	£13.00-£20.50
(19)	£190.00-£450.00

120 touring pitches

Popular family site in delightful National Trust setting on Exmoor, just 2 miles from the Coast. Surrounding moors and woods provide a walker's paradise. Children can play and explore safely. Riding stables offer pony-trekking for all abilities. Heated shower block with disabled and baby-changing facilities, laundrette and pot wash.

Directions: From Minehead, A39 towards Porlock; 1st left after Allerford to Horner and West Luccombe; Burrowhayes is 0.25 miles along on right before hump-backed bridge.

Open: Mid-March to end of October.

Payment: 💷 ☼ **Leisure:** ♿ ♪ ♆ **Catering:** ⛽ **Park:** 🐕 🔲 📖 🌿 **Touring:** 🚰 ♻ 🚿 🎵

PORLOCK, Somerset   Map ref 1D1

SatNav TA24 8ND

Porlock Caravan Park
High Bank, Porlock TA24 8ND
T: (01643) 862269 **F:** (01643) 862269 **E:** info@porlockcaravanpark.co.uk
W: www.porlockcaravanpark.co.uk

🚐 (40)
🚕 (14)
🏕 (7)
40 touring pitches

Delightful, family run, award winning park situated within walking distance of quaint village of Porlock. Luxury holiday homes for hire. Touring caravans, motor homes and tents welcome. Spotless facilities. Prices on Application. **Directions:** A39 from Minehead, in Porlock village take B3225 to Porlock Weir, site signposted. **Open:** March to October.

Payment: 🏧 ☼ **Leisure:** ♪ ∪ **Park:** 🐕 🚮 📺 ⛽ ℝ **Touring:** 🚿 ⊙ 💧

TAUNTON, Somerset   Map ref 1D1

SatNav TA3 5NW

Ashe Farm Caravan and Campsite
Ashe Farm Caravan and Campsite, Thornfalcon, Taunton TA3 5NW
T: (01823) 443764 **E:** info@ashefarm.co.uk
W: www.ashefarm.co.uk

🚐 (20)   £12.00-£15.00
🚕 (10)   £12.00-£15.00
🏕 (10)   £12.00-£14.00
🏠 (3)   £170.00-£220.00
30 touring pitches

Quiet farm site, lovely views, easy access. Central for touring. Easy reach coast and hills. Family run and informal. **Directions:** Leave M5 at Jnt 25, take A358 eastwards for 2.5 miles, turn right at Nags Head pub towards West Hatch. Site 0.25 miles on RHS. **Open:** 1st April to 31st October.

Payment: ☼ **Leisure:** ♪ ⏵ ∪ ⚲ **Children:** 🛝 ⛰ **Park:** 🐕 📺 ℝ **Touring:** 🚿 ⊙

WATERROW, Somerset   Map ref 1D1

SatNav TA4 2AZ

Waterrow Touring Park
Wiveliscombe, Nr Taunton, Somerset TA4 2AZ
T: (01984) 623464 **E:** info@waterrowpark.co.uk
W: www.waterrowpark.co.uk **£ BOOK ONLINE**

🚐 (38)   £16.00-£27.00
🚕 (38)   £16.00-£27.00
🏕 (8)   £16.00-£27.00
46 touring pitches

Attractively landscaped park with good access, situated in beautiful river valley. All pitches are level with hardstanding or grass plus electric. Ideal base from which to explore this unspoilt area. Elizabethan cottage also for rent. Adults only. **Directions:** M5 Junction 25, A358 round Taunton. B3227 through Wiveliscombe to Waterrow. Park 500 yds after Rock Inn. Do not use Sat Nav directions. **Open:** All year.

Payment: 🏧 ☼ **Leisure:** ♪ ⏵ ∪ **Park:** 🐕 🚮 📺 ⛽ ℝ **Touring:** 🚿 ⊙ 💧 ♫

WESTON-SUPER-MARE, Somerset   Map ref 1D1

SatNav BS22 9UJ

Country View Holiday Park
29 Sand Road, Sand Bay, Weston-super-Mare BS22 9UJ
T: (01934) 627595 **E:** info@cvhp.co.uk
W: www.cvhp.co.uk

🚐 (90)
🚕 (90)
🏕 (30)
120 touring pitches

Country View is surrounded by countryside and just 200yds from Sand Bay Beach. Heated pool, bar, shop and children's play area. Fantastic toilet and shower facilities. Holiday Homes for sale. Please contact us for prices. **Directions:** Exit 21 of M5, follow signs for Sand Bay along Queensway into Lower Norton Lane, take right into Sand Road. **Open:** March to January.

Site: 🏠 **Payment:** 🏧 ☼ **Leisure:** ⚲ ♪ ⏵ ∪ ⚲ ⚓ **Children:** 🛝 ⛰ **Catering:** 🍴 **Park:** 🐕 📺 ⛽ ℝ
Touring: 🚿 ⊙ 💧 ♫

WESTON-SUPER-MARE, Somerset   Map ref 1D1

SatNav BS24 0JQ

Dulhorn Farm Holiday Park

Weston Road, Lympsham, Weston Super Mare, Somerset BS24 0JQ
T: (01934) 750298 **F:** (01934) 750913 **E:** dfhp@btconnect.com
W: www.dulhornfarmholidaypark.co.uk

🚐 (100)	£14.00-£28.00
🚍 (10)	£14.00-£28.00
⛺ (60)	£8.00-£28.00
🏠 (4)	£160.00-£420.00
🏚 (1)	£202.00-£420.00
100 touring pitches	

A familly site on a working farm set in the countryside. Between Weston-S-M and Burnham on Sea. Ideal for touring. Close to Cheddar Gorge & Quantock Hills. Secure caravan storage available. S/C Cottages available. Seasonal Pitches and Statics. **Directions:** M5 Junction 22, then North on A38, at next roundabout A370 towards Weston-Super-Mare, 1.5 miles on left. **Open:** March to October.

Site: ⛺🅿 **Payment:** 💷 ☼ **Leisure:** ♪ ▶ ∪ 🎣 **Children:** 🛝 ⚠ **Catering:** 🍴 **Park:** 🐕 🖥 🖨 🏧 **Touring:** 🚽 🚿 🔌 ♨

WINSFORD, Somerset   Map ref 1D1

SatNav TA24 7JL

Halse Farm Caravan & Tent Park

Halse Farm Caravan & Tent Park, Winsford, Exmoor, Somerset TA24 7JL
T: (01643) 851259 **E:** brit@halsefarm.co.uk
W: www.halsefarm.co.uk

🚐 (22)	£14.00-£19.00
🚍 (22)	£14.00-£19.00
⛺ (22)	£14.00-£19.00
44 touring pitches	

Exmoor National Park, small, peaceful, working farm with spectacular views. Walkers and country lovers paradise. David Bellamy Gold Conservation Award. One mile to Winsford with shop, thatched pub and tea gardens. Overnight holding area available. **Directions:** Signposted from A396. In Winsford turn left and bear left past Royal Oak Inn. One mile up hill. Entrance immediately after cattle grid on left. **Open:** 14th March to 31st October.

Site: ⛺🅿 **Payment:** 💷 **Children:** 🛝 ⚠ **Park:** 🐕 🖥 🖨 🏧 **Touring:** 🚽 ♨

LACOCK, Wiltshire   Map ref 2B2

SatNav SN15 2LP

Piccadilly Caravan Park Ltd

Folly Lane (West), Lacock, Chippenham SN15 2LP
T: (01249) 730260 **E:** piccadillylacock@aol.com

🚐 (39)	£18.00-£20.00
🚍 (39)	£18.00-£20.00
⛺ (4)	£18.00-£23.50
43 touring pitches	

This peaceful site stands in countryside 0.5 miles from the historic National Trust village of Lacock. The site is well-screened and beautifully-maintained. An ideal location for exploring the west country. **Directions:** Turn off A350 between Chippenham and Melksham, into Folly Lane West signposted Gastard and with Caravan symbol. **Open:** April to October.

Payment: ☼ **Leisure:** ♪ **Children:** ⚠ **Park:** 🐕 🖥 🏧 🏧 **Touring:** 🚽 🚿 ♨

SALISBURY, Wiltshire   Map ref 2B3

SatNav SP5 4LP

Summerlands Caravan Park

College Farm, Rockbourne Road, Coombe Bissett, Salisbury SP5 4LP
T: (01722) 718259 **E:** enquiries@summerlandscaravanpark.co.uk
W: www.summerlandscaravanpark.co.uk

🚐 (20)	£13.50-£18.00
🚍 (20)	£13.50-£18.00
⛺ (28)	£13.50-£18.00
28 touring pitches	

A small family run campsite, ideal for those seeking a quiet place for their caravan, motorhome or tent, which is off the beaten track. The site affords level grass pitches, peace and tranquillity, with superb panoramic views. **Directions:** Off the A354 (Salisbury to Blandford Road) signposted towards Rockbourne, south of Coombe Bissett. After 300m turn left onto track and follow signs. **Open:** 1st April - 31st October.

Site: ⛺🅿 **Payment:** ☼ **Children:** 🛝 **Park:** 🐕 🏧 **Touring:** 🚽 ♨

South East

Miles of delightful coastline and countryside, the historic cities of Oxford and Winchester, and the naval centres of Portsmouth and Southampton make the South East one of the country's most popular areas to visit. The region boasts a plethora of some of the best attractions and outdoor pursuits anywhere in the country. Come rain or shine, there are endless options when you're looking for things to do. And once you've toured the mainland you can take a ferry trip to the Isle of Wight and explore.

Highlights

Blenheim Palace

Standing in a romantic park created by 'Capability' Brown, Blenheim Palace was presented to John Churchill, first Duke of Marlborough, in recognition of his victory in 1704 over French and Bavarian troops.

Canterbury Cathedral

The cathedral exhibits Romanesque and Gothic architecture, and is the seat of the Church of England. St Martin's Church and St Augustine's Abbey were founded during the early stages of Christianity among Anglo-Saxons.

Chilterns

The Chiltern Hills stretch from the River Thames in Oxfordshire to Hitchin in Hertfordshire and are nationally-protected as some of the finest countryside in the UK. They're a fantastic place to explore all year round.

New Forest

The New Forest was England's first official visitor destination, named by William the Conqueror way back in 1079AD. Over 3000 ponies, 3000 cattle and 2500 deer wander freely around this National Park.

Oxford

The world famous city of Oxford, with its university, colleges, and library, has always been at the forefront of achievement – shaping so many national leaders, scientists, writers and philosophers.

South Downs

Combining a biodiverse landscape with bustling towns and villages, the South Downs National Park is recognised as an area of outstanding beauty.

White Cliffs of Dover

Known as the Garden of England, Kent has an extensive and varied coastline, encompassing some stunning landscapes, including the White Cliffs of Dover.

Winchester

Winchester is a historic city and former capital city of England. Its major landmark is Winchester Cathedral, one of the largest in Europe, with the distinction of having the longest nave and overall length of all Gothic cathedrals in Europe.

Windsor

Windsor is home to two of the UK's Top 20 visitor attractions – Windsor Castle and Legoland Windsor. It also feature boat trips on the River Thames and romantic horse-drawn carriage rides through Windsor Great Park.

SHOE REPAIRS

SHOE
REPAIRS
—
KEY
CUTTING
—
WATCH
REPAIRS

Café Mauresque

GAP

Coffee
Shop
&
Take
Away

Coffee
Shop

THE
CITY ARMS
INN

Cover
Designs

CASEY'S

GUY

TO LET

Blacks

JAEGER

CITY ARMS

FOOD Sr WED
12 -6
COFFEE

Editor's Picks

Take a guide with you

By booking a guided city tour you will discover things about places like Oxford or Windsor that you will never discover if you go it alone.

Climb aboard a boat trip

South East England is blessed with a multitude of picturesque waterways, and there's no better way to explore and relax than on an organised boat trip.

Raise a glass

As this region is one of the main hop-growing counties in the country, take a tour of the 300-year-old Shepherd Neame Brewery in Kent and sample their ales.

High speed action

If you want to experience the thrills of high speed action then head for Buckmore Park International Kart Circuit near Chatham in Kent where Lewis Hamilton learned his trade.

Step back in time

Discover the fascinating world of animals and plants from millions of years ago to the present day at Paradise Park in East Sussex.

Things to do

 Attractions with this sign participate in the Places of Interest Quality Assurance Scheme.

 Attractions with this sign participate in the Visitor Attraction Quality Assurance Scheme.

Both schemes recognise high standards in all aspects of the visitor experience (see page 7)

Entertainment & Culture

Beaulieu National Motor Museum
Hampshire SO42 7ZN
(01590) 612123
www.beaulieu.co.uk
Beaulieu featuring the world famous National Motor Museum, Palace House home of the Montagu family and Abbey Ruins containing an exhibition of monastic life.

City Sightseeing Windsor and Eton
Berkshire SL4 1NJ
(01708) 866000
www.city-sightseeing.com
Enjoy the dignified tranquillity of Windsor, including Windsor Castle, home of the British monarchy for centuries, and Eton College.

Dinosaur Isle
Sandown,
Isle of Wight PO36 8QA
(01983) 404344
www.dinosaurisle.com
In a spectacular pterosaur shaped building on Sandown's blue flag beach walk back through fossilised time and meet life sized replica dinosaurs.

Museum of English Rural Life
Reading, Berkshire RG1 5EX
(0118) 378 8660
www.merl.org.uk
MERL houses one of England's most fascinating collections relating to life and work in the countryside over the last 200 years.

REME Museum of Technology
Reading, Berkshire RG2 9NJ
(0118) 976 3375
www.rememuseum.org.uk
The museum shows the developing technology used by the Royal Electrical and Mechanical Engineers in maintaining and repairing the army's equipment since 1942.

Roald Dahl Museum and Story Centre
Great Missenden,
Buckinghamshire HP16 0AL
(01494) 892192
www.roalddahlmuseum.org
Where Roald Dahl (1916-1990) lived and wrote many of his well-loved books.

Family Fun

Aerial Extreme Milton Keynes
Buckinghamshire MK15 0DS
0845 652 1736
www.aerialextreme.co.uk/courses/willen-lake
Amaze yourself as you take each of the challenges head on.

Bekonscot Model Village and Railway
Beaconsfield,
Buckinghamshire HP9 2PL
(01494) 672919
www.bekonscot.com
Use your imagination in this unique world of make-believe that has delighted generations of visitors.

Blackgang Chine
Chale, Isle of Wight PO38 2HN
(01983) 730330
www.blackgangchine.com
Set in over 40 acres of spectacular cliff-top gardens.

Gulliver's Land
Milton Keynes,
Buckinghamshire MK15 0DT
(01908) 609001
www.gulliversfun.co.uk
Family theme park with 40 rides aimed at children between 2 and 12 years.

Go Ape! High Wire Forest Adventure - Bracknell
Berkshire RG12 7QW
0845 643 9215
www.goape.co.uk
Go Ape! and tackle a high-wire forest adventure course of rope bridges, Tarzan swings and zip slides up to 35 feet above the forest floor.

LEGOLAND® Windsor
Berkshire SL4 4AY
0870 504 0404
www.legoland.co.uk
With over 55 interactive rides and attractions, there's just too much to experience in one day!

The Look Out Discovery Centre
Bracknell, Berkshire RG12 7QW
(01344) 354400
www.bracknell-forest.gov.uk/be
A hands-on, interactive science exhibition with over 80 exhibits, set in 1,000 hectares of Crown woodland.

Thorpe Park
Chertsey, Surrey KT16 8PN
0871 663 1673
www.thorpepark.com
New in 2010, prepare for SAW Alive, the world's most extreme live action horror maze.

Food & Drink

Denbies Wine Estate
Dorking, Surrey RH5 6AA
(01306) 876616
www.denbiesvineyard.co.uk
Established in 1986, Denbies Wine Estate is England's largest single estate vineyard with 265 acres of vines.

Heritage

1066 Battle Abbey and Battlefield
East Sussex TN33 0AD
(01424) 775705
www.english-heritage.org.uk/daysout/properties/1066-battle-of-hastings-abbey-and-battlefield/
An abbey founded by William the Conqueror on the site of the Battle of Hastings.

Bateman's
Etchingham,
East Sussex TN19 7DS
(01435) 882302
www.nationaltrust.org.uk/batemans/
A 17th century Ironmaster's house which was the home of Rudyard Kipling between 1902-35. His study and Rolls Royce can be seen. Garden with working watermill.

Blenheim Palace
Woodstock,
Oxfordshire OX20 1PX
(01993) 811091
www.blenheimpalace.com
Birthplace of Sir Winston Churchill and home to the Duke of Marlborough, Blenheim Palace, one of the finest baroque houses in England, is set in over 2,000 acres of landscaped gardens.

Brighton Pier
East Sussex BN2 1TW
(01273) 609361
www.brightonpier.co.uk
A Victorian pier with various food and drink outlets, fairground attractions and Palace of Fun arcade.

Chichester Cathedral
West Sussex PO19 1RP
(01243) 782595
www.chichestercathedral.org.uk
A magnificent Cathedral with treasures ranging from medieval stone carvings to world famous 20th century artworks.

Didcot Railway Centre
Oxfordshire OX11 7NJ
(01235) 817200
www.didcotrailwaycentre.org.uk
Living museum recreating the golden age of the Great Western Railway. Steam locomotives and trains, Brunel's broad gauge railway, engine shed and small relics museum.

Frogmore House
Windsor, Berkshire SL4 1NJ
(020) 7766 7305
www.royalcollection.org.uk
Late 17th century royal residence, particularly associated with Queen Charlotte and Queen Victoria.

Guildford Cathedral
Surrey GU2 7UP
(01483) 547860
www.guildford-cathedral.org
New Anglican Cathedral, the foundation stone of which was laid in 1936. Notable sandstone interior and marble floors. Restaurant and shops.

Hever Castle and Gardens
Edenbridge, Kent TN8 7NG
(01732) 865224
www.hevercastle.co.uk
Romantic 13th century moated castle, once Anne Boleyn's childhood home. Magnificently furnished interiors, spectacular award winning gardens. Miniature Model House Exhibition, Yew Maze, unique Splashing Water Maze.

Kent & East Sussex Railway
Tenterden, Kent TN30 6HE
(01580) 765155
www.kesr.org.uk
England's finest rural light railway enables visitors to experience travel and service from a bygone age aboard beautifully restored Victorian coaches and locomotives.

Loseley Park
Guildford, Surrey GU3 1HS
(01483) 405112
www.loseley-park.com
A beautiful Elizabethan mansion, is set in stunning gardens and parkland. Built in 1562 it has a fascinating history and contains a wealth of treasures.

Osborne House
East Cowes,
Isle of Wight PO32 6JX
(01983) 200022
www.english-heritage.org.uk/daysout/properties/osborne-house
Step into Queen Victoria's favourite country home and experience a world unchanged since the country's longest reigning monarch died here just over 100 years ago.

Oxford Castle Unlocked
Oxfordshire OX1 1AY
(01865) 260666
www.oxfordcastleunlocked.co.uk
For the first time in 1000 years, the secrets of Oxford Castle have been 'unlocked', revealing episodes of violence, executions, great escapes, betrayal and even romance. Visit Oxford Castle and uncover the secrets for yourself.

Petworth House and Park
West Sussex GU28 0AE
(01798) 342207
www.nationaltrust.org.uk/petworth
Discover the National Trust's finest art collection displayed in a magnificent 17th century mansion within a beautiful 700-acre park. Petworth House contains works by artists such as Van Dyck, Reynolds and Turner.

Portsmouth Historic Dockyard
Hampshire PO1 3LJ
(023) 9272 8060
www.historicdockyard.co.uk
Be a part of your history at Portsmouth Historic Dockyard.

Rochester Castle
Kent ME1 1SW
(01634) 335882
www.visitmedway.org/site/
attractions/rochester-castle-p44583
One of the finest keeps in England. Also the tallest, partly built on the Roman city wall. Good views from the battlements over the River Medway.

Shanklin Chine
Shanklin Isle of Wight PO37 6BW
(01983) 866432
www.shanklinchine.co.uk
Historic gorge with dramatic waterfalls and nature trail.

Spinnaker Tower
Portsmouth, Hampshire PO1 3TT
(023) 9285 7520
www.spinnakertower.co.uk
The Spinnaker Tower is a national icon. It is a striking viewing tower on the south coast offering the public spectacular views from three platforms.

The Historic Dockyard Chatham
Kent ME4 4TZ
(01634) 823807
www.thedockyard.co.uk
A unique, award-winning maritime heritage destination with a fantastic range of attractions, iconic buildings and historic ships to explore, plus a fabulous programme of touring exhibitions at No.1 Smithery.

Waddesdon Manor
Aylesbury,
Buckinghamshire HP18 0JH
(01296) 653226
www.waddesdon.org.uk
This National Trust property houses the Rothschild Collection of art treasures and wine cellars. It also features spectacular grounds with an aviary, parterre and woodland playground, licensed restaurants, gift and wine shops.

Windsor Castle
Berkshire SL4 1NJ
(020) 7766 7304
www.royalcollection.org.uk
The oldest and largest inhabited castle in the world and The Queen's favourite weekend home.

Nature & Wildlife

Arundel Wetland Centre
West Sussex BN18 9PB
(01903) 883355
www.wwt.org.uk/visit/arundel
WWT Arundel Wetland Centre is a 65-acre reserve in an idyllic setting, nestled at the base of the South Downs National Park.

Bedgebury National Pinetum & Forest
Cranbrook, Kent TN17 2SL
(01580) 879820
www.forestry.gov.uk/bedgebury
Visit the world's finest conifer collection at Bedgebury National Pinetum.

British Wildlife Centre
Lingfield, Surrey RH7 6LF
(01342) 834658
www.britishwildlifecentre.co.uk
The best place to see and learn about Britain's own wonderful wildlife, with over 40 different species including deer, foxes, otters, badgers, pine martens and red squirrels.

Chiltern Sculpture Trail
Watlington, Oxfordshire
(01865) 778918
www.chilternsculpturetrail.co.uk
Woodland trail with sculpture sited around the forest. Artists work at the site during some months of the year.

Denmans Garden
Fontwell, West Sussex BN18 0SU
(01243) 542808
www.denmans-garden.co.uk
Beautiful 4 acre garden designed for year round interest through use of form, colour and texture. Beautiful plant centre, award-winning and fully licensed Garden Cafe.

Drusillas Park
Alfriston, East Sussex BN26 5QS
(01323) 874100
www.drusillas.co.uk
Widely regarded as the best small zoo in the country Drusillas Park offers an opportunity to get nose to nose with nature with hundreds of exotic animals from monkeys and crocodiles to penguins and meerkats.

Exbury Gardens and Steam Railway

Beaulieu, Hampshire SO45 1AZ
(023) 8089 1203
www.exbury.co.uk
World famous woodland garden, home to the Rothschild Collection of rhododendrons, azaleas, camellias, rare trees and srubs, with its own steam railway.

Fishers Adventure Farm Park

Billingshurst, West Sussex RH14 0EG
(01403) 700063
www.fishersfarmpark.co.uk
Award-winning Adventure Farm Park and open all year. Ideally suited for ages 2-11 years. Huge variety of animals, rides and attractions from the skating rink, to pony rides, toboggan run, bumper boats, theatre shows and much much more!

Marwell Wildlife

Winchester, Hampshire SO21 1JH
(01962) 777407
www.marwell.org.uk
A visit to Marwell Wildlife is a chance to get close to the wonders of the natural world – and play a big part in helping to save them.

Great Dixter House and Gardens
Rye, East Sussex TN31 6PH
(01797) 252878
www.greatdixter.co.uk
An example of a 15th century manor house with antique furniture and needlework. The house is restored and the gardens were designed by Lutyens.

Pashley Manor Gardens
Wadhurst, East Sussex TN5 7HE
(01580) 200888
www.pashleymanorgardens.com
Pashley Manor Gardens offer a blend of romantic landscaping, imaginative plantings and fine old trees, fountains, springs and large ponds with an exciting programme of special events for garden and art lovers.

Paultons Family Theme Park

Romsey, Hampshire SO51 6AL
(023) 8081 4455
www.paultonspark.co.uk
A great family day out with over 60 different attractions and rides included in the price!

RHS Garden Wisley

Woking, Surrey GU23 6QB
0845 260 9000
www.rhs.org.uk/wisley
Stretching over 240 acres of glorious garden.

RSPB Pulborough Brooks

West Sussex RH20 2EL
(01798) 875851
www.rspb.org.uk/pulboroughbrooks
Set in the scenic Arun Valley with views to the South Downs, the two mile circular nature trail leads around this beautiful reserve.

Stowe Landscape Gardens
Buckinghamshire MK18 5DQ
(01280) 822850
www.nationaltrust.org.uk/stowegardens
Over 40 temples and monuments, laid out against an inspiring backdrop of lakes and valleys.

Ventnor Botanic Gardens
St. Lawrence, Isle of Wight PO38 1UL
(01983) 855397
www.botanic.co.uk
The Botanic Garden on the Isle of Wight is a place where the pleasure of plants can be enjoyed to the fullest.

Outdoor Activities

French Brothers Ltd
Windsor, Berkshire SL4 5JH
(01753) 851900
www.boat-trips.co.uk
Large range of public trips on weather-proof vessels from Windsor, Runnymede and Maidenhead.

Guildford Boat House
Surrey GU1 3XJ
(01483) 504494
www.guildfordboats.co.uk
Regular trips operate from Guildford along this tranquil stretch of the River Wey.

Xscape
Milton Keynes, Buckinghamshire MK9 3XS
0871 200 3220
www.xscape.co.uk
Xscape, Milton Keynes offers a unique combination of extreme sports and leisure activities for all ages.

Events 2014

Brighton & Hove Food & Drink Festival

April 17-April 21, Brighton

This spring event celebrates local producers, growers, restaurants, bars and food retailers and showcases fantastic food, drink and hospitality, with events across the city.

www.brightonfoodfestival.com

Eastbourne Festival

April 19-May 11, Eastbourne

Eastbourne Festival is an Open Access Arts Festival which takes place annually for three weeks from Easter Saturday each year. Now in its fifth year it has become recognised as an annual showcase for local professional and amateur talent.

www.eastbournefestival.co.uk

End of the Pier Film Festival

April-May, Worthing

The festival is a short and feature film competition for independent, low-budget and new film makers.

www.eotpfilmfestival.co.uk

Tulip Festival at Pashley Manor

April-May, Wadhurst

Now in its 18th year, the festival gives visitors the chance to lose themselves among the 25,000 blooms gracing this quintessential English garden.

www.pashleymanorgardens.com

Brighton Marathon

April 6, Brighton

Having grown enormously in just two years, the Brighton Marathon is now one of the top 12 running events in the UK.

www.brightonmarathon.co.uk

Brighton Fringe

May-June, Brighton

One of the largest fringe festivals in the world, offering cabaret, comedy, classical concerts, club nights, theatre and exhibitions, as well as street performances.

www.brightonfestivalfringe.org.uk

Isle of Wight Walking Festival

May

The festival boasts 16 days of unbeatable, informative and healthy walks.

www.isleofwightwalkingfestival.co.uk

Artists' Open Houses

Weekends throughout May, Brighton

The biggest free arts event in Britain with over 1,000 artists exhibiting in 200 houses and studios across the city.

www.aoh.org.uk

Brighton Festival

May 3-25, Brighton

The Brighton Festival continues to grow each year, with its sensational programme of art, theatre, dance, music, literature and family shows. The festival is started with a Children's Parade, which winds its way through the city.

www.brightonfestival.org

The Great Escape
May 8-10, Brighton
This city-wide music festival showcases over 350 new local, national and international bands in various venues throughout the city taking place over three days.
www.escapegreat.com

Glyndebourne Festival
May 1-August 31, Lewes
An English opera festival held at Glyndebourne, an English country house near Lewes.
www.glyndebourne.com

Surrey County Show
May 26, Stoke Park
Surrey County Show attracts up to 40,000 visitors and features hundreds of top quality animals from giant beef bulls to bantam hens.
www.surreycountyshow.co.uk

Alton Summer Beer Festival
May 30-May 31, Alton
Celebrating the cultural heritage of Alton as a traditional area for brewing, based on the clear waters rising from the source of the River Wey, and locally grown hops.
www.altonbeerfestival.co.uk

Investec Derby
June 7, Epsom Racecourse
The biggest horse race in the flat-racing calendar.
www.epsomderby.co.uk

South of England Show
June 5-7, Haywards Heath
The South of England Agricultural Society's flagship event.
www.seas.org.uk

Folkestone Airshow
June 7, Folkestone
The airshow will include ground displays, exhibitions, entertainment, family fun and children's activities.
www.folkestoneairshow.com

Isle of Wight Festival
June 12-15, Newport
A music festival featuring some of the UK's top acts and bands.
www.isleofwightfestival.com

Marlow Regatta
June 21, Eton Dorney
Marlow Regatta is one of the multi-lane regattas in the British Rowing calendar.
www.themarlowregatta.com

London to Brighton Bike Ride
June 15, Ends on Madeira Drive, Brighton
The annual bike ride from the capital to the coast in aid of the British Heart Foundation. The UK's largest charity bike ride with 27,000 riders.
www.bhf.org.uk/london-brighton

Reading Real Ale and Jazz Festival
June 26-29, Reading
This year's festival is going to be the biggest and best yet, featuring some of the best jazz acts on the circuit.
www.raaj.info

Deal Festival of Music and the Arts
June 27-Jul 6, Deal
Experience great classical and contemporary music from some of the world's finest music-makers, as well as theatre, opera, cinema and dance – in the beautiful and historic surroundings of Deal and Dover on England's south coast.
www.dealfestival.co.uk

Henley Royal Regatta
July 2-6, Henley
Attracting thousands of visitors over a five-day period and spectators will be thrilled by over 200 races of international standard.
www.hrr.co.uk

Winchester Hat Fair
July, Winchester
Named after the tradition of throwing donations into performance hats, it's Britain's longest running festival of street theatre and outdoor arts.
www.hatfair.co.uk

Roald Dahl Festival
July, Aylesbury Town Centre
An annual celebration of the famous author, including a 500-strong parade of pupils, teachers and musicians with puppets and artwork based on the Roald Dahl stories.
www.aylesburyvaledc.gov.uk/dahl

Paddle Round the Pier
July, Brighton & Hove seafront
A weekend of beach events which gets bigger every year, Paddle Round the Pier invites all kinds of vessels to take to the sea and spectators to enjoy the festivities on land.
www.paddleroundthepier.com

Hampton Court Palace Flower Show
July 8-13, Hampton Court
One of the biggest events in the horticulture calendar.
www.rhs.org.uk

Swan Upping
Starts third week of July
This is the annual census of the swan population on stretches of the Thames in the counties of Middlesex, Surrey, Buckinghamshire, Berkshire and Oxfordshire. This historic ceremony dates from the 12th century, when the Crown claimed ownership of all mute swans.
www.royalswan.co.uk

Lammas Festival
July-26-27, Eastbourne
A friendly family-oriented free festival of music, dance and entertainment.
www.lammasfest.org

Glorious Goodwood
July 29-Aug 2, Chichester
Bursting with fabulous fashions, succulent strawberries, chilled Champagne and top horse racing stars, as well as music and dancing.
www.goodwood.com

New Forest and Hampshire Show
July 29-31, New Park, Brockenhurst
The show attracts, on average, 95,000 visitors every year and brings together a celebration of traditional country pursuits, crafts, produce and entertainment.
www.newforestshow.co.uk

Cowes Week
August 2-8, Cowes
Cowes Week is one of the longest-running regular regattas in the world.
www.aamcowesweek.co.uk

Isle of Wight Garlic Festival
August 16-17, Newchurch
Garlic is of course, at the heart of this event – coming in all shapes and forms, some of them traditional, some surprising.
www.garlic-festival.co.uk

Arundel Festival
August 16-25, Arundel
Ten days of the best music, theatre, art and comedy.
www.arundelfestival.co.uk

England's Medieval Festival
August 23-25,
Herstmonceux Castle
A celebration of the Middle Ages.
www.mgel.com

Wings & Wheels
August 23-24,
Dunsfold Aerodrome
Outstanding variety of dynamic aviation, motoring displays and iconic cars.
www.wingsandwheels.net

Reading Festival
August 22-24, Reading
The Reading and Leeds Festivals are a pair of annual music festivals that take place simultaneously.
www.readingfestival.com

Shoreham Airshow 2014
August 30-31, Shoreham-by-Sea
One of the UK's finest airshows with a fantastic air display and excting attractions.
www.shorehamairshow.co.uk

Brighton Digital Festival
September, Brighton
With a month of exhibitions, performances, workshops and outdoor events, Brighton & Hove is certainly a leading digital destination. There will be workshops, interactive demonstrations and displays throughout the city.
www.brightondigitalfestival.co.uk

Southampton Boat Show
September 12-21, Southampton
See the best boats and marine brands gathered together in one fantastic water-based show.
www.southamptonboatshow.com

Kop Hill Climb
September 20-21,
Princes Risborough
In the 1900s Kop Hill Climb was one of the most popular hill climbs in the country for cars and motorcycles. Now the spirit of the climb is being revived.
www.kophillclimb.org.uk

Brighton Comedy Festival
October, Brighton Dome
The land of one-liners, whimsical thoughts, innuendo, ridiculous characters, clever puns and hand over mouth dirty jokes descends on Brighton for three weeks of laughter, mirth and merriment.
www.brightoncomedyfestival.com

Eastbourne Beer Festival
October 9-11,
Winter Gardens, Eastbourne
Eastbourne's annual beer festival features over 120 cask ales, plus wines, international bottled beers, ciders and perries. Each session features live music.
www.visiteastbourne.com/beer-festival

Burning the Clocks
December,
Brighton Winter Solstice Parade
Started in 1993, Burning the Clocks represents an alternative to the commercial Christmas. Thousands of people gather to make paper and willow lanterns to carry through the city before burning them on the beach as a token for the end of the year and to greet the lengthening days.
www.burningtheclocks.co.uk

Tourist Information Centres

When you arrive at your destination, visit an Official Partner Tourist Information Centre for quality assured help with accommodation and information about local attractions and events, or email your request before you go. To find a Tourist Information Centre visit www.visitengland.com

Ashford	Ashford Gateway Plus	01233 330316	tourism@ashford.gov.uk
Aylesbury	The Kings Head	01296 330559	tic@aylesburyvaledc.gov.uk
Banbury	Castle Quay Shopping Centre	01295 753752	banbury.tic@cherwell-dc.gov.uk
Bicester	Bicester Village	01869 369055	bicestervisitorcentre@valueretail.com
Brighton	Royal Pavilion Shop	01273 290337	visitorinfo@visitbrighton.com
Burford	33a High Street	01993 823558	burford.vic@westoxon.gov.uk
Canterbury	Canterbury Heritage Museum	01227 378100	canterburyinformation@canterbury.gov.uk
Chichester	The Novium	01243 775888	chitic@chichester.gov.uk
Dover	Market Square	01304 201066	tic@doveruk.com
Gravesend	Towncentric	01474 337600	info@towncentric.co.uk
Guildford	155 High Street	01483 444333	tic@guildford.gov.uk
Hastings	Queens Square	01424 451111	hic@hastings.gov.uk
Lewes	187 High Street	01273 483448	lewes.tic@lewes.gov.uk
Maidstone	Maidstone Museum	01622 602169	tourism@maidstone.gov.uk
Marlow	55a High Street	01628 483597	tourism_enquiries@wycombe.gov.uk
Newbury	The Wharf	01635 30267	tourism@westberks.gov.uk
Oxford	15/16 Broad Street	01865 252200	info@visitoxfordshire.org
Portsmouth	Clarence Esplanade	023 9282 6722	vis@portsmouthcc.gov.uk
Rochester	95 High Street	01634 338141	visitor.centre@medway.gov.uk
Romsey	13 Church Street	01794 512987	romseytic@testvalley.gov.uk
Royal Tunbridge Wells	The Old Fish Market	01892 515675	touristinformationcentre@tunbridgewells.gov.uk
Rye	4/5 Lion Street	01797 229049	ryetic@tourismse.com
Swanley	Library & Information Centre	01322 614660	touristinfo@swanley.org.uk
Thanet	The Droit House	01843 577577	visitorinformation@thanet.gov.uk
Winchester	Guildhall	01962 840500	tourism@winchester.gov.uk
Windsor	Old Booking Hall	01753 743900	windsor.tic@rbwm.gov.uk
Witney	3 Welsh Way	01993 775802	witney.vic@westoxon.gov.uk
Worthing	22a Marine Parade	01903 239868	tic@dur-worthing.gov.uk

Regional Contacts and Information

For more information on accommodation, attractions, activities, events and holidays in South East England, contact the regional or local tourism organisations. Their websites have a wealth of information and many produce free publications to help you get the most out of your visit.

The following publications are available from Tourism South East by logging on to www.visitsoutheastengland.com, emailing enquiries@tourismse.com or by calling (023) 8062 5400.

- E-Brochures
- Family Fun
- Time for Us

South East England – We know just the place...

Visit our 2014 guide websites...

- Detailed information
- Up-to-date availability
- Book your accommodation online

Includes over 20,000 places to stay, all of them star rated.

Win amazing prizes, every month...

Enter our monthly competition at
www.visitor-guides.co.uk/prizes

Entries appear alphabetically by town name in each county. A key to symbols appears on page 7

HURLEY, Berkshire   Map ref 2C2
SatNav SL6 5NN

Hurley Riverside Park
Hurley, Maidenhead, Near Henley SL6 5NE
T: (01628) 824493 **E:** info@hurleyriversidepark.co.uk
W: www.hurleyriversidepark.co.uk **£ BOOK ONLINE**

🚐 (138) £15.00-£30.00
🚍 (138) £15.00-£30.00
⛺ (130) £13.00-£26.00
🚐 (10) £300.00-£550.00
200 touring pitches

SPECIAL PROMOTIONS
Touring Park Loyalty Card. Membership Card. Giveaways and offers on Facebook and Twitter. Short breaks available in Hire Caravan Holiday Homes and ReadyTents one week prior to arrival.

Family-run park alongside the river Thames, ideal for visiting LEGOLAND® Windsor, Henley-on-Thames, Oxford & London. Tents, tourers, motorhomes & RVs are welcome. Caravan Holiday Homes and ReadyTents for hire. Free heated shower blocks, laundry, shop, nature trail, children's trim trail, riverside picnic grounds, slipway, fishing in season and Wi-Fi. 2 day LEGOLAND® tickets are available at a great rate.

Directions: M4 J8/9 or M40 J4, onto A404(M), third exit to Henley (A4130). Past Hurley Village, turn right into Shepherds Lane.   **Open:** March to October.

Payment: **Leisure:** **Children:** **Catering:** **Park:** **Touring:**

READING, Berkshire   Map ref 2C2
SatNav RG7 1SP

Wellington Country Park - Touring Caravan & Campsite
Odiham Road, Riseley, Nr Reading RG7 1SP
T: (0118) 932 6444 **F:** (0118) 932 6445 **E:** info@wellington-country-park.co.uk
W: www.wellington-country-park.co.uk **£ BOOK ONLINE**

🚐 (57) £17.00-£36.00
🚍 (57) £17.00-£36.00
⛺ (30) £15.50-£29.50
87 touring pitches

Set within beautiful woodlands, fees include 2 people and free unlimited access to Country Park with nature trails, animal farm, play areas, miniature railway, sand pits and mini golf. Easy access from both M3 & M4. **Directions:** Hampshire/Berkshire border between Reading/Basingstoke. Do not use Sat Nav. M4 junction 11 A33 to Basingstoke. M3 junction 5 B3349 to Reading. **Open:** March to November.

Payment: **Leisure:** **Children:** **Catering:** **Park:** **Touring:**

LYMINGTON, Hampshire   Map ref 2C3
SatNav SO41 0LH

Downton Holiday Park
Shorefield Road, Milford-on-Sea, Lymington SO41 0LH
T: (01425) 476131 **F:** (01590) 642515 **E:** info@downtonholidaypark.co.uk
W: www.downtonholidaypark.co.uk

🚐 (74) £130.00-£685.00

Downton Holiday Park is a small, peaceful park, close to the New Forest and less than 5 minutes drive from the beach at Milford-on-Sea. **Directions:** By road, leave the M27 at Junction 1 and follow the A337 to Lyndhurst. Keeping on the A337, drive through Brockenhurst and Lymington and on to Downton. **Open:** March to October.

Payment: **Leisure:** **Property:** **Children:**

The Official Tourist Board Guide to *Camping, Touring & Holiday Parks 2014*

OWER, Hampshire   Map ref 2C3
SatNav SO51 6AJ

Green Pastures Caravan Park
Green Pastures Farm, Whitemoor Lane, Romsey SO51 6AJ
T: (023) 8081 4444 E: enquiries@greenpasturesfarm.com
W: www.greenpasturesfarm.com

🚐 £19.00-£24.00
🚏 £19.00-£24.00
⛺ £14.00
100 touring pitches

Located on the outskirts of the New Forest, Green Pastures Farm is ideal for families as there is plenty of space for children to play in full view of the caravans and tents. However, it is also peaceful enough to be able to unwind after a busy working week. **Directions:** Drive Off A3090 between Romsey and Cadnam. From M27 junction 2 follow signs for Salisbury until our own brown signs are seen at big roundabout. **Open:** 15th March - 3rd November.

Site: Payment: Leisure: Children: Catering: Park: Touring:

ROMSEY, Hampshire   Map ref 2C3
SatNav SO51 6FH

Hill Farm Caravan Park
Branches Lane, Sherfield English, Romsey SO51 6FH
T: (01794) 340402 F: (01794) 342358 E: gjb@hillfarmpark.com
W: www.hillfarmpark.com

🚐 (70) £15.00-£35.00
🚏 (70) £15.00-£35.00
⛺ (30) £15.00-£35.00
🏠 (6) £280.00-£550.00
100 touring pitches

In countryside on the edge of the New Forest, our quiet family-run site provides an ideal base for mature visitors and families with younger children to visit the area. **Directions:** Directions can be found on our website. **Open:** Touring & camping March to October, statics February to December.

Site: Payment: Leisure: Children: Catering: Park: Touring:

New Forest and Dorset Holidays
Perfect locations by Forest and Coast

Our parks offer pitches for touring caravans, motorhomes or tents. There are great leisure facilities and lots of fun entertainment for everyone. Explore the New Forest and the Jurassic Coast, or relax on Bournemouth's sandy beaches.

Ref VET

SHOREFIELD HOLIDAYS LIMITED
Tel **01590 648 331**
holidays@shorefield.co.uk
www.shorefield.co.uk
follow us on @shorefieldparks

HAMPSHIRE
Forest Edge Holiday Park, BH24 2SD
Oakdene Forest Park, BH24 2RZ (tents only)
Lytton Lawn Touring Park, SO41 0TX
DORSET
Swanage Coastal Park, BH19 2RS
Merley Court Touring Park, BH21 3AA

NITON, Isle of Wight   Map ref 2C3   SatNav PO38 2NS

Meadow View Caravan Site
Newport Road, Niton, Ventnor, Isle of Wight PO38 2NS
T: (01983) 730015 / 07977 856795 **E:** info@meadowviewniton.co.uk
W: www.meadowviewniton.co.uk

⊡ (7)   £200.00-£330.00

Small family run site with panoramic views over surrounding countryside, adjacent to owners working farm of cattle and sheep. 2 mins from village and friendly pubs within walking distance. **Directions:** See website or call for details. **Open:** April to November.

Payment: ☼ **Leisure:** ♪ ♣ **Children:** ⚲ ⚑ **Park:** ⚐ ▣

RYDE, Isle of Wight   Map ref 2C3   SatNav PO33 1QL

Whitefield Forest Touring Park
Brading Road, Ryde PO33 1QL
T: (01983) 617069 **E:** pat&louise@whitefieldforest.co.uk
W: www.whitefieldforest.co.uk

⊡ (50)   £16.50-£24.00
⊟ (50)   £16.50-£24.00
▲ (50)   £16.50-£24.00
100 touring pitches

Award winning campsite in the picturesque woodland of Whitefield Forest. Near to the sandy beaches of Ryde & Sandown on a good bus route, ideal for caravans, motor homes and tents. Special offers available on ferry travel & for over 50's. **Directions:** Just off A3055 follow to Brading, at Tesco's roundabout straight accross, site approx half mile on left hand side. **Open:** 28th March - 6th October.

Payment: £ ☼ **Leisure:** ♪ ▶ ∪ **Children:** ⚲ ⚑ **Catering:** ⚱ **Park:** ⚐ ▭ ▣ ⚲ **Touring:** ⚑ ♲ ▣ ♪

Looking for something else?

The official and most comprehensive guide to independently inspected, star rated accommodation.

B&Bs and Hotels - B&Bs, Hotels, farmhouses, inns, serviced apartments, campus and hostel accommodation in England.

Self Catering - Self-catering holiday homes, approved caravan holiday homes, boat accommodation and holiday cottage agencies in England.

Camping, Touring and Holiday Parks - Touring parks, camping holidays and holiday parks and villages in Britain.

Now available in all good bookshops and online at **www.hudsons.co.uk/shop**

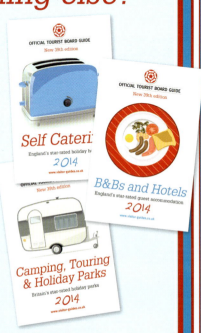

Need more information?

Visit our new 2014 guide websites for detailed information, up-to-date availability and to book your accommodation online. Includes over 20,000 places to stay, all of them star rated.

www.visitor-guides.co.uk

2014 Official Tourist Board Guides

100 touring pitches

Carpenters Farm Campsite

Carpenters Road, St Helens PO33 1YN
T: (01983) 874557 **E:** info@carpentersfarms.co.uk
W: www.carpentersfarm.co.uk

Family campsite with beautiful views in picturesque rural setting, adjacent to RSPB Reserve and SSSI. Close to beaches and attractions. Relaxed atmosphere on site. Family groups and pets very welcome. Overnight holding area available. Electric hookup, bookings advised for high season, please check our website for up to date tariffs. **Directions:** Please contact us for directions. **Open:** May - September.

Site: **Payment:** **Leisure:** **Children:** **Catering:** **Park:**
Touring:

(70)   £15.95-£30.95
(30)   £15.95-£30.95
(30)   £15.95-£26.95
(40)   £215.00-£830.00

Appuldurcombe Gardens Holiday Park

Appuldurcombe Road, Wroxall, Nr. Ventnor, Isle of Wight PO38 3EP
T: (01983) 852597 **F:** 01983 856225 **E:** info@appuldurcombegardens.co.uk
W: www.appuldurcombegardens.co.uk

Picturesque holiday park located within an Area of Outstanding Natural Beauty. Situated within 14 acres of lush secluded grounds & only minutes by car to glorious beaches and attractions. There are 40 static caravans within a walled orchard and 130 pitches with a selection of pitch options.

Directions: Head to Newport and take A3020 turning off towards Shanklin and Ventnor. Travel through Blackwater and onto Rookley, Godshill and Sandford. Once you reach Whiteley Bank roundabout, turn right towards Wroxall village.

Open: February-November.

Site: **Payment:** **Leisure:** **Children:** **Catering:**
Park: **Touring:**

BIRCHINGTON, Kent   Map ref 3C3   SatNav CT7 0NH

St Nicholas Camping Site

Streete Farm House, Court Road, St Nicholas-at-Wade, Birchington, Kent CT7 0NH
T: (01843) 847245

(12)	£19.00-£21.00
(8)	£19.00-£21.00
(55)	£16.00-£19.00

75 touring pitches

The site - flat, grassy and well-sheltered, is on the outskirts of the village, close to the village shop. The resort of Thanet is within easy reach and we are also close to Canterbury, Whitstable, and Holme Bay. **Directions:** The site is signposted from the A299 and A28. **Open:** Easter to 31st October.

Site: ▲🅿 Payment: € ☼ Leisure: ♿ ♪ ▶ ∪ Children: 🐾 ⚠ Park: 🐕 🐾 Touring: 🚿 🚻 ♨ ♪

KINGSDOWN, Kent   Map ref 3C4   SatNav CT14 8EU

Kingsdown Park Holiday Village

Upper Street, Kingsdown, Deal CT14 8EU
T: (01304) 361205 **F:** (01304) 380125 **E:** info@kingsdownpark.net
W: www.kingsdownpark.net **£ BOOK ONLINE**

(50)	£275.00-£770.00

This picturesque park provides the perfect base for exploring Kent. Comfortable lodges and excellent leisure facilities ensure you are not disappointed. Short breaks available on request. **Directions:** Please see our website for directions. **Open:** March to October and 20th December to 2nd January.

Site: 🏠 Payment: 💳 Leisure: ♿ ♪ ▶ ∪ ♦ ♒ ♙ Property: ♫ 🖥 🗐 📱 Children: 🐾 ⚠ Catering: ✕

BANBURY, Oxfordshire   Map ref 2C1   SatNav OX17 1AZ

Anita's Touring Caravan Park

The Yews, Church Farm, Banbury OX17 1AZ
T: (01295) 750731 / 07966 171959 **F:** (01295) 750731 **E:** bookings@anitascampsite.co.uk
W: www.oxfordshirecamping.com

(36)	£18.00-£20.00
(36)	£18.00-£20.00
(20)	£14.00-£17.00
	£30.00-£50.00

Anita's is a friendly family run site in North Oxon on the edge of Mollington village. Clean facilities, shop, reception, hard and grass pitches, camping, camping pods and cottages. **Directions:** M40 Junction 11 Banbury take 3rd roundabout to Southam for 4 miles, 150yds past Mollington, turn-off on left. Brown signs. **Open:** All year.

Site: ▲🅿 Payment: 💳 Leisure: ♪ ▶ ∪ Children: 🐾 Catering: 🛒 Park: 🐕 🚜 🐾 Touring: 🚿 🚻 ♨

STANDLAKE, Oxfordshire   Map ref 2C1   SatNav OX29 7PZ

Hardwick Parks

Downs Road, Standlake, Witney OX29 7PZ
T: (01865) 300501 **F:** (01865) 300037 **E:** info@hardwickparks.co.uk
W: www.hardwickparks.co.uk **£ BOOK ONLINE**

(214)	£21.50-£23.75
(214)	£26.50
(214)	£16.00-£19.00
(7)	£275.00-£585.00

214 touring pitches

Rural park near Witney with lakes and river. Licensed clubhouse serving food and drinks. Shower/toilet block and shop. Tents, caravans and motorhomes welcome. Holiday caravans for hire and sale. Watersports available. Dogs on leads welcome. **Directions:** Four and a half miles from Witney, signposted from the A415. **Open:** April to October.

Site: 🏕 ⚲🅿 **Payment:** 💳 ☀ **Leisure:** 🎵 **Children:** 🛝 ⛰ **Catering:** ✕ 🛒 **Park:** 🐕 🖥 🔲 📱 ☂
Touring: 🚿 ♿ 🚐 ♪

WITNEY, Oxfordshire   Map ref 2C1   SatNav OX29 7RH

Lincoln Farm Park Oxfordshire

High Street, Standlake, Witney, Oxon OX29 7RH
T: (01865) 300239 **F:** (01865) 300127 **E:** info@lincolnfarmpark.co.uk
W: www.lincolnfarmpark.co.uk **£ BOOK ONLINE**

(90)	£18.30-£32.40
(44)	£18.30-£32.40
(16)	£18.30-£29.30

90 touring pitches

Set in eight acres of beautiful Oxfordshire countryside, Lincoln Farm park offers you the opportunity to explore, or simply relax. **Open:** 1st February to Mid November.

Site: 🏕 ⚲🅿 **Payment:** 💳 € ☀ **Leisure:** 🎵 ⚑ ♻ ☂ **Children:** 🛝 ⛰ **Catering:** 🛒 **Park:** 🐕 🖥 🔲 📱
Touring: 🚿 ♿ 🚐 ♪

BRACKLESHAM BAY, Sussex   Map ref 2C3   SatNav PO20 8JE

South Downs Holiday Village

Bracklesham Lane, Bracklesham Bay, Chichester PO20 8JE
T: (01692) 582277 **E:** info@richardsonsgroup.net
W: www.richardsonsholidayvillages.co.uk

	£275.00-£500.00

South Downs Holiday Village is a small and friendly location for adults. Providing full board breaks with regular entertainment. Chalets are all ground floor. Hotel over two floors. The Village has facilities including an outdoor swimming pool, amusements, ballroom, bar, hairdressing and beauty salon, gym, bowls and much more.

Directions: Six miles south of Chichester, on the outskirts of Bracklesham Bay.   **Open:** All year.

Payment: 💳 **Leisure:** ⚲ ♻ **Property:** 🎵 🖥 📱 **Catering:** ✕

Fairfields Farm Caravan & Camping Park

Eastbourne Road, Westham, Pevensey BN24 5NG
T: (01323) 763165 F: (01323) 469175 E: enquiries@fairfieldsfarm.com
W: www.fairfieldsfarm.com

🚐 (60)   £17.00-£24.00
🚌 (60)   £17.00-£24.00
⛺ (60)   £17.00-£24.00
60 touring pitches

SPECIAL PROMOTIONS
Special promotions
available throughout
the season, please
contact us for more
details.

A quiet country touring site on a working farm. Clean facilities, lakeside walk with farm pets and free fishing for campers. Close to the beautiful seaside resort of Eastbourne, and a good base from which to explore the diverse scenery and attractions of South East England. Overnight holding area available. Free Wi-Fi is also available on site.

Directions: From A27 Pevensey roundabout, travel through Pevensey towards castle, then through Westham. Turn left (B2191) towards Eastbourne. Over level crossing and we are on left.

Open: April to October.

Site: ⚐🅿 Payment: 💳 ☼ Leisure: 🎣 ▶ ♫ Children: 🛝 Catering: 🍴 Park: 🐕 🚉 🗑 🏕 Touring: 🚰 🚰 🚐 🎵

Bay View Park Ltd

Old Martello Road, Pevensey Bay, Pevensey BN24 6DX
T: (01323) 768688 F: (01323) 769637 E: holidays@bay-view.co.uk
W: www.bay-view.co.uk £ BOOK ONLINE

🚐 (94)   £16.00-£25.00
🚌 (94)   £16.00-£25.00
⛺ (75)   £16.00-£25.00
🏠 (9)   £165.00-£770.00
94 touring pitches

Family site on a private road next to the beach. Play area. New showers and laundry. Small, well-stocked shop. On site 9 hole golf course and refreshments. **Directions:** On A259 coast road between Pevensey Bay and Eastbourne. **Open:** March to October.

Site: ⚐🅿 Payment: 💳 ☼ Leisure: 🎣 ▶ Children: 🛝 ⛰ Catering: 🍴 Park: 🐕 🚉 🗑 🏕 Touring: 🚰 🚰 🚐 🎵

Green Lawns Holiday Park
Paddock Lane, Selsey, Chichester, West Sussex PO20 9EJ
T: (01243) 606080 **F:** (01243) 606068 **E:** holidays@bunnleisure.co.uk
W: www.bunnleisure.co.uk

(1) £690.00-£1650.00
(20) £168.00-£1055.00

Offers leafy lanes, duck ponds and open green spaces for privacy, peace and quiet but with access to all Bunn Leisure's facilities and a courtesy bus to take you around. **Directions:** From A27 Chichester by-pass take B2145 to Selsey. Green Lawns is clearly signed on right once you are in town. **Open:** March to January.

Site: **Payment:** **Leisure:** **Property:** **Children:** **Catering:**

Warner Farm Camping & Touring Park
Warner Lane, Selsey, Chichester, West Sussex PO20 9EL
T: (01243) 604499 **E:** touring@bunnleisure.co.uk
W: www.warnerfarm.co.uk

(80) £20.00-£45.00
(50) £20.00-£45.00
(120) £18.00-£33.00
250 touring pitches

Great value, quality, fun filled family camping & touring holidays. Well maintained standard, electric & full service pitches. Stay here & enjoy all Bunn Leisure's great facilities and entertainment. Overnight holding area available. **Directions:** From A27 Chichester by-pass take B2145 to Selsey. Warner Farm is clearly signed on the right once you are in town. **Open:** March to January.

Site: **Payment:** **Leisure:** **Children:** **Catering:** **Park:** **Touring:**

West Sands Holiday Park
Mill Lane, Selsey, Chichester, West Sussex PO20 9BH
T: (01243) 606080 **F:** (01243) 606068 **E:** holidays@bunnleisure.co.uk
W: www.bunnleisure.co.uk

(5)   £440.00-£1600.00
(150) £168.00-£1055.00

Image

The liveliest of our parks on the South Coast offering family fun in a fantastic seaside location. Famous for the best entertainment with top acts, live performances and kids entertainment. **Directions:** From A27 Chichester by-pass take B2145 to Selsey. West Sands is clearly signed on right once you are in the town. **Open:** March to January.

Site: **Payment:** **Leisure:** **Property:** **Children:** **Catering:**

White Horse Holiday Park
Paddock Lane, Selsey, Chichester, West Sussex PO20 9EJ
T: (01243) 606080 **F:** (01243) 606068 **E:** holidays@bunnleisure.co.uk
W: www.bunnleisure.co.uk

(20) £168.00-£1055.00

With its coveted award for its traditional atmosphere, White Horse Holiday Park is perfect for families. Offering a relaxed holiday, though never far from all the facilities and entertainment. **Directions:** From A27 Chichester bypass take B2145 to Selsey. White Horse is clearly signed on the right once you are in town. **Open:** March to January.

Site: **Payment:** **Leisure:** **Property:** **Children:** **Catering:**

London

Historical landmarks, museums, theatres, sporting venues...the list goes on. The capital of the UK has everything a tourist could ever want. Whether it's a visit to the Tower of London or a ride on the London Eye, this city will not disappoint. You can spend a day sightseeing and then sample one of the world-famous West End shows in the evening. A single trip to London will not be enough to take in the most popular attractions – you'll leave with the intention of returning quickly to see what else the capital has in store.

Highlights

Art galleries

Don't miss out on the best London art exhibitions, from sculpture and installations to painting and photography.

Buckingham Palace

The official London residence and principal workplace of the British monarch, the palace is a setting for state occasions and royal hospitality. The changing of the guard is a popular visitor attraction.

Hampton Court Palace

Discover the magnificence of Henry VIII's favourite royal residence. Immerse yourself in the sights and sounds of the bustling Base Court and marvel at the breath taking grandeur of Henry's State Rooms.

London Eye

Get a fantastic view of the capital from the London Eye, a giant Ferris wheel on the South Bank of the River Thames. The entire structure is 135 metres tall and the wheel has a diameter of 120 metres.

London Zoo

Set in leafy Regent's Park amid iconic architecture and beautiful gardens, London Zoo is an oasis in the heart of the city. With over 760 animal species, exciting and innovative new exhibits and heritage-listed building almost as famous as their inhabitants, a visit to the zoo is a great day out.

Maritime Greenwich

The area is significant for the Royal Observatory where the understanding of astronomy and navigation were developed. The complex was until recently the Royal Naval College.

Museums

Visitors to London are able to enjoy access to some of the greatest museums in the world, including the Natural History Museum, Victoria & Albert Museum and the National Maritime Museum.

Royal Botanic Gardens, Kew

The gardens house botanic collections that have been considerably enriched through the centuries.

Tower of London

Started in 1066 by William the Conqueror during the Norman conquest of England, the Tower of London is a symbol of power and an example of Norman military architecture that spread across England.

Westminster

Westminster Palace is an example of neo-Gothic architecture. The site comprises the Church of Saint Margaret and Westminster Abbey, where all the sovereigns since the 11th century have been crowned.

Editor's Picks

Take in the view

For unrivalled views of the capital, hop on the London Eye. The UK's top paid-for visitor attraction provides a magical and entertaining way to experience the city.

Discover another angle

The view from the top of Primrose Hill is one of London's best, affording a fantastic panorama across the city.

Fit for a princess

Explore Kate Middleton's London haunts including the National Portrait Gallery, Kensington Palace and Bluebird restaurant.

Step back in time

Leave modern London behind with a visit to one of the city's historic houses. Learn about the people who lived there, find out about historic interiors and design, or get inspiration from their exquisite gardens.

Explore London's maritime history

Venture aboard the Cutty Sark, one of the world's most famous ships and last surviving tea clipper. Visits to the Golden Hinde and HMS Belfast are also worthwhile.

Things to do

Attractions with this sign participate in the Places of Interest Quality Assurance Scheme.

Attractions with this sign participate in the Visitor Attraction Quality Assurance Scheme.

Both schemes recognise high standards in all aspects of the visitor experience (see page 7)

Entertainment & Culture

Apsley House
Westminster W1J 7NT
(020) 7499 5676
www.english-heritage.org.uk/daysout/properties/apsley-house/
This great 18th century town house pays homage to the Duke's dazzling military career, which culminated in his victory at Waterloo in 1815.

British Museum
Camden WC1B 3DG
(020) 7323 8299
www.thebritishmuseum.ac.uk
Founded in 1753, the British Museum's remarkable collections span over two million years of human history and culture, all under one roof.

Down House - Home of Charles Darwin
Bromley BR6 7JT
(01689) 859119
www.english-heritage.org.uk/daysout/properties/home-of-charles-darwin-down-house/
The family home and workplace of Charles Darwin.

Estorick Collection of Modern Italian Art

Islington N1 2AN
(020) 7704 9522
www.estorickcollection.com
World-famous collection of Italian Futurists, Modigliani, Morandi and others in a beautiful Georgian house. Also temporary exhibitions, events, library and shop.

Greenwich Heritage Centre

Greenwich SE18 4DX
(020) 8854 2452
www.greenwich.gov.uk
Local history museum with displays of archaeology, natural history and geology. Also temporary exhibitions, schools service, sales point and Saturday club.

London Transport Museum

Westminster WC2E 7BB
(020) 7379 6344
www.ltmuseum.co.uk
The history of transport for everyone, from spectacular vehicles, special exhibitions, actors and guided tours to film shows, gallery talks and children's craft workshops

Lord's Tour

Westminster NW8 8QN
(020) 7616 8595
www.lords.org/history/tours-of-lords/
Guided tour of Lord's Cricket Ground including the Long Room, MCC Museum, Real Tennis Court, Mound Stand and Indoor School.

Imperial War Museum

Southwark SE1 6HZ
(020) 7416 5320
www.iwm.org.uk
This award-winning museum tells the story of conflict involving Britain and the Commonwealth since 1914. See thousands of imaginatively displayed exhibits, from art to aircraft, utility clothes to U-boats.

Museum of London
City of London EC2Y 5HN
(020) 7001 9844
www.museumoflondon.org.uk
Step inside Museum of London for an unforgettable journey through the capital's turbulent past.

National Gallery
Westminster WC2N 5DN
(020) 7747 2888
www.nationalgallery.org.uk
The National Gallery houses one of the greatest collections of Western European painting in the world. Discover inspiring art by Botticelli, Caravaggio, Leonardo da Vinci, Monet, Raphael, Rembrandt, Titian, Vermeer and Van Gogh.

Natural History Museum
Kensington and Chelsea SW7 5BD
(020) 7942 5000
www.nhm.ac.uk
The Natural History Museum reveals how the jigsaw of life fits together. Animal, vegetable or mineral, the best of our planet's most amazing treasures are here for you to see - for free.

National Maritime Museum

Greenwich SE10 9NF
(020) 8858 4422
www.nmm.ac.uk
Britain's seafaring history housed in an impressive modern museum. Themes include exploration, Nelson, trade and empire, passenger shipping, luxury liners, maritime London, costume, art and the sea, the future and environmental issues.

National Portrait Gallery
Westminster WC2H 0HE
(020) 7306 0055
www.npg.org.uk
The National Portrait Gallery houses the world's largest collection of portraits. Visitors come face to face with the people who have shaped British history from Elizabeth I to David Beckham. Entrance is free.

Royal Air Force Museum Hendon

Barnet NW9 5LL
(020) 8205 2266
www.rafmuseum.org
Take off to the Royal Air Force Museum and flypast the history of aviation with an exciting display of suspended aircraft, touch screen technology, simulator rides, hands-on section, film shows, licensed restaurant.

Science Museum

Kensington and Chelsea SW7 2DD
0870 870 4868
www.sciencemuseum.org.uk
The Science Museum is world-renowned for its historic collections, awe-inspiring galleries, family activities and exhibitions - and it's free!

Southbank Centre

Lambeth SE1 8XX
0871 663 2501
www.southbankcentre.co.uk
A unique arts centre with 21 acres of creative space, including the Royal Festival Hall, Queen Elizabeth Hall and The Hayward.

St Bartholomew's Hospital Archives and Museum

City of London EC1A 7BE
(020) 7601 8152
www.bartsandthelondon.nhs.uk/aboutus/st_bartholomews_hospital.asp
The museum tells the inspiring story of Bart's Hospital. Founded nearly 9 centuries ago, it is one of the oldest hospitals in Britain.

Tate Britain
Westminster SW1P 4RG
(020) 7887 8888
www.tate.org.uk
Tate Britain presents the world's greatest collection of British art in a dynamic series of new displays and exhibitions.

Tate Modern
Southwark SE1 9TG
(020) 7887 8888
www.tate.org.uk/modern
The national gallery of international modern art and is one of London's top free attractions. Packed with challenging modern art and housed within a disused power station on the south bank of the River Thames.

Tower Bridge Exhibition

Southwark SE1 2UP
(020) 7403 3761
www.towerbridge.org.uk
Inside Tower Bridge Exhibition you will travel up to the high-level walkways, located 140 feet above the Thames and witness stunning panoramic views of London before visiting the Victorian Engine Rooms.

Victoria and Albert Museum
Kensington and Chelsea SW7 2RL
(020) 7942 2000
www.vam.ac.uk
The V&A is the world's greatest museum of art and design, with collections unrivalled in their scope and diversity.

Wallace Collection
Westminster W1U 3BN
(020) 7563 9551
www.wallacecollection.org
The Wallace Collection is a national museum, displaying superb works of art in an historic London town house.

Wembley Stadium Tours
Brent HA9 0WS
0844 800 2755
www.wembleystadium.com/wembleystadiumtour/default.aspx
Until your dream comes true, there's only one way to experience what it's like winning at Wembley - take the tour.

Wimbledon Lawn Tennis Museum
Merton SW19 5AG
(020) 8944 1066
www.wimbledon.org
A fantastic collection of memorabilia dating from 1555, including Championship Trophies, Art Gallery, and special exhibitions, reflecting the game and championships of today.

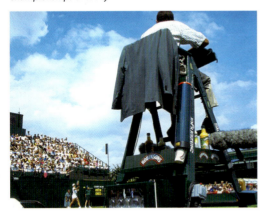

Family Fun

Chessington World of Adventures
Kingston upon Thames KT9 2NE
0870 444 7777
www.chessington.com
Explore Chessington - it's a whole world of adventures! Soar on the Vampire rollercoaster or discover the mystery of Tomb Blaster. Take a walk on the wild side in the Trails of the Kings or visit the park's own SEA LIFE Centre.

London Eye
Lambeth SE1 7PB
0870 500 0600
www.londoneye.com
Get the best view of London when you visit The London Eye, a top London attraction and the world's largest observation wheel.

Royal Observatory Greenwich
Greenwich SE10 9NF
(020) 8858 4422
www.nmm.ac.uk/places/royal-observatory/
Stand on the Greenwich Meridian Line, Longitude Zero, which divides East and West. Watch the time-ball fall at 1 o'clock. Giant refracting telescope.

Heritage

Chiswick House
Hounslow W4 2RP
(020) 8995 0508
www.english-heritage.org.uk/daysout/properties/chiswick-house/
The celebrated villa of Lord Burlington with impressive grounds featuring Italianate garden with statues, temples, obelisks and urns.

Churchill Museum and Cabinet War Rooms
Westminster SW1A 2AQ
(020) 7930 6961
www.iwm.org.uk
Learn more about the man who inspired Britain's finest hour at the highly interactive and innovative Churchill Museum, the world's first major museum dedicated to life of the 'greatest Briton'. Step back in time and discover the secret.

Eltham Palace
Greenwich SE9 5QE
(020) 8294 2548
www.elthampalace.org.uk
A spectacular fusion of 1930s Art Deco villa and magnificent 15th century Great Hall. Surrounded by period gardens.

Hampton Court Palace
Richmond upon Thames KT8 9AU
0870 752 7777
www.hrp.org.uk
This magnificent palace set in delightful gardens was famously one of Henry VIII's favourite palaces.

HMS Belfast
Southwark SE1 2JH
(020) 7940 6300
www.iwm.org.uk
HMS Belfast, launched 1938, served throughout WWII playing a leading part in the destruction of the German battle cruiser Scharnhorst and in the Normandy Landings.

Kensington Palace State Apartments

Kensington and Chelsea W8 4PX
0870 751 5170
www.hrp.org.uk
Home to the Royal Ceremonial Dress Collection, which includes some of Queen Elizabeth II's dresses worn throughout her reign, as well as 14 of Diana, Princess of Wales' evening dresses.

Kenwood House

Camden NW3 7JR
(020) 8348 1286
www.english-heritage.org.uk/daysout/properties/kenwood-house/
Beautiful 18th century villa with fine interiors, and a world class collection of paintings. Also fabulous landscaped gardens and an award-winning restaurant.

Queen Elizabeth's Hunting Lodge

Waltham Forest E4 7QH
(020) 8529 6681
www.cityoflondon.gov.uk
Timber-framed hunting grandstand built in 1543 for Henry VIII. It still stands in a beautiful part of Epping Forest overlooking the old hunting field for which it was designed.

Southwark Cathedral

Southwark SE1 9DA
(020) 7367 6700
www.southwark.anglican.org/cathedral
Oldest Gothic church in London (c.1220) with interesting memorials connected with the Elizabethan theatres of Bankside.

Somerset House

Westminster WC2R 1LA
(020) 7845 4670
www.somerset-house.org.uk
This magnificent 18th century building houses the celebrated collections of the Courtauld Institute of Art Gallery, Gilbert Collection and Hermitage Rooms.

Tower of London

Tower Hamlets EC3N 4AB
0870 756 6060
www.hrp.org.uk
The Tower of London spans over 900 years of British history. Fortress, palace, prison, arsenal and garrison, it is one of the most famous fortified buildings in the world, and houses the Crown Jewels, armouries, Yeoman Warders and ravens.

Nature & Wildlife

London Wetland Centre

Richmond upon Thames SW13 9WT
(020) 8409 4400
www.wwt.org.uk
The London Wetland Centre is a unique wildlife visitor attraction just 25 minutes from central London. Run by the Wildfowl and Wetlands Trust (WWT), it is acclaimed as the best urban site in Europe to watch wildlife.

ZSL London Zoo

Westminster NW1 4RY(020) 7722 3333
www.londonzoo.co.uk
Come face to face with some of the hairiest, scariest, tallest and smallest animals on the planet - right in the heart of the capital.

Outdoor Activities

Bateaux London Restaurant Cruisers

Westminster WC2N 6NU
(020) 7695 1800
www.bateauxlondon.com
Bateaux London offers lunch and dinner cruises, combining luxury dining, world-class live entertainment and five-star customer care.

London Eye River Cruise Experience

Lambeth E1 7PB
0870 500 0600
www.londoneye.com
See London from a different perspective and enjoy a unique 40 minute circular sightseeing cruise on the river Thames.

Events 2014

London Ice Sculpting Festival at Canary Wharf
January, date TBC
At this super-cool, free annual event, talented sculptors from around the world compete against the clock to create chilly artworks from two-metre glistening blocks of ice in a nail-biting competition.

Burns Night in London
January 25, Various venues
Celebrate Scotland's favourite son on Burns Night in London. Burns Night is the anniversary of the Scottish poet Robert Burns' birthday. Many London restaurants and bars hold special Burns Night events.

Chinese New Year
February, date TBC Various venues
London's Chinese New Year celebrations are the largest outside Asia, with parades, performances and fireworks.
www.visitlondon.com

Vodafone London Fashion Weekend
February, dates TBC, Somerset House
London's largest and most exclusive designer shopping event.
www.londonfashionweekend.co.uk

The Boat Race
April 6, Putney Bridge
Boat crews from the universities of Oxford and Cambridge battle it out on the Thames.
www.theboatrace.org

Virgin London Marathon
April 13, Various venues
Whether you run, walk or cheer from the sidelines, this is a London sporting institution you won't want to miss.
www.virginlondonmarathon.com

Covent Garden May Fayre and Puppet Festival
May 11, The Actors' Church, St Paul's Covent Garden
Enjoy a day of traditional British entertainment at the Actor's Church in Covent Garden.

Museums At Night 2014
May 15-17, Various venues
Explore arts and heritage after dark at museums across London. Packed with special events, from treasure trails to pyjama parties, Museums at Night is a great opportunity to explore culture in a new light.

RHS Chelsea Flower Show
May 20-24, Royal Hospital Chelsea
Experience the greatest flower show in the world at London's Royal Hospital Chelsea.
www.rhs.org.uk/Chelsea-Flower-Show

Taste of London
June 19-22, Regent's Park and Primrose Hill
Taste of London is the capital's largest open-air food and drink festival, bringing together big-name chefs, popular restaurants and top-notch food.
www.tastefestivals.com/london

Greenwick+Docklands International Festival

June, dates TBC, Various venues

The Greenwich+Docklands International Festival returns with a ten-day rollercoaster of theatre, dance and spectacle. The best of UK and international street arts brings extraordinary sights and sounds to Greenwich and East London.
www.festival.org

London Festival of Architecture

June 13-July 26

See London's buildings in a new light during the Festival of Architecture.
www.visitlondon.com

City of London Festival

June-July, Various venues

The City of London Festival is an annual extravaganza of music, dance, art, film, poetry, family and participation events that takes place in the city's Square Mile.
www.visitlondon.com

Wimbledon Lawn Tennis Championships

June 23-July 6, Wimbledon

The world of tennis descends on Wimbledon in South West London every summer for two weeks of tennis, strawberries and cream, and good-natured queuing.
www.wimbledon.com

RideLondon

August 9-10, Various venues

A world class festival of cycling in London, it includes four main cycling events. Even if you can't ride as fast as Bradley Wiggins, you can still take part riding in the Freecycle and the 100 races through central London. As a spectator, you'll love cheering on the expert riders in the Classic race and Grand Prix.
www.ridelondon.co.uk

Notting Hill Carnival

August 24-25, Various venues

The streets of West London come alive every August Bank Holiday weekend as London celebrates Europe's biggest street festival.
www.thenottinghillcarnival.com

The Mayor's Thames Festival

September

A spectacular weekend of free events celebrating London and its river.
www.visitlondon.com

London Design Festival

September, Various venues

A celebration of international design, with talks, seminars, exhibitions, parties and private views.
www.visitlondon.com

Tour of Britain

September, Various venues

Celebrating its 10th anniversary this year, the Tour of Britain is a multi-stage cycling race that takes place across the UK.
www.tourofbritain.com

London Film Festival

October, Various venues

A two-week showcase of the world's best new films, the BFI London Film Festival is one of the most anticipated events in London's cultural calendar.
www.bfi.org.uk/lff

ATP World Tour Finals

November, O2 Arena

See the world's top eight singles players and doubles teams in London for the prestigious season-ending tennis tournament.
www.atpworldtour.com

Tourist Information Centres

When you arrive at your destination, visit an Official Partner Tourist Information Centre for quality assured help with accommodation and information about local attractions and events, or email your request before you go. To find a Tourist Information Centre visit www.visitengland.com

City of London	St Paul's Churchyard	020 7606 3030	stpauls.informationcentre@cityoflondon.gov.uk
Greenwich	2 Cutty Sark Gardens	0870 608 2000	tic@greenwich.gov.uk

Regional Contacts and Information

For more information on accommodation, attractions, activities, events and holidays in London, contact Visit London.

The publications listed are available from the following organisations:

Go to visitlondon.com for all you need to know about London. Look for inspirational itineraries with great ideas for weekends and short breaks.

Or call 0870 1 LONDON (0870 1 566 366) for:

• A London visitor information pack
• Visitor information on London
• Accommodation reservations

Speak to an expert for information and advice on museums, galleries, attractions, riverboat trips, sightseeing tours, theatre, shopping, eating out and much more! Or simply go to visitlondon.com

Entries appear alphabetically by town name in each county. A key to symbols appears on page 7

LONDON E4, Inner London Map ref 2D2 SatNav E4 7RA

enjoyEngland.com ★★★★ TOURING & CAMPING PARK

Caravan	(65)	£13.50-£19.20
Motorhome	(65)	£13.50-£19.20
Tent	(35)	£13.50-£19.20
Holiday accommodation	(17)	£25.00-£50.00

65 touring pitches

Lee Valley Campsite - Sewardstone

Sewardstone Road, Chingford, London E4 7RA
T: (020) 8529 5689 **F:** (020) 8559 4070 **E:** sewardstonecampsite@leevalleypark.org.uk
W: www.visitleevalley.org.uk/wheretostay **£ BOOK ONLINE**

Lee Valley Campsite, Sewardstone is less than 40 minutes from central London and is close to the scenic Hertfordshire and Essex countryside. Come camping, caravanning or stay in one of our cosy cocoons or woodland cabins – it's perfect for families, couples or groups of friends looking for affordable accommodation in London.

Directions: The campsite is situated on the A112 between Chingford and Waltham Abbey to the South of the M25. Leave M25 at junction 26 and follow the signs.

Open: Open 1st March - 31st January.

Payment: **Leisure:** **Children:** **Catering:** **Park:** **Touring:**

LONDON N9, Inner London Map ref 2D2 SatNav N9 0AR

enjoyEngland.com ★★★ TOURING & CAMPING PARK

Caravan	(100)	£13.50-£19.20
Motorhome	(100)	£13.50-£19.20
Tent	(60)	£13.50-£19.20
Holiday accommodation	(12)	£25.00-£50.00

100 touring pitches

Lee Valley Camping and Caravan Park - Edmonton

Meridian Way, Edmonton, London N9 0AR
T: (020) 8803 6900 **F:** (020) 8884 4975 **E:** edmontoncampsite@leevalleypark.org.uk
W: www.visitleevalley.org.uk/wheretostay **£ BOOK ONLINE**

A peaceful site that puts you in easy each of both central London and the many attractions of Lee Valley Regional Park. With excellent facilities including an on-site shop and children's play area, plus a golf course, athletics centre, cinema and restaurant all located within the complex. Overnight holding area available.

Directions: Leave M25 at J25, follow signs for City. Turn left for Freezywater at traffic lights, follow signs for Lee Valley Leisure Complex.

Open: All year.

Payment: **Leisure:** **Children:** **Catering:** **Park:** **Touring:**

HUDSONS HERITAGE *Explorer*

Hatfield House, Hertfordshire

An exciting touring pass

Opening the door to the country's heritage attractions

2014

www.hudsons-explorer.com

- 3, 7, 14 or 28-day passes
- Visit as many participating attractions as you wish during the fixed-day period
- Prices start from just £49.00 per Adult
- Complimentary full-colour guidebook
- Available to buy online and in person at selected outlets

Amazing value! Visit heritage attractions for less than £6.40 per day* SAVE MORE WITH EVERY VISIT!

HS Garden Wisley, Surrey   Bamburgh Castle, Northumberland   Roman Baths, Somerset   Portsmouth Historic Dockyard

STATELY HOMES • HISTORIC HOUSES • CASTLES • GARDENS • ABBEYS & CATHEDRALS • WORLD HERITAGE SITES

East of England

Bedfordshire, Cambridgeshire, Essex, Hertfordshire, Norfolk, Suffolk

Explore East Anglia and you'll discover a diverse mixture of vibrant cities, individual towns and villages, beautiful countryside and idyllic seaside – and all attractions are within easy reach. Based around the ancient kingdom of East Anglia, the area is made up of the six counties of Norfolk, Suffolk, Bedfordshire, Cambridgeshire, Essex and Hertfordshire to form the well-known 'hump' on England's eastern side. Directly to the north of London, the region has preserved much of its unspoiled character, rural landscape, architecture and traditions.

Highlights

Cambridge

An elegant yet compact city, Cambridge boasts a blend of history, scientific discovery, hi-tech innovation, culture and beauty. Try some punting along the River Cam, passing age-old colleges.

Ely Cathedral

A magnificent Norman Cathedral, which attracts visitors from all over the world. It dominates the Cambridgeshire skyline and can be seen for miles.

Fenland

A naturally marshy region, most of the fens were drained several centuries ago, resulting in a flat, damp, low-lying agricultural region. It is home to a wide range of wildlife.

Huntingdon

This Cambridgeshire market town was chartered by King John in 1205 and was the birthplace in 1599 of Oliver Cromwell. Huntingdon is an important bridge-head where the Great North Road, crosses the River Great Ouse near to Hinchingbrooke House, once home to Cromwell.

Ipswich

Ipswich enjoys a wonderful position on the meandering River Orwell and is known as East Anglia's premier waterfront town. For centuries, the river has been the lifeblood of the town – even today it acts as the social focal point for both residents and visitors.

Knebworth House

One of England's most beloved stately homes, Knebworth House is famous worldwide for its rock concerts and as the home of Victorian novelist Edward Bulwer Lytton – author of the words "The pen is mightier than the sword".

Norfolk Broads

The Broads is Britain's largest protected wetland and third largest inland waterway, and is home to some of the rarest plants and animals in the UK.

Norwich

This medieval city, on the banks of the River Wensum is bursting with cultural vibrancy and heritage buildings, plus stunning 1000 year old architecture. From the medieval period until the start of the Industrial Revolution, Norwich was England's second city, enormously prosperous and culturally active.

Norfolk and Suffolk Coast

Mile upon mile of stunning beaches and unspoiled coastline can be found in these two counties. One of the best beaches is at Holkham near Wells-on-Sea, and there are numerous nature reserves along the coastal path.

Woburn Abbey

Set in a beautiful 3000 acre deer park, Woburn Abbey is home to The Duke of Bedford. It is also well-known for its safari park. to man's interaction with his environment.

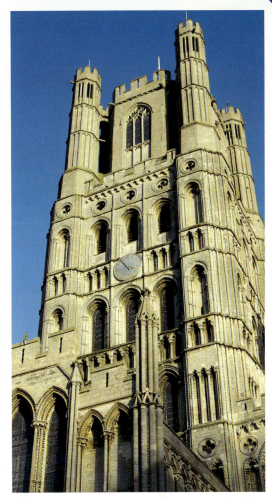

Editor's Picks

Take a punt

The best way to soak up the heritage and culture of Cambridge is to take a punt on the River Cam.

Binoculars at the ready

Take in the fresh air, see stunning views and set your eyes on some of the region's rare wildlife.

Enjoy a festival

Suffolk is the UK's festival county with an event for all tastes – music, comedy, theatre and dance are all covered.

Jump on your bicycle

Explore the countryside, with some of the best cycle routes in the country…and they're suitable for everyone.

Learn about our aviation heritage

From the very beginnings of flight with balloons and airships, to the present day airfields of the RAF, this region is steeped in aviation history.

Things to do

Attractions with this sign participate in the Places of Interest Quality Assurance Scheme.

Attractions with this sign participate in the Visitor Attraction Quality Assurance Scheme.

Both schemes recognise high standards in all aspects of the visitor experience (see page 7)

Entertainment & Culture

Central Museum and Planetarium
Southend-on-Sea, Essex SS2 6ES
(01702) 434449
www.southendmuseums.co.uk
An Edwardian building housing displays of archaeology, natural history, social and local history.

Gainsborough's House
Sudbury, Suffolk CO10 2EU
(01787) 372958
www.gainsborough.org
Gainsborough's House is the only museum situated in the birthplace of a great British artist. The permanent collection is built around the works of Thomas Gainsborough.

Hitchin Museum and Art Gallery
Hertfordshire SG5 1EH
(01462) 434476
www.north-herts.gov.uk/art_museums_and_heritage.htm
Local history museum and art gallery which tells the story of Hitchin. Two art galleries. Victorian pharmacy, costume gallery, and more.

Imperial War Museum Duxford
Cambridge CB22 4QR
(01223) 835000
www.iwm.org.uk/duxford
With its air shows, unique history and atmosphere, nowhere else combines the sights, sounds and power of aircraft quite like Duxford.

National Horseracing Museum and Tours
Newmarket, Suffolk CB8 8JH
(01638) 667333
www.nhrm.co.uk
Discover the stories of racing from its early origins at Newmarket to its modern-day heroes

Norwich Castle Museum and Art Gallery
Norfolk NR1 3JU
(01603) 493625
www.museums.norfolk.gov.uk
Ancient Norman keep of Norwich Castle dominates the city and is one of the most important buildings of its kind in Europe.

Peterborough Museum and Art Gallery

Cambridgeshire PE1 1LF
(01733) 864663
www.peterborough.gov.uk/leisure_and_culture/museum_and_galleries.aspx
Discover the rich & varied history of the Peterborough area -from Jurassic Sea Monsters to Napoleonic Prisoners of War to the haunted Museum building.

Royal Gunpowder Mills

Waltham Abbey, Essex EN9 1JY
(01992) 707370
www.royalgunpowdermills.com
A spectacular 170-acre location for a day of family fun. Special events including Spitfire flypast, award winning Secret History exhibition, tranquil wildlife walks, guided land train tours and rocket science gallery.

Family Fun

Adventure Island

Southend-on-Sea, Essex SS1 1EE
(01702) 443400
www.adventureisland.co.uk
One of the best value 'theme parks' in the South East with over 60 great rides and attractions for all ages. No admission charge you only 'pay if you play'.

Bodyflight Bedford

Clapham, MK41 6AE
0845 200 2960
www.bodyflight.co.uk
Indoor Skydiving! Learn to fly like a skydiver on a vertical column of air! Offering lessons for all abilities.

Go Ape! High Wire Forest Adventure - Thetford
Santon Downham, Suffolk IP27 0AF
0845 643 9215
www.goape.co.uk
Take to the trees and experience an exhilarating course of rope bridges, tarzan swings and zip slides... all set high above the forest floor.

Go Ape! High Wire Forest Adventure - Woburn Safari Park
Milton Keynes, Bedfordshire MK17 9QN
0845 643 9215
www.goape.co.uk
Take to the trees and experience an exhilarating course of rope bridges, tarzan swings and zip slides...all set high above the forest floor.

Sea-Life Adventure

Southend-on-Sea, Essex SS1 2ER
(01702) 442200
www.sealifeadventure.co.uk
With more than 30 display tanks and tunnels to explore, there are loads of fishy residents to discover at Sea-Life Adventure.

The National Stud
Newmarket, Cambridgeshire CB8 0XE
(01638) 663464
www.nationalstud.co.uk
The beautiful grounds & facilities are a recognised tourist attraction in the eastern region.

Heritage

Audley End House and Gardens

Saffron Walden, Essex CB11 4JF
(01799) 522842
www.english-heritage.org.uk/audleyend
Audley End is one of England's most magnificent stately homes.

Blickling Hall, Gardens and Park
Norwich, Norfolk NR11 6NF
(01263) 738030
www.nationaltrust.org.uk/blickling
A Jacobean redbrick mansion with a garden, orangery, parkland and lake. Spectacular long gallery, plasterwork ceilings and fine collections of furniture, pictures and books. Walks.

Bressingham Steam and Gardens
Diss, Norfolk IP22 2AA
(01379) 686900
www.bressingham.co.uk
World-renowned gardener and horticulturalist Alan Bloom combined his passion for plants and gardens with his love of steam, to create a truly unique attraction at Bressingham.

Cathedral and Abbey Church of St Alban

St. Albans, Hertfordshire AL1 1BY
(01727) 860780
www.stalbanscathedral.org
St Alban is Britain's first Christian martyr and the Cathedral, with its shrine, is its oldest place of continuous worship.

Holkham Hall
Wells-next-the-Sea, Norfolk NR23 1AB
(01328) 710227
www.holkham.co.uk
Magnificent Palladian hall. Rolling parkland. A wealth of wildlife. The best beach in England.

Ickworth House, Park and Gardens
Bury St. Edmunds, Suffolk
IP29 5QE
(01284) 735270
www.nationaltrust.org.uk/ickworth
Fine paintings, a beautiful collection of Georgian silver, an Italianate garden and stunning parkland.

Kings College Chapel
Cambridge CB2 1ST
(01223) 331212
www.kings.cam.ac.uk
It's part of one of the oldest Cambridge colleges sharing a wonderful sense of history and tradition with the rest of the University.

Knebworth House
Hertfordshire SG1 2AX
(01438) 812661
www.knebworthhouse.com
Historic house, home to the Lytton family since 1490.

Oliver Cromwell's House
Ely, Cambridgeshire CB7 4HF
(01353) 662062
www.olivercromwellshouse.co.uk
Visit the former Lord Protector's family's home and experience an exhibition on 17th Century life.

Sandringham
King's Lynn, Norfolk PE35 6EN
(01485) 545408
www.sandringhamestate.co.uk
H.M. The Queen. A fascinating house, an intriguing museum and the best of the Royal gardens.

Somerleyton Hall and Gardens

Lowestoft, Suffolk NR32 5QQ
(01502) 734901
www.somerleyton.co.uk
12 acres of landscaped gardens to explore including our famous 1864 Yew hedge maze. Guided tours of the Hall.

Nature & Wildlife

Banham Zoo

Norwich, Norfolk NR16 2HE
(01953) 887771
www.banhamzoo.co.uk
Wildlife spectacular which will take you on a journey to experience tigers, leopards and zebra plus some of the world's most exotic, rare and endangered animals.

Colchester Zoo
Essex CO3 0SL
(01206) 331292
www.colchester-zoo.com
Enjoy daily displays, feed elephants and giraffes and see over 260 species in over 60 acres of parkland!

Fritton Lake Country World
Great Yarmouth,
Norfolk NR31 9HA
(01493) 488288
A woodland and lakeside haven with a children's assault course, putting, an adventure playground, golf, fishing, boating, wildfowl, heavy horses, cart rides, falconry and flying displays.

The Raptor Foundation
Huntingdon, Cambridgeshire PE28 3BT
(01487) 741140
www.raptorfoundation.org.uk
Bird of prey centre, offering 3 daily flying displays with audience participation, gift shop, Silent Wings tearoom, Raptor crafts shop.

RHS Garden Hyde Hall
Chelmsford, Essex CM3 8AT
(01245) 400256
www.rhs.org.uk/hydehall
A garden of inspirational beauty with an eclectic range of horticultural styles from traditional to modern providing year round interest.

RSPB Minsmere Nature Reserve
Saxmundham, Suffolk IP17 3BY
(01728) 648281
www.rspb.org.uk/minsmere
One of the UK's premier nature reserves, offering excellent facilities for people of all ages and abilities.

WWT Welney Wetland Centre
Wisbech, Norfolk PE14 9TN
(01353) 860711
www.wwt.org.uk/welney
A wetland nature reserve of 1,000 acres attracting large numbers of ducks and swans in winter and waders in spring and summer plus a range of wild plants and butterflies.

ZSL Whipsnade Zoo
Dunstable, Bedfordshire LU6 2LF
(01582) 872171
www.zsl.org/zsl-whipsnade-zoo
ZSL Whipsnade Zoo is one of Europe's largest wildlife conservation parks.

Woburn Safari Park
Bedfordshire MK17 9QN
(01525) 290407
www.woburn.co.uk
Drive through the safari park with 30 species of animals in natural groups just a windscreen's width away.

Events 2014

Essex Book Festival
March 1-31, Various locations throughout Essex
Venues throughout the county fill with people eager to listen to some of their favourite authors.
www.essexbookfestival.org.uk

Maldon Mud Race
May 25, Maldon
The annual Maldon Mud Race is a wacky fun competition in which participants race to become the first to finish a 400m dash over the bed of the River Blackwater.
www.maldonmudrace.com

Hertfordshire County Show
May 24-25, Redbourn
County show with all the usual attractions.
www.hertsshow.com

Suffolk Show
May 28-29, Ipswich
Animals, food and drink, shopping…there's lots to see and do at this popular county show.
www.suffolkshow.co.uk

King's Lynn
May Garland Procession
May, King's Lynn
The King's Morris dancers carry the May Garland around the town.
www.thekingsmorris.co.uk

Luton International Carnival
May, Luton
The highlight is the spectacular carnival parade – an eye-catching, breathtaking procession through the town centre, superbly reflecting the diverse mix of cultures in Luton.
www.luton.gov.uk

Colchester Medieval Fayre
June 7-8, Lower Castle Park, Colchester
This medieval style fair remembers a time when folk from the countryside and neighbouring villages would travel to the 'Big Fair' in the town.
www.oysterfayre.flyer.co.uk

Cambridgeshire County Show
June 1, Royston
Featuring traditional crafts, livestock, food hall, rural crafts and displays, vintage tractors, fairground, children's corner and ring events.
www.cambscountyshow.co.uk

Peterborough Dragon Boat Festival

June 14, Peterborough Rowing Lake, Thorpe Meadows

Teams of up to 11 people, dragon boats and all equipment provided, no previous experience required. Family entertainment and catering stalls

www.dragonboatfestivals.co.uk/peterborough

Royal Norfolk Show

June 25-26, Norwich

The Royal Norfolk Show celebrates everything that's Norfolk. It offers 10 hours of entertainment each day from spectacular grand ring displays, traditional livestock and equine classes, to a live music stage, celebrity guests and over 650 stands.

www.royalnorfolkshow.co.uk

Bedfordshire County Show

July, Biggleswade

Held in the beautiful grounds of Shuttleworth the Bedfordshire County Show is a showcase of town meets country.

www.bedfordshirecountyshow.co.uk

Rhythms of the World

July, dates TBC, Hitchin

This is a festival of world music.

www.rotw.org.uk

Latitude Festival

July, dates TBC, Southwold

Primarily a music festival but also has a full spectrum of art including film, comedy, theatre, cabaret, dance and poetry.

www.latitudefestival.com

Cambridge Folk Festival

July 31- August 3, Cherry Hinton

Top acts make this a must-visit event for folk fans.

www.cambridgefolkfestival.co.uk

Dunstable Downs Kite Festival

July, Dunstable

Kite enthusiasts from around the UK converge on Dunstable.

www.dunstablekitefestival.co.uk

Southend Carnival

August, Southend-on-Sea

A wide range of events held over eight days. www.southend-on-seacarnival.org.uk

Clacton Airshow

August 21-22, Clacton Seafront

Impressive aerobatic displays take to the skies while a whole host of exhibition, trade stands, food court and on-site entertainment are available at ground level.

www.clactonairshow.com

Chilli Festival

August 24-25, Benington Lordship Gardens, Stevenage

A popular family event attracting thousands of visitors over two days, offering a chance to buy Chilli plants, products and sample foods from around the world.

www.beningtonlordship.co.uk

Duxford Air Show

September 6-7, Duxford, nr Cambridge

Set within the spacious grounds of the famous former First and Second World War airfield, the Duxford Air Show features an amazing array of aerial displays.

www.iwm.org.uk/duxford

Great Yarmouth Maritime Festival

September 6-7, Great Yarmouth

A mix of traditional and modern maritime vessels will be moored on South Quay for visitors to admire and go aboard.

www.maritime-festival.co.uk

Essex Country Show

September 13-14, Barleylands, Billericay

The show, with an emphasis on agricultural history and rural crafts, is now in its 27th year.

www.barleylands.co.uk/essex-country-show

Aldeburgh Food & Drink Festival

September 27-28, Aldeburgh

A two-week celebration of the abundance of good local food and drink to be found in East Suffolk.

www.aldeburghfoodanddrink.co.uk

World Conker Championship

October, Oundle

A picturesque corner of Northamptonshire hosts the World Conker Championships on the second Sunday in October every year. Thousands flock to the venue to watch this great spectacle as modern day gladiators fight for glory armed only with a nut and 12 inches of string.

www.worldconkerchampionships.com

Britten Centenary

November, Snape Maltings

Benjamin Britten was the most celebrated British composer of the 20th century. The centenary of Benjamin Britten (1913-1976), born in Lowestoft, Suffolk, will be marked by special events.

www.aldeburgh.co.uk

Tourist Information Centres

When you arrive at your destination, visit an Official Partner Tourist Information Centre for quality assured help with accommodation and information about local attractions and events, or email your request before you go. To find a Tourist Information Centre visit www.visitengland.com

Aldeburgh	48 High Street	01728 453637	atic@suffolkcoastal.gov.uk
Bedford	St Pauls Square	01234 718112	TouristInfo@bedford.gov.uk
Bishop's Stortford	2 Market Square	01279 655831	tic@bishopsstortford.org
Bury St Edmunds	6 Angel Hill	01284 764667	tic@stedsbc.gov.uk
Cambridge	Peas Hill	0871 226 8006	info@visitcambridge.org
Colchester	1 Queen Street	01206 282920	vic@colchester.gov.uk
Diss	Meres Mouth	01379 650523	dtic@s-norfolk.gov.uk
Ely	Oliver Cromwell's House	01353 662062	tic@eastcambs.gov.uk
Felixstowe	91 Undercliff Road West	01394 276770	ftic@suffolkcoastal.gov.uk
Great Yarmouth	25 Marine Parade	01493 846346	gab@great-yarmouth.gov.uk
Hunstanton	Town Hall	01485 532610	info@visithunstanton.info
Ipswich	St Stephens Church	01473 258070	tourist@ipswich.gov.uk
King's Lynn	The Custom House	01553 763044	kings-lynn.tic@west-norfolk.gov.uk
Lavenham	Lady Street	01787 248207	lavenhamtic@babergh.gov.uk
Letchworth Garden City	33-35 Station Road	01462 487868	tic@letchworth.com
Lowestoft	East Point Pavilion	01502 533600	touristinfo@waveney.gov.uk
Luton	Luton Central Library	01582 401579	tourist.information@lutonculture.com
Maldon District	Wenlock Way	01621 856503	tic@maldon.gov.uk

Newmarket	63 The Guineas	01638 719749	tic.newmarket@forest-heath.gov.uk
Norwich	The Forum	01603 213999	tourism@norwich.gov.uk
Peterborough	9 Bridge Street	01733 452336	tic@peterborough.gov.uk
Saffron Walden	1 Market Place	01799 524002	tourism@saffronwalden.gov.uk
Southend-on-Sea	Pier Entrance	01702 215620	vic@southend.gov.uk
Southwold	69 High Street	01502 724729	southwold.tic@waveney.gov.uk
St Albans	Old Town Hall	01727 864511	tic@stalbans.gov.uk
Stowmarket	The Museum of East Anglian Life	01449 676800	tic@midsuffolk.gov.uk
Sudbury	Sudbury Library	01787 881320	sudburytic@sudburytowncouncil.co.uk
Witham	61 Newland Street	01376 502674	tic@witham.gov.uk
Woodbridge	New Street	01394 446510	felixstowetic@suffolkcoastal.gov.uk

Regional Contacts and Information

For more information on accommodation, attractions, activities, events and holidays in East of England, contact the regional or local tourism organisations. Their websites have a wealth of information and many produce free publications to help you get the most out of your visit.

East of England Tourism
Tel: (01284) 727470
Email: info@eet.org.uk
Web: www.visiteastofengland.com

The comprehensive website is updated daily. Online brochures and information sheets can be downloaded including Whats's New; Major Events; Stars and Stripes (connections with the USA) and a range of Discovery Tours around the region.

East of England
Where to Stay

Entries appear alphabetically by town name in each county. A key to symbols appears on page 7

CAMBRIDGE, Cambridgeshire Map ref 2D1   SatNav CB23 7DG

Highfield Farm Touring Park

Long Road, Comberton, Cambridge CB23 7DG
T: (01223) 262308 **F:** (01223) 262308 **E:** enquiries@highfieldfarmtouringpark.co.uk
W: www.highfieldfarmtouringpark.co.uk

🚐 (60)	£18.50-£23.50	
🚏 (60)	£18.50-£23.50	
⛺ (60)	£13.00-£16.50	

120 touring pitches

A popular, family-run park with excellent facilities close to the University City of Cambridge and Imperial War Museum, Duxford. Ideally situated for touring East Anglia within easy access of the Cambridge park and rides. Prices for Caravans and motorvans are based on two people with electric included. Please view our website for further information.

Directions: From Cambridge take the A1303 to Bedford. After 3 miles, left at roundabout, follow sign to Comberton. From M11 jct 12, A603 to Sandy. Then B1046 to Comberton.

Open: April to October.

Site: ⛺🅿 **Payment:** € ☀ **Leisure:** ♪ ▶ ∪ **Children:** 🛝 ⚠ **Catering:** 🍴 **Park:** 🐕 🗑 🏠 📶
Touring: 🚿 ♿ 🔌 ♨

HUNTINGDON, Cambridgeshire Map ref 3A2   SatNav PE28 9AJ

Quiet Waters Caravan Park (Touring)

Hemingford Abbots, Huntingdon, Cambridgeshire PE28 9AJ
T: (01480) 463405 **F:** (01480) 463405 **E:** quietwaters.park@btopenworld.com
W: www.quietwaterscaravanpark.co.uk

🚐 (18)	£15.50-£19.50	
🚏 (18)	£15.50-£19.50	
⛺ (2)	£15.50-£19.50	
🏠 (9)	£295.00-£425.00	

18 touring pitches

A quiet, family owned riverside park in the centre of a picturesque village. Fishing, boating & excellent walking area. Luxury holiday static caravans and touring pitches, seasonal pitches also available. Disabled facilities available. **Directions:** Junction 25 off the A14, 13 miles from Cambridge, 5 miles from Huntingdon. **Open:** 1st April to 30th October.

Site: ⛺🅿 **Payment:** 💷 ☀ **Leisure:** ♪ ▶ **Children:** 🛝 **Park:** 🐕 🗑 🏠 📶 **Touring:** 🚿 ♿ 🔌 ♨

HUNTINGDON, Cambridgeshire Map ref 3A2   SatNav PE28 2AA

Wyton Lakes Holiday Park

Banks End, Wyton, Huntingdon, Cambridgeshire PE28 2AA
T: (01480) 412715 / 07785 294419 **E:** loupeter@supanet.com
W: www.wytonlakes.com

🚐 (60)	£19.00	
🚏 (60)	£19.00	
⛺ (20)	£16.00	

80 touring pitches

Adult-only park. Some pitches beside the on-site carp and coarse-fishing lakes. River frontage. Close to local amenities. **Directions:** Exit 23 off A14. Follow signs A141 March. Go past 4 roundabouts. At 4th roundabout take A1123 to St Ives. Park approx 1 mile on right. **Open:** April to October.

Leisure: ♪ **Property:** 🐕 🛏

COLCHESTER, Essex   Map ref 3B2

SatNav CO5 8FE

Fen Farm Camping and Caravan Site

Moore Lane, East Mersea, Colchester, Essex CO5 8FE
T: (01206) 383275 **F:** 01206 386316 **E:** havefun@fenfarm.co.uk
W: www.fenfarm.co.uk

🚐 (30)	£18.00-£30.00
🚍 (30)	£18.00-£30.00
⛺ (30)	£18.00-£30.00

Celebrating 90 years of Camping, peaceful family run caravan & camping park on the Essex Coast. Excellent for families. Modern facilities. No hire vans. We welcome tents, tourers and motorhomes of any size. Dogs welcome. **Directions:** Follow the B1025 to Mersea, take left fork onto Island. Follow road to 'Dog and Pheasant' pub, 1st turn on right leads to Fen Farm. **Open:** March - November.

Site: ⚎🅿 **Payment:** 💷 ☀ **Leisure:** 🎵 ⚑ **Children:** 🐾 ⛰ **Catering:** 🍴 **Park:** 🐕 ⛭ 🚽 🗐 📻 **Touring:** 🔌 🚰 🚿 🎵

COLCHESTER, Essex   Map ref 3B2

SatNav CO5 8SE

Waldegraves Holiday Park

Waldegraves Lane, West Mersea, Colchester, Essex CO5 8SE
T: (01206) 382898 **F:** (01206) 385359 **E:** holidays@waldegraves.co.uk
W: www.waldegraves.co.uk

🚐 (60)	£18.00-£30.00
🚍 (60)	£18.00-£30.00
⛺ (60)	£18.00-£30.00
🏠 (26)	£120.00-£750.00
60 touring pitches	

🇫 🐦

Ideal family park. Private Beach. Grassland sheltered with trees and four fishing lakes, boating lake, undercover golf driving range, heated swimming pool, pitch and put and crazy golf. Family entertainment. Licensed bar and restaurant. **Directions:** Junction 26 off A12 join B1025 to Mersea Island cross the Strood take left folk to East Mersea, 2nd right. **Open:** 1 March to 30 November.

Site: 🏪 ⚎🅿 **Payment:** 💷 ☀ **Leisure:** 🎵 ⚑ 🎣 ⚓ **Children:** 🐾 ⛰ **Catering:** ✗ 🍴 **Park:** 🐕 🎵 🚽 🗐 📻 **Touring:** 🔌 🚰 🚿 🎵

ST. LAWRENCE, Essex   Map ref 3B3

SatNav CM0 7LY

St Lawrence Holiday Park

10 Main Road, St. Lawrence Bay, Southminster CM0 7LY
T: (01621) 779434 **F:** (01621) 778311 **E:** office@slcaravans.co.uk
W: www.slcaravans.co.uk

Over the last ten years there has been major reinvestment and redevelopment of the park with the installation of a new launderette, Wi-Fi, a launching ramp for the beach and expansion of the St Lawrence Inn to include a children's room and an Indian restaurant offering fine cuisine and take-away menu. This quality graded park was a finalist in the 2010 & 2013 Caravan Park Essex Tourism awards. Please contact for prices.

Directions: On the A130 turn exit at Rettendon turnpike, take A132 towards South Woodham Ferrers. Then take the B1012 to Latchingdon. At the Church turn left into Bradwell Road, follow our brown tourism signs, though Mayland and Steeple, turn left into Main Road. The park is 1km on the right hand side.

Open: March - November.

🇫

Site: 🏪 **Leisure:** 🎵 ⚑ 🎣 **Property:** 🐕 🎵 📖 **Catering:** ✗

Lee Valley Caravan Park - Dobbs Weir

Charlton Meadows, Essex Road, Hoddesdon, Hertfordshire EN11 0AS
T: (08456) 770609 **E:** dobbsweircampsite@leevalleypark.org.uk
W: www.visitleevalley.org.uk/wheretostay **£ BOOK ONLINE**

🚐 (46)	£13.50-£19.20
🚎 (46)	£13.50-£19.20
⛺ (138)	£13.50-£19.20

Lee Valley Caravan Park, Dobbs Weir is just 30 minutes from London by train and is surrounded by the picturesque countryside of Hertfordshire and Essex. Perfect for camping and caravanning. Enjoy a short break in the Lee Valley or stay for longer and buy a luxury holiday home.

Directions: From the A10 take the Hoddesdon turn off, then at the second roundabout, turn left signposted Dobbs Weir. Lee Valley Caravan Park is on the right within 1 mile.

Open: From 1st March - 31st January.

Payment: 💳 ☼ **Children:** 🛝 ⛏ **Catering:** 🍴 **Park:** 🐕 🚻 📶 🔥 **Touring:** 🚿 🛢 🚐 ⚡

CAISTER-ON-SEA, *Norfolk*   *Map ref 3C1*   SatNav NR30 5DH

Wentworth Holidays

Bultitudes Loke, Caister on Sea, Great Yarmouth, Norfolk NR30 5DH
T: (01493) 720382 **F:** (01493) 377573 **E:** donaldpeers@hotmail.co.uk
W: www.grasmere-wentworth.co.uk

(12)   £160.00-£395.00

Wentworth is a small family run chalet site adjacent to Grasmere Caravan Park. All chalets are fully equipped including towels and bedding, also four wheelchair friendly units. **Directions:** From A149 Great Yarmouth enter at Stadium roundabout ½ mile concealed turning just after blue house on the left. **Open:** March-October.

Payment: **Property:** **Children:**

GREAT YARMOUTH, *Norfolk*   *Map ref 3C1*   SatNav NR30 5DH

Grasmere Caravan Park

9 Bultitudes Loke, Caister on Sea, Great Yarmouth, Norfolk NR30 5DH
T: (01493) 720382 **F:** (01493) 377573 **E:** donaldpeers@hotmail.co.uk
W: www.grasmere-wentworth.co.uk

(40)   £16.00-£20.00
(6)   £16.00-£20.00
(1)   £185.00-£400.00
(11)   £125.00-£415.00
40 touring pitches

Grasmere is a family run business suitable for those looking for a quieter holiday. Touring pitches and static vans for hire are available. **Directions:** From A149 Great Yarmouth enter at Stadium roundabout 0.5 miles concealed turning just after blue house on the left. **Open:** April to October.

Site: **Payment:** **Children:** **Park:** **Touring:**

GREAT YARMOUTH, *Norfolk*   *Map ref 3C1*   SatNav NR29 4HR

Seacroft Holiday Village

Beach Road, Hemsby, Norfolk NR29 4HR
T: (01692) 582277 **E:** info@richardsonsgroup.net
W: www.richardsonsgroup.net

£240.00-£450.00

Seacroft in Hemsby near Great Yarmouth is only a 10 minute walk from the beach. Offers themed breaks and full entertainment programme. Catered, adult only site. We offer themed breaks from February – December including Christmas and New Year, so whether it's Comedy, 60's, 70's or Star Cabarets that you like, we have something to suit all.

Directions: Please contact us for directions.   **Open:** February to December.

Site: **Payment:** **Leisure:** **Property:** **Catering:**

GREAT YARMOUTH, *Norfolk* Map ref 3C1

SatNav NR29 3NW

★★★★
HOLIDAY PARK

🏠 £150.00-£700.00
🚐 £265.00-£580.00

Summerfields Holiday Park

Beach Road, Scratby, Great Yarmouth NR29 3NW
T: (01692) 582277 **F:** (01493) 730292 **E:** info@richardsonsgroup.net
W: www.richardsonsholidayparks.co.uk **£ BOOK ONLINE**

Featuring an indoor heated pool with sauna, spa bath and solarium. Amusements and entertainment for children and adults. Chalet and caravan accommodation. Eight hundred yards from the beach. Children's club with Ellie the Elephant and Richie the Monkey plus evening entertainment for all the family.

Directions: Please contact us.   **Open:** April-October.

Site: 🏕 Payment: 💳 Leisure: ♦ ☎ Property: 🐾 🚐 🛋 Children: 🛝 ⛰ Catering: ✗

GREAT YARMOUTH, *Norfolk* Map ref 3C1

SatNav NR30 1TB

★★★★★
HOLIDAY &
TOURING PARK

🚐 (213)
🚐 (213)
⛺ (213)
🏠 (5)
🏠 (48)
🚐 (389)

213 touring pitches

[f] [t]

Vauxhall Holiday Park

Acle New Road, Great Yarmouth, Norfolk NR30 1TB
T: (01493) 857231 **F:** 01493 331122 **E:** info@vauxhallholidays.co.uk
W: www.vauxhall-holiday-park.co.uk **£ BOOK ONLINE**

Vauxhall Holiday Park in Great Yarmouth, Norfolk is a long established holiday park in a convenient location. Offering superb accommodation and welcomes tents and touring vans. Offers family holidays, short breaks and music weekender events. Please contact for prices. **Directions:** Please contact us for directions.
Open: All Year.

Site: 🏕 ⛺🅿 Payment: 💳 Leisure: ⛳ ⚑ ♦ ☎ ⚲ Children: 🛝 ⛰ Catering: ✗ 🛒 Park: 🎵 🖥 🛋 🎣 Touring: 🚿 🔌 ♨ 🎵

Need more information?

Visit our new 2014 guide websites for detailed information, up-to-date availability and to book your accommodation online. Includes over 20,000 places to stay, all of them star rated.

www.visitor-guides.co.uk

HEMSBY, Norfolk   Map ref 3C1

SatNav NR29 4HT

Hemsby Beach Holiday Park

Beach Road, Hemsby, Great Yarmouth NR29 4HT
T: (01692) 582277 **E:** info@richardsonsgroup.net
W: www.richardsonsholidayparks.co.uk **£ BOOK ONLINE**

(200) £160.00-£950.00

Family holiday park with on-site facilities, children's club with loads of activities & daily entertainment. Just minutes from the sandy beach, arcades & diners on Beach Road. Hemsby Beach has acres of green lawns providing open spaces for everyone to play and never feel crowded. The facilities at Hemsby Beach include a heated pool and play areas.

Directions: Please contact us for directions.

Open: April to October.

Site: ⌂ **Payment:** 💳 **Leisure:** ◆ ⚲ **Property:** ⌂ ♫ ▣ 📺 🏠 **Children:** 🛝 ⛰

HUNSTANTON, Norfolk   Map ref 3B1

SatNav PE36 5BB

Searles Leisure Resort

South Beach Road, Hunstanton PE36 5BB
T: (01485) 534211 **F:** (01485) 533815 **E:** bookings@searles.co.uk
W: www.searles.co.uk **£ BOOK ONLINE**

(157)
(50)
(125)
(156)
332 touring pitches

SPECIAL PROMOTIONS
Superb themed breaks every autumn. Beauty breaks, music weekends, Turkey and Tinsel breaks. Please check website for more details.

Creating happiness for all ages. Family-run, established for fifty years, Searles has something for everyone: superb range of accommodation, award winning touring park, bars, restaurants, entertainment, swimming pools, 27 hole golf, fishing lake and more - all 200yds from a sandy beach. The ideal base for exploring the Norfolk coast. Overnight holding area available. Please contact us for prices.

Directions: From King's Lynn take the A149 to Hunstanton. Upon entering Hunstanton follow B1161 to South Beach.

Open: Touring - all year. Holiday hire - Feb to Nov.

Site: ⌂ **Payment:** 💳 ☼ **Leisure:** 🚲 ♪ ♪ ∪ ◆ ⚲ ⚲ ⚲ **Children:** 🛝 ⛰ **Catering:** ✕ 🍴
Park: ⌂ ♫ ▣ 📺 🏠 **Touring:** 🚿 🚽 🔌 ⚡

Sunnymead Holiday Park Ltd

2 Kirkgate, Holme-next-the-Sea, Hunstanton, Norfolk PE36 6LH
T: (01485) 525381 **E:** sunnymeadholpark@aol.com
W: www.sunnymeadcorner.co.uk

 (8)   £225.00-£525.00

SPECIAL PROMOTIONS
Small Party Reduction all season: £50 off any full week if only 1 or 2 sharing. Off Peak Fortnight Special: cheapest week half price! Available 15th March - 24th May & 27th September - 1st November.

Location, Location, Location! Escape the constraints of city life and holiday in an Area of Outstanding Natural Beauty. Easily accessible from the A149, we are a small, family-run park nestling between meadows, the village church and adjacent to a bird reserve. If you are seeking a tranquil holiday in serene surroundings, you have found the ideal holiday. Perfect for bird watchers & nature lovers.

Directions: Upon reaching Holme-Next-Sea (A149), turn into Eastgate. At the bottom of this road there is a sharp bend to the left, do not follow the bend; to find us go straight ahead down the small unmade lane.

Open: 15th March - 1st November.

Payment: € **Leisure:** ↑ **Property:** 🐾 **Children:** 🛝

🏳 (180) £225.00-£450.00

Mundesley Holiday Village

Paston Road, Norwich NR11 8BT
T: (01692) 582277 **E:** info@richardsonsgroup.net
W: www.richardsonsholidayvillages.co.uk

Adult only, catered holiday village, providing a programme of entertainment & activities. Just a few minutes walk from Mundesley Beach & close to the seaside villages of Cromer & Sheringham. Many people come to Mundesley Holiday Village year after year and call it a home from home.

Directions: Please contact us for directions.   **Open:** April-December.

Site: 🏠 **Payment:** 💷 **Leisure:** ♣ 🎋 **Property:** 🎵 🍴 **Catering:** ✗

🚐 (40)   £15.00-£26.00
🚙 (40)   £12.00-£25.00
🏕 (2)   £250.00-£465.00
40 touring pitches

SPECIAL PROMOTIONS
New & used holiday caravans for sale. Luxury caravans to hire with panoramic sea views.

Sandy Gulls Caravan Park

Cromer Road, Mundesley, Norfolk NR11 8DF
T: (01263) 720513 / 07876 594699 **E:** info@sandygulls.co.uk
W: www.sandygulls.co.uk

The area's only cliff-top touring park. Located just south of Cromer. All pitches have panoramic sea views, electric/TV hook-ups. Free access to superb shower facilities. Miles of clean, sandy beaches and rural footpaths. Managed by the owning family for thirty years. Gold David Bellamy Conservation Award. Adults only.

Directions: From Cromer drive south along coast road for 5 miles.   **Open:** 1st March - 30th November.

Payment: € ☼ **Leisure:** 🎵 ▶ ∪ **Catering:** 🛒 **Park:** 🐾 📺 📖 📷 **Touring:** 🚽 🚿 🔌 ♪

NORTH RUNCTON, *Norfolk*   Map ref 3B1   *SatNav PE33 0RA*

Kings Lynn Caravan & Camping Park
New Road, North Runcton, King's Lynn, Norfolk PE33 0RA
T: (01553) 840004 **E:** klcc@btconnect.com
W: www.kl-cc.co.uk **£ BOOK ONLINE**

🚐 (150)   £18.00
🚐 (150)   £18.00
⛺ (150)   £11.00
🏠 (4)   £350.00
150 touring pitches

Set in approximately ten acres of beautiful mature parkland, the site is ideal for touring Norfolk and the Fens. Modern eco facility block. Camping Mega Pods and Holiday Lodges now available. **Directions:** Situated on the edge of the village North Runcton. Approximately one mile from the Hardwick roundabout where the A47, A10, A149 and A17 meet. **Open:** All year.

Site: 🅰🅿 Payment: 💷 € ☼ Leisure: ♪ ▶ ∪ Children: 🛝 Catering: 🍴 Park: 🐕 🚰 🖥 🛁 ⛱
Touring: 🚽 ⏱ 🚿 ♪

NORWICH, *Norfolk*   Map ref 3C1   *SatNav NR12 0EW*

Cable Gap Holiday Park
Coast Road, Bacton, Norfolk NR12 0EW
T: (01692) 650667 **E:** holiday@cablegap.co.uk
W: www.cablegap.co.uk

🚐 (1)   £405.00-£675.00
🚐 (17)   £195.00-£665.00

Cable Gap Holiday Park is a friendly, family run 5 star park providing first class facilities. **Directions:** Follow B1150 from Norwich or B1159 from Cromer. **Open:** March to November.

Payment: 💷 Leisure: ♿ ♪ ▶ ∪ Property: 🐕 🚰 🖥 🛁 Children: 🛝

SHERINGHAM, *Norfolk*   Map ref 3B1   *SatNav NR25 7HW*

Weybourne Forest Lodges
Sandy Hill Lane, Weybourne, Holt, Norfolk NR25 7HW
T: (01263) 588440 **F:** 01263 588588 **E:** info@weybourneforestlodges.co.uk
W: www.weybourneforestlodges.co.uk

🏠 (7)   £250.00-£950.00

There is nowhere else like this in North Norfolk. Well hidden in a forest glade, a small cluster of Self-catering lodges surrounded by woodland. Warm, comfortable, well equipped. Wildlife, wonderful walks and rare breeds. Owners on site. Local shop and pub located 1.5 miles away. Lodges available Christmas & New Year. **Directions:** 3 miles from Sheringham and Holt. 5 minutes drive from the coast at Weybourne. **Open:** All Year.

Payment: 💷 Leisure: ♿ ♪ ▶ ∪ ☂ Property: 🐕 🚰 🖥 🛁 Children: 🛝

STANHOE, Norfolk   Map ref 3B1 — SatNav PE31 8PU

The Rickels Caravan and Camping Park
Bircham Road, Stanhoe, King's Lynn PE31 8PU
T: (01485) 518671 **E:** therickelscaravanandcampingpark@hotmail.co.uk

£14.00-£16.00
£14.00-£16.00
£14.00-£16.00
24 touring pitches

The Rickels is a quiet, friendly, high-quality family-run park in 3 acres of grassland. A peaceful, relaxed atmosphere where you can enjoy a pleasant and restful holiday. Adults only. **Directions:** Please contact us for directions. **Open:** April to end October.

Payment: Leisure: Park: Touring:

BUNGAY, Suffolk   Map ref 3C1 — SatNav NR35 1HG

Outney Meadow Caravan Park
Outney Meadow, Bungay, Suffolk NR35 1HG
T: (01986) 892338 **E:** info@outneymeadow.co.uk
W: www.outneymeadow.co.uk

(45) £14.00-£21.00
(45) £14.00-£21.00
(45) £14.00-£21.00
45 touring pitches

Easy walking distance to Bungay market town. Situated between the River Waveney (canoe trail) and golf course, ideal base for exploring the beautiful countryside. Fishing, bikes and canoes available. Overnight holding area available. **Directions:** The Park entrance is sign posted from the roundabout, junction A143 and A144. **Open:** March to October.

Payment: Leisure: Children: Park: Touring:

LOWESTOFT, Suffolk   Map ref 3C1 — SatNav NR33 7BQ

Pakefield Caravan Park
Arbor Lane, Pakefield, Lowestoft NR33 7BQ
T: (01502) 561136 **F:** (01502) 539264 **E:** info@pakefieldcaravanpark.co.uk
W: www.pakefieldpark.co.uk

(12)
(12)
12 touring pitches

Set on the Sunrise coast, with fantastic sea views, this park is an ideal location to explore all that Suffolk and the Norfolk coast has to offer. Please contact us for prices. **Directions:** From the A12 take the Pakefield exit and pass the water tower on left. Turn right Grayson Drive, then right down Grayson Avenue. **Open:** March - October.

Site: Payment: Leisure: Property: Children: Catering:

WOODBRIDGE, Suffolk   Map ref 3C2 — SatNav IP12 3NF

Forest Camping Limited
Tangham Campsite, Rendlesham Forest Centre, Woodbridge, Suffolk IP12 3NF
T: (01394) 450707 **E:** admin@forestcamping.co.uk
W: www.forestcamping.co.uk

£16.00-£19.00
£16.00-£19.00
£16.00-£19.00
90 touring pitches

Spacious & well drained site in Forestry Commission wood, 5 miles along B1084 road between Woodbridge & Orford. Ideal for young families. Shower and toilet facilities. Site shop. Ideal for cycling and walking in forest. **Directions:** By Road: From A12 follow A1152 - Brown tourist signs 'Rendlesham Forest Centre'. B1084 towards Orford. **Open:** 1st April to 31st October.

Site: Payment: Children: Catering: Park: Touring:

East Midlands

Derbyshire, Leicestershire, Lincolnshire,
Northamptonshire, Nottinghamshire, Rutland

The East Midlands offer an exciting and
varied landscape. From the Lincolnshire
Wolds to the majestic Robin Hood
country of Sherwood Forest, and from
the honeycomb villages of Rutland
and Northamptonshire to the famous
hunting county of Leicestershire,
there is much to be seen and admired.
The region is a treasure trove of
magnificent castles and historic houses,
thriving cities and market towns.

Highlights

Chatsworth House

Chatsworth is home to the Duke and Duchess of Devonshire, and has been passed down through 16 generations of the Cavendish family. The house architecture has been evolving for five centuries, and it has one of Europe's most significant art collections.

Derwent Valley Mills

The cotton mills provide an industrial landscape of high historical and technological interest. The modern factory owes its origins to the mills where Richard Arkwright's inventions were first put into production.

Lincolnshire Wolds

The Lincolnshire Wolds is a range of hills designated an Area of Outstanding Natural Beauty, and is the highest area of land in Eastern England between Yorkshire and Kent.

National Forest

The National Forest is a forest in the making, an inspiring example for the country in the face of climate change and other environmental pressures. From one of the country's least wooded regions, the ambitious goal is to increase tree cover to about a third of all the land within its boundary.

Nottingham

Renowned around the world as the home of Robin Hood, Nottingham today is a destination for culture, heritage, shopping, sport and the arts.

Peak District

The stunning scenery may be the area's biggest free attraction, but there are plenty of other places to visit, including caves, ancient druidic stone circles and hilltop forts.

RAF Scampton

Lincolnshire has a proud history of aviation, having been an important base during World War Two. RAF Scampton was the home of the Dambusters and is the current base for the Red Arrows.

Rutland Water

This internationally famous nature reserve is managed by the Leicestershire & Rutland Wildlife Trust in partnership with Anglian Water, and provides one of the most important wildfowl sanctuaries in the UK, regularly holding in excess of 20,000 waterfowl. It is a Site of Special Scientific Interest.

Editor's Picks

Enjoy a bike ride

Cycling around Rutland Water is a favourite activity among locals and visitors – the off-road circular route is 23 miles.

Discover aviation history

During the Second World War Lincolnshire was known as 'Bomber County' because of the number of bomber bases dotted around the flatter countryside. Bring those days to life at the Lincolnshire Aviation Heritage Centre.

Enter the caves

Nottingham has a network of over 400 caves running beneath its streets. Many of are hidden below private homes but there are a few places where you can get a glimpse of what lies beneath.

Take the cable car

The Heights of Abraham has become one of the Peak District's most popular destinations. The observation cars transport you to the hilltop and stunning views of the Derwent Valley.

Things to do

 Attractions with this sign participate in the Places of Interest Quality Assurance Scheme.

 Attractions with this sign participate in the Visitor Attraction Quality Assurance Scheme.

Both schemes recognise high standards in all aspects of the visitor experience (see page 7)

Entertainment & Culture

Derby Museum and Art Gallery

Derby DE1 1BS
(01332) 716659
www.derby.gov.uk/museums
Derby Museum and Art Gallery holds collections and displays relating to the history, culture and natural environment of Derby and its region.

Galleries of Justice Museum

Nottingham NG1 1HN
(0115) 952 0555
www.galleriesofjustice.org.uk
You will be delving in to the dark and disturbing past of crime and punishment.

Mansfield Museum

Mansfield, Nottinghamshire NG18 1NG
(01623) 463088
www.mansfield.gov.uk/museum
Our dynamic museum and art gallerys permanent displays house a fascinating mix of local art and artefacts. Come and explore Mansfields social history or investigate 21st Century challenges facing our planet.

Newark Castle and Conflict
Newark, Nottinghamshire NG24 1BG
(01636) 655765
www.newark-sherwood.gov.uk
Newark Castle has been at the heart of the town for many centuries and has played an important role in historical events.

National Waterways Museum - Stoke Bruerne

Towcester, Northamptonshire NN12 7SE
(01604) 862229
www.stokebruernecanalmuseum.org.uk
Stoke Bruerne is an ideal place to explore the story of our waterways.

Newark Air Museum

Nottinghamshire NG24 2NY
(01636) 707170
www.newarkairmuseum.org
The museum is open to the public every day except December 24th, 25th, 26th and January 1st.

Northampton Museum & Art Gallery

Northampton NN1 1DP
(01604) 838111
www.northampton.gov.uk/museums
Displays include footwear and related items, paintings, ceramics and glass and the history of Northampton.

Silk Mill - Derby's Museum of Industry and History
Derby DE1 3AF
(01332) 255308
www.derby.gov.uk/museums
The Silk Mill was completed around 1723 and the rebuilt Mill now contains displays on local history and industry.

Family Fun

Foxton Locks
Market Harborough LE16 7RA
(01908) 302500
www.foxtonlocks.com
A great day out for all the family.

Gulliver's Theme Park
Matlock Bath, Derbyshire DE4 3PG
(01629) 580540
www.gulliversfun.co.uk
With more than 40 rides & attractions, Gulliver's provides the complete family entertainment experience. Fun & adventure with Gully Mouse, Dora the explorer, Diego and "The Lost World".

National Space Centre
Leicester LE4 5NS
0845 605 2001
www.spacecentre.co.uk
The award winning National Space Centre is the UK's largest attraction dedicated to space. From the moment you catch sight of the Space Centre's futuristic Rocket Tower, you'll be treated to hours of breathtaking discovery & interactive fun.

Sherwood Pines Forest Park
Edwinstowe, Nottinghamshire NG21 9JL
(01623) 822447
www.forestry.gov.uk
The largest forest open to the public in the East Midlands and centre for a wide variety of outdoor activities.

Wicksteed Park
Kettering, Northamptonshire NN15 6NJ
(01536) 512475
www.wicksteedpark.co.uk
Wicksteed Park remains Northamptonshire's most popular attraction and entertainment venue

Heritage

78 Derngate
Northampton NN1 1UH
(01604) 603407
www.78derngate.org.uk
Charles Rennie Mackintosh transformed a typical terraced house into a startlingly modern house for local model maker W.J. Bassett-Lowke. It was his last major commission and his only work in England.

Althorp
Northampton NN7 4HQ
(01604) 770107
www.althorp.com
Come and visit one of England's finest country houses, home of the Spencer family for over 500 years and ancestral home of Diana, Princess of Wales.

Ashby-de-le-Zouch Castle
Leicestershire LE65 1BR
(01530) 413343
www.english-heritage.org.uk/daysout/properties/ashby-de-la-zouch-castle
Visit Ashby-de-la-Zouch Castle where you will see the ruins of this historical castle, the original setting for many of the scenes of Sir Walter Scott's classic tale 'Ivanhoe'.

Belton House
Belton, Lincolnshire NG32 2LS
(01476) 566116
www.nationaltrust.org.uk/main/w-beltonhouse
Belton, is a perfect example of an English Country House.

Belvoir Castle
Melton Mowbray, Leicestershire NG32 1PE
(01476) 871002
www.belvoircastle.com
Home to the Duke and Duchess of Rutland, Belvoir Castle offers stunning views of the Vale of Belvoir.

Bosworth Battlefield Heritage Centre

Market Bosworth, Leicestershire CV13 0AD
(01455) 290429
www.bosworthbattlefield.com
Delve into Leicestershire's fascinating history at Bosworth Battlefield Country Park - the site of the 1485 Battle of Bosworth.

Chatsworth
Bakewell, Derbyshire DE45 1PP
(01246) 582204
www.chatsworth.org
One of Britain's best loved historic houses and estates.

Creswell Crags

Chesterfield, Derbyshire S80 3LH
(01909) 720378
www.creswell-crags.org.uk
A world famous archaeological site, home to Britain's only known Ice Age cave art.

Doddington Hall
Lincoln LN6 4RU
(01522) 694308
www.doddingtonhall.com
A superb Elizabethan mansion by the renowned architect Robert Smythson. The hall stands today as it was completed in 1600 with walled courtyards, turrets and gatehouse.

Great Central Railway

Leicester LE11 1RW
(01509) 230726
www.gcrailway.co.uk
The Great Central Railway is Britain's only double track main line steam railway. Enjoy an exciting calendar of events, a footplate ride or dine in style on board one of the steam trains.

Haddon Hall
Bakewell, Derbyshire DE45 1LA
(01629) 812855
www.haddonhall.co.uk
Haddon Hall is conveniently situated on the A6 between Bakewell and Matlock, Derbyshire.

Hardwick Hall
Chesterfield, Derbyshire S44 5QJ
(01246) 850430
www.nationaltrust.org.uk/hardwick
Owned by the National Trust the Estate includes Hardwick Hall, Stainsby Mill and a Park. The Hall is one of Britain's greatest Elizabethan houses, the water-powered Mill is fully functioning, the Park has a fishing lake and circular walks.

Kedleston Hall
Derby DE22 5JH
(01332) 842191
www.nationaltrust.org.uk/main/w-kedlestonhall
A fine example of a neo-classical mansion built between 1759-65 by the architecht Robert Adam and set in over 800 acres of parkland and landscaped pleasure grounds. Administered by The National Trust.

Lamport Hall and Gardens
Northamptonshire NN6 9HD
(01604) 686272
www.lamporthall.co.uk
Grade 1 listed building that was home to the Isham family and their collections for over four centuries.

Normanby Hall Museum and Country Park

Scunthorpe, Lincolnshire DN15 9HU
(01724) 720588
www.northlincs.gov.uk/normanby
Set in 300 acres of gardens, parkland, deer park, woods, ornamental and wild birds, well-stocked gift shop.

Nottingham Castle

Nottingham NG1 6EL
(0115) 915 3700
www.nottinghamcity.gov.uk/museums
Situated on a high rock, Nottingham Castle commands spectacular views over the city and once rivalled the great castles of Windsor and the Tower of London.

Papplewick Hall & Gardens
Nottinghamshire NG15 8FE
(0115) 963 3491
www.papplewickhall.co.uk
A fine Adam house, built in 1787 and Grade I listed building with a park and woodland garden.

Prebendal Manor Medieval Centre
Nassington, Northamptonshire PE8 6QG
(01780) 782575
www.prebendal-manor.co.uk
Visit a unique medieval manor and enjoy the largest recreated medieval gardens in Europe.

Rockingham Castle
Market Harborough, Northamptonshire LE16 8TH
(01536) 770240
www.rockinghamcastle.com
Rockingham Castle stands on the edge of an escarpment giving dramatic views over five counties and the Welland Valley below.

Sudbury Hall

Ashbourne, Derbyshire DE6 5HT
(01283) 585305
www.nationaltrust.org.uk/sudburyhall/
Explore the grand 17th Century hall with its richly decorated interior and see life below stairs.

Sulgrave Manor

Northamptonshire OX17 2SD
(01295) 760205
www.sulgravemanor.org.uk
A Tudor manor house and garden, the ancestral home of George Washington's family with authentic furniture shown by friendly guides

Tattershall Castle
Lincolnshire LN4 4LR
(01526) 342543
www.nationaltrust.org.uk/tattershall
Tattershall Castle was built in the 15th Century to impress and dominate by Ralph Cromwell, one of the most powerful men in England. The castle is a dramatic red brick tower.

Nature & Wildlife

Ayscoughfee Hall Museum and Gardens

Spalding, Lincolnshire PE11 2RA
(01775) 764555
www.ayscoughfee.org
Ayscoughfee Hall Museum is housed in a beautiful wool merchant's house built in 1451 on the banks of the River Welland.

Castle Ashby Gardens
Northamptonshire NN7 1LQ
(01604) 695200
www.castleashbygardens.co.uk
A haven of tranquility and beauty in the heart of Northamptonshire. Take your time to explore these beautiful gardens and enjoy the fascinating attractions from the rare breed farmyard to the historic orangery.

Conkers Discovery Centre
Ashby-de-la-Zouch, Leicestershire DE12 6GA
(01283) 216633
www.visitconkers.com/thingstodo/discoverycentre
Enjoy the great outdoors and explore over 120 acres of the award winning parkland.

Hardys Animal Farm
Ingoldmells, Lincolnshire PE25 1LZ
(01754) 872267
www.hardysanimalfarm.co.uk
An enjoyable way to learn about the countryside and how a farm works. There are animals for the children to enjoy as well as learning about the history and traditions of the countryside.

Renishaw Hall and Gardens
Dronfield, Derbyshire S21 3WB
(01246) 432310
www.renishaw-hall.co.uk
The Gardens are Italian in design and were laid out over 100 years ago by Sir George Sitwell. The garden is divided into 'rooms' with yew hedges, flanked with classical statues.

Salcey Forest
Hartwell, Northamptonshire NN17 3BB
(01780) 444920
www.forestry.gov.uk/salceyforest
Get a birds eye view of this wonderful woodland on the tremendous Tree Top Way.

Sherwood Forest Farm Park
Nottinghamshire NG21 9HL
(01623) 823558
www.sherwoodforestfarmpark.co.uk
Meet over 30 different rare farm breeds, plus other unusual species!

Sherwood Forest Country Park
Nottinghamshire NG21 9HN
(01623) 823202
www.nottinghamshire.gov.uk/sherwoodforestcp
Sherwood Forest Country Park covers 450 acres and incorporates some truly ancient areas of native woodland.

Twycross Zoo
Hinckley, Leicestershire CV9 3PX
(01827) 880250
www.twycrosszoo.com
Meet Twyford's famous orangutans, gorillas and chimpanzees plus many other mammals, birds and reptiles.

Events 2014

Dave's Comedy Festival
February 7-23, various venues
Confirmed acts are Alan Davies, Milton Jones, Russell Kane, Carl Donnelly, Doc Brown, Terry Alderton, Jenny Éclair, Seann Walsh, Al Murray and An Ideal Night Out hosted by Johnny Vegas.
www.comedy-festival.co.uk

Festival of Words
February date TBC, Nottingham
Celebrating Nottingham's Love of Words. This inaugural Festival of Words takes its inspiration from Nottingham's lace industry, an important thread in the city's heritage. nottwords.org.uk

Space Fiction
**February,
National Space Centre, Leicester**
Meet your favourite authors, discover new stories, champion a book and help us discover the greatest space fiction story ever written.
www.spacecentre.co.uk

Lincoln Music and Drama Festival
March (first two weeks), Lincoln
A competitive festival for children and adults of all ages, groups or individuals from schools or private entries. www.lincolnmdfest.org.uk

International Antiques & Collectors Fair
April, Newark Showground
The Newark International Antiques and Collectors Fair is the largest event of its kind in Europe – a world-wide phenomenon, this is one IACF event that needs to be experienced to be believed.
www.iacf.co.uk/newark

Easter Vintage Festival
April 18-21, Great Central Railway
A real treat for all this Easter with traction engines, classic cars and buses, fairground rides, trade stands, a beer tent as well as lots of action on the double track. www.gcrailway.co.uk

Brigstock International Horse Trials
May 2-4, Rockingham Castle
The Brigstock International Horse Trials is relocating to Rockingham Castle with a brand new course designed by International acclaimed designer Philip Herbert.
www.rockinghamcastle.com

Artisan Cheese Fair
May 3-4, Melton Mowbray
A chance to taste the huge range of cheeses that are made locally and further afield.
www.artisancheesefair.co.uk

Nottinghamshire County Show
May 10-11, Newark Showground
A fantastic traditional county show promoting farming, food, rural life and heritage in Nottinghamshire and beyond.
www.newarkshowground.com

Derbyshire Food & Drink Festival
May 17-18, Derby
Over 150 stalls will showcase the best local produce from Derbyshire and the Peak District region, as well as unique and exotic foods from further afield.
www.derbyshirefoodfestival.co.uk

Lincolnshire Wolds Walking Festival
May 17- June 1, Louth
Over 90 walks, taking place in an Area of Outstanding Natural Beauty and surrounding countryside.
www.woldswalkingfestival.co.uk

Lincolnshire Show
June 18-19,
Lincolnshire Showground
Agriculture remains at the heart of the Lincolnshire Show with livestock and equine competitions, machinery displays and the opportunity not only to find out where your food comes from but to taste a lot of it too!
www.lincolnshireshow.co.uk

Earth & Fire International Ceramics Fair
June 20-22,
Rufford Abbey Country Park
Earth and Fire is one of the country's premier ceramic events, and takes place in the historic grounds of Rufford Abbey.
www.nottinghamshire.gov.uk/earthandfire

Armed Forces Weekend
June 28, Wollaton Park, Nottingham
Nottingham welcomes the annual national event celebrating our Armed Forces past and present.
www.mynottingham.gov.uk/armedforces

British Grand Prix
June 30, Silverstone
Chance to see the world's best Formula One drivers in action.
www.silverstone.co.uk

RAF Waddington Air Show
July 5-6, Waddington, Lincoln
The largest of all RAF air shows, regularly attended by over 125,000 visitors.
www.waddingtonairshow.co.uk

Buxton Festival
July, Buxton
A summer celebration of the best opera, music and literature, at the heart of the beautiful Peak District.
www.buxtonfestival.co.uk

Robin Hood Festival
August 4-10, Sherwood Forest
Celebrate our most legendary outlaw in Sherwood Forest's medieval village.
www.nottinghamshire.gov.uk/robinhoodfestival/

Burghley Horse Trials
September, date TBC,
Burghley House, Lincs
One of the most popular events in the equestrian calendar.
www.burghley-horse.co.uk

Robin Hood Beer Festival
October, Nottingham Castle
Set in the stunning grounds of Nottingham Castle, the Robin Hood Beer Festival offers the world's largest selection of real ales and ciders.
www.beerfestival.nottinghamcamra.org

Robin Hood Pageant
October, Nottingham Castle
Nottingham Castle transforms into a medieval village for a weekend of celebrations in honour of Robin Hood and his merry men.
www.nottinghamcity.gov.uk

GameCity
October, Nottingham
Now in its 8th year, GameCity is the largest festival dedicated to the videogame culture in Europe.
festival.gamecity.org

Tourist Information Centres

When you arrive at your destination, visit an Official Partner Tourist Information Centre for quality assured help with accommodation and information about local attractions and events, or email your request before you go. To find a Tourist Information Centre visit www.visitengland.com

Ashbourne	13 Market Place	01335 343666	ashbourneinfo@derbyshiredales.gov.uk
Ashby-de-la-Zouch	North Street	01530 411767	ashby.tic@nwleicestershire.gov.uk
Bakewell	Old Market Hall	01629 813227	bakewell@peakdistrict.gov.uk
Buxton	The Pavillion Gardens	01298 25106	tourism@highpeak.gov.uk
Castleton	Buxton Road	01433 620679	castleton@peakdistrict.gov.uk
Chesterfield	Rykneld Square	01246 345777	tourism@chesterfield.gov.uk
Derby	Assembly Rooms	01332 255802	tourism@derby.gov.uk
Leicester	51 Gallowtree Gate	0844 888 5181	info@goleicestershire.com
Lincoln Castle Hill	9 Castle Hill	01522 545458	visitorinformation@lincolnbig.co.uk
Newark	Keepers Cottage, Riverside Park	01636 655765	newarktic@nsdc.info
Northampton	Sessions House, County Hall	01604 367997/8	tic@northamptonshire.gov.uk
Nottingham City	1-4 Smithy Row	08444 775 678	tourist.information@nottinghamcity.gov.uk
Sherwood	Sherwood Heath	01623 824545	sherwoodheath@nsdc.info
Silverstone	Silverstone Circuit	0844 3728 200	Elicia.Bonamy@silverstone.co.uk
Swadlincote	Sharpe's Pottery Museum	01283 222848	gail.archer@sharpespotterymuseum.org.uk

Regional Contacts and Information

The publications listed are available from the following organisations:

East Midlands Tourism
Web: www.eastmidlandstourism.com
- Discover East Midlands

Experience Nottinghamshire
Tel: 0844 477 5678
Web: www.experiencenottinghamshire.com
- Nottinghamshire Essential Guide
- Where to Stay Guide, City Breaks
- The City Guide
- Robin Hood Breaks

Peak District and Derbyshire
Web: www.visitpeakdistrict.com
- Peak District and Derbyshire Visitor Guide
- Well Dressing
- Camping and Caravanning Guide
- Walking Festivals Guide and Visitor Guide

Discover Rutland
Tel: (01572) 722577
Web: www.discover-rutland.co.uk
- Discover Rutland
- Eat drink Rutland
- Attractions
- Uppingham
- Oakham
- Oakham Heritage Trail

Lincolnshire
Tel: (01522) 545458
Web: www.visitlincolnshire.com
- Visit Lincolnshire – Destination Guide
- Great Days Out
- Good Taste
- Keep up with the flow

Explore Northamptonshire
Tel: (01604) 838800
Web: www.britainonshow.co.uk
- Northamptonshire Visitor Guide
- Northamptonshire presents Britain on show
- County Map

Leicestershire
Tel: 0844 888 5181
Web: www.goleicestershire.com
- Leicestershire City Guide
- Stay, Play, Explore
- Great Days Out in Leicestershire

East Midlands
Where to Stay

Entries appear alphabetically by town name in each county. A key to symbols appears on page 7

Rivendale Caravan & Leisure Park

Buxton Road, Nr Alsop En Le Dale, Ashbourne DE6 1QU
T: (01335) 310311 **F:** (01335) 310100 **E:** enquiries@rivendalecaravanpark.co.uk
W: www.rivendalecaravanpark.co.uk **£ BOOK ONLINE**

🚐 (81)	£18.50-£26.00	
🚃 (81)	£18.50-£26.00	
⛺ (30)	£18.00-£26.00	
🏠 (12)	£40.00-£50.00	
🏚 (2)	£490.00-£910.00	

111 touring pitches

SPECIAL PROMOTIONS
Stay Sunday - Thursday
& get 5 nights for the
price of 4.

Surrounded by spectacular Peak District scenery, convenient for Alton Towers, Chatsworth, Dove Dale and Carsington Water. Ideal for cyclists and ramblers with the Tissington Trail 100 metres away and footpaths running directly from site into Dove Dale and Mill Dale. Choice of all-grass, hardstanding or 50/50 pitches. Yurts, Camping Pods and Fly fishing lake. Overnight holding area available.

Directions: From A515, Rivendale is situated 6.5 miles north of Ashbourne, directly off the A515 Buxton road on the right-hand side, travelling north.

Open: All year except 3rd Jan - 28th Jan.

Site: 🏢 **Payment:** 💳 ☼ **Leisure:** ♿ ♪ ♾ **Children:** 🛝 ⚠ **Catering:** ✗ 🛒 **Park:** 🐕 🚏 🗄 🏚 🛎 **Touring:** 🚰 ♲ 🔌 ♪

Beech Croft Farm Caravan & Camping Park

Blackwell-in-the-Peak, Nr Buxton, Derbyshire SK17 9TQ
T: (01298) 85330 **E:** mail@beechcroftfarm.co.uk
W: www.beechcroftfarm.co.uk

🚐 (30)	£18.00-£22.00	
🚃 (30)	£18.00-£22.00	
⛺ (40)	£6.00-£16.00	

30 touring pitches

In the heart of the Peak District, Beech Croft is a small family run site, alongside their small sheep farm. Southerly facing. On the Pennine Bridleway with Monsal Trail & Limestone Way close by. All hardstandings have 16 amp EHU, water tap & TV aerial socket. **Directions:** Midway between Buxton & Bakewell being 6 miles to each town. Signposted & easily accessible from the A6. **Open:** All Year.

🌱 **Site:** ⛺🅿 **Payment:** 💳 ☼ **Children:** 🛝 **Catering:** 🛒 **Park:** 🐕 🚏 🗄 🛎 **Touring:** 🚰 ♲ 🔌

Book your accommodation online

Visit our new 2014 guide websites for detailed information, up-to-date availability and to book your accommodation online. Includes over 20,000 places to stay, all of them star rated.

www.visitor-guides.co.uk

BUXTON, Derbyshire   Map ref 4B2

SatNav SK17 0DT

HOLIDAY, TOURING & CAMPING PARK

Newhaven Caravan and Camping Park

Newhaven, Buxton SK17 0DT
T: (01298) 84300 **F:** (01332) 726027 **E:** newhavencaravanpark@btconnect.com
W: www.newhavencaravanpark.co.uk

🚐 (73)   £11.25-£18.75
🚍 (14)   £14.75-£18.75
⛺ (30)   £11.00-£18.75
95 touring pitches

Halfway between Ashbourne and Buxton in the Peak District National Park. Well-established park with modern facilities, close to the Tissington and High Peak trails, local towns and villages, historic houses and Derbyshire Dales. **Directions:** Half way between Ashbourne and Buxton on the A515 at junction with A5012. **Open:** March to October.

Payment: ⊞ ☼ Leisure: 🎣 🎿 Children: 🎠 🎢 Catering: 🍴 Park: 🐕 🗑 🎦 Touring: 🚿 🚾 💧

ANDERBY, Lincolnshire   Map ref 4D2

SatNav PE24 5YB

TOURING & CAMPING PARK

Manor Farm Caravan Park

Sea Road, Anderby, Skegness PE24 5YB
T: (01507) 490372 **E:** manorfarmtina@aol.com
W: www.manorfarmcaravanpark.co.uk

🚐 (130)
🚍 (10)
⛺ (50)
140 touring pitches

A peaceful and relaxed atmosphere await those who choose our park as their base to enjoy the East Coast and surrounding countryside. Overnight holding area available. Please contact us for prices. **Directions:** Turn right off A52 Skegness to Mablethorpe into Anderby 1.5 miles on the left. **Open:** March to November.

Site: ⛺🅿 Payment: ⊞ ☼ Leisure: 🎣 ⛵ ♻ Children: 🎠 🎢 Park: 🐕 🗑 🎦 Touring: 🚿 💧 🎣

BURGH-LE-MARSH, Lincolnshire   Map ref 4D2

SatNav PE24 5LN

TOURING & CAMPING PARK

Sycamore Lakes Park

Skegness Road, Burgh le Marsh PE24 5LN
T: (01754) 811411 **F:** (01754) 811411 **E:** info@sycamorelakes.co.uk
W: www.sycamorelakes.co.uk

🚐 (54)
🚍 (54)
⛺ (54)
🏠 (4)
🛖 (5)
54 touring pitches

SPECIAL PROMOTIONS
Out of season short breaks in cottages or cabins available.

Set in landscaped grounds with four fishing lakes (well stocked with carp, tench, rudd, roach and perch). Spacious, level pitches (hard standing and grass) with hook-ups. Dog walks. Superb amenity block. Lakeside cafeteria, Sunday lunches. Tackle shop. Lakeside holiday cottages and cabins. Sycamore lakes premier static caravan park, sales office. Overnight holding area available. Please contact us for prices.

Directions: Situated on the A158 between Burgh-le-Marsh and Skegness at Sycamore Lakes roundabout.

Open: March to November.

Payment: ☼ Leisure: 🎣 ⛵ ♻ Children: 🎠 🎢 Catering: ✕ 🍴 Park: 🐕 🗑 🎦 Touring: 🚿 🚾 🎣

LINCOLN, Lincolnshire Map ref 4C2
SatNav LN6 0EY

Hartsholme Country Park
Skellingthorpe Road, Lincoln LN6 0EY
T: (01522) 873578 **E:** hartsholmecp@lincoln.gov.uk
W: www.lincoln.gov.uk/hartsholmecampsite

🚐	£15.60-£22.00
🚏	£15.60-£22.00
⛺ (8)	£8.60-£18.00
26 touring pitches	

Our 3 star English Tourism rated site offers flat, level grassy pitches set in mature wooded parkland. Easy access to city centre and local attractions. **Directions:** Main entrance is on the B1378 (Skellingthorpe Road). It is signposted from the A46 (Lincoln Bypass) and from the B1003 (Tritton Road). **Open:** 1st March to 31st October.

Payment: 🆔 ☼ **Leisure:** 🎵 **Children:** 🐾 ⛰ **Catering:** ✕ 🍴 **Park:** 🐕 🐾 **Touring:** 🚿 🍴

MARKET RASEN, Lincolnshire Map ref 4C2
SatNav LN8 2DB

Lincolnshire Lanes
Manor Farm, East Firsby, Market Rasen LN8 2DB
T: (01673) 878258 **F:** (01673) 878310 **E:** info@lincolnshire-lanes.com
W: www.lincolnshire-lanes.com

🚐 (15)	£12.00-£17.00
🚏 (15)	£12.00-£17.00
⛺ (8)	£8.00-£16.00
🏠 (2)	£250.00-£400.00

Small, quiet touring caravan and camping site with two self-catering log cabins, two tipis, gypsy caravan and pod for hire. Ideal for The Wolds and Lincoln. 3 star rating. **Directions:** Mid way between Lincoln and Market Rasen. North from Lincoln on A15 2.5 miles north of RAF Scampton, turn right signposted Spridlington and follow brown tourist signs. **Open:** All year.

Site: 🏢 ⛺🅿 **Payment:** 🆔 **Leisure:** 🚲 🎵 ▶ **Children:** 🐾 ⛰ **Catering:** 🍴 **Park:** 🐕 📶 🐾 **Touring:** 🚿 ♿ 🍴

SKEGNESS, Lincolnshire Map ref 4D2
SatNav PE25 1JF

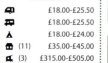

Skegness Water Leisure Park
Walls Lane, Skegness PE25 1JF
T: (01754) 899400 **F:** (01754) 897867 **E:** enquiries@skegnesswaterleisurepark.co.uk
W: www.skegnesswaterleisurepark.co.uk **£ BOOK ONLINE**

🚐	£18.00-£25.50
🚏	£18.00-£25.50
⛺	£18.00-£24.00
🏠 (11)	£35.00-£45.00
🚗 (3)	£315.00-£505.00
250 touring pitches	

Family-orientated caravan and camping site 'Where the coast meets the countryside'. Ten-minute walk to award-winning beaches with scenic, rural views. Close to Butlins and Fantasy Island. **Directions:** A52 north from Skegness 2.5 miles. Turn left at Cheers pub into Walls Lane. Site entrance is 400 yards on the left hand side. **Open:** March to November.

Site: 🏢 **Payment:** 🆔 ☼ **Leisure:** 🎵 ▶ **Catering:** ✕ **Park:** 🐕 🎵 📶 📶 🐾 **Touring:** ♿ 🍴 🎵

Need more information?
Visit our new 2014 guide websites for detailed information, up-to-date availability and to book your accommodation online. Includes over 20,000 places to stay, all of them star rated.
www.visitor-guides.co.uk

WOODHALL SPA, *Lincolnshire*   *Map ref 4D2*   *SatNav LN10 6UJ*

⛟ (80)   £20.00-£24.00
🚐 (80)   £20.00-£24.00
⛺ (25)   £15.00-£17.00
80 touring pitches

Woodhall Country Park
Stixwould Road, Woodhall Spa LN10 6UJ
T: (01526) 353710 **E:** info@woodhallcountrypark.co.uk
W: www.woodhallcountrypark.co.uk **£ BOOK ONLINE**

Woodhall Country Park is a unique 5 star camping and touring experience, set in tranquil woodlands in the heart of a conservation area in Lincolnshire. You will enjoy the natural surroundings of the park and feel close to nature, surrounded by woodland and wildlife. The new facilities offered here are ideal for touring caravans and tents – with pitches set in wooded areas, hard standing ground for caravans and spacious washroom facilities. AA Campsite of the Year for Central England for 2013.

Directions: Woodhall Country Park is located on the outskirts of Woodhall Spa, Lincolnshire.   **Open:** 1st March - 30th November.

Site: 🏧 ⛺🅿 **Payment:** 💳 ☀ **Leisure:** ♿ 🎵 ▶ **Children:** 🎠 **Park:** 🐾 🗑 🎦 **Touring:** 🚿 💷 ♪

NOTTINGHAM, *Nottinghamshire*   *Map ref 4C2*   *SatNav NG12 2LU*

⛟ (52)   £10.50-£14.00
🚐 (52)   £14.00-£16.00
⛺ (360)   £8.00-£29.00
52 touring pitches

SPECIAL PROMOTIONS
Electric hook-up available for £4.00 per night.
Special Easter & Halloween weekend events available to book.

National Water Sports Centre Caravan & Camping Park
Adbolton Lane, Holme Pierrepont, Nottingham NG12 2LU
T: 0115 982 1212 **E:** info.nwsc@serco.com
W: nwscnotts.com

Our 18 acre Campsite is rated as a 2 star facility with Enjoy England and welcomes vans, tents and campers; with on-site shower facilities, 136 electrical hook-ups, 40 hard standing pitches and 24-hour warden service. We have a shop on the campsite, where you are able to purchase a cup of tea and camping supplies ranging from gas for your cooker to toys and games and basic food provisions.
Our Campsite enjoys easy access to the city centre, rail network and East Midlands Airport. For the kids there are loads to do, with a sandpit, outdoor table tennis, football, netball and volleyball area. There is also a children's play area both on the campsite and in the main country park and within a short walking distance from the campsite you can find a nature trail. All this in addition to the fantastic range of activities available across our 270 acre site.

Directions: 3 miles from city centre on A52. (Please See Website).   **Open:** All year

Site: 🏧 **Payment:** 💳 ☀ **Leisure:** 🎵 ▶ ∪ **Children:** 🎠 🎪 **Catering:** ✗ 🛒 **Park:** 🐾 🖶 🗑 🎦 **Touring:** 🚿 💷 ♪

Heart of England

Herefordshire, Shropshire, Staffordshire,
Warwickshire, West Midlands, Worcestershire

Take time to visit the Cotswolds – beautiful countryside dotted with honey-coloured villages with limestone cottages – or soak up the stunning landscape of the Malvern hills. Discover places that inspired the likes of Tolkien, George Eliot and William Shakespeare. There's also a wide selection of ancient and modern cathedrals and historic houses to visit. Birmingham has recently undergone substantial regeneration and offers a world-class cultural scene as well as superb shopping - an ideal location to explore the region… and don't forget the Jewellery Quarter and Cadbury's Bournville.

Highlights

Birmingham

With a fantastic network of transport links to the rest of the country, Birmingham is a cosmopolitan, bustling city. The city played a central role in the West Midlands' transport manufacturing heritage.

Cotswolds

The Cotswolds area is one of England's favourite destinations – famous for hundreds of honey-colour limestone villages in a beautiful rural setting.

Ironbridge Gorge

From mines to railway lines, Ironbridge is a symbol of the Industrial Revolution. The blast furnace of Coalbrookdale is a reminder of the discovery of coke while the bridge was the first to be built from iron.

Malvern Hills

The Malvern Hills have been described as a mountain range in miniature; the eight mile ridge contains some of the oldest rocks in Britain and their craggy outline is reminiscent of the uplands further west into Wales.

Potteries

At the Potteries Museum and Art Gallery, Stoke-on-Trent, you can travel back in time and discover the area's history and view the world's greatest collection of Staffordshire ceramics.

Stratford-upon-Avon

Stratford-upon-Avon is world famous as the birthplace of William Shakespeare and one of the country's leading heritage places to visit. It is home to the Royal Shakespeare Company and Theatre.

Worcester Cathedral

Before the English Reformation it was known as Worcester Priory. Today it's an Anglican cathedral situated on a bank overlooking the River Severn.

Editor's Picks

Go back in time

Immerse yourself in a thousand years of jaw-dropping history at Warwick Castle. The castle promises an experience where ancient myths and spell-binding tales will set your imagination.

Have an undersea experience

At Birmingham's National Sea Life Centre, you can walk through a glass tunnel surrounded by an enormous ocean tank where giant turtles, sharks and tropical reef fish swim inches from your head.

Discover the history of iron

It was at Ironbridge in Shropshire that first large scale production of cast iron was developed using a process pioneered by Abraham Darby. Find out more by visiting one of the many museums.

Taste the chocolate

Experience the magic, making and history of confectionery at Cadbury World in Birmingham.

Put on your walking boots

The Cotswolds Area of Outstanding Natural Beauty spans nearly 800 square miles and contains many outstanding walking trails and footpaths.

Things to do

Entertainment & Culture

Barber Institute of Fine Arts

Edgbaston, West Midlands B15 2TS
(0121) 414 7333
www.barber.org.uk
British and European paintings, drawings and sculpture from the 13th century to mid 20th century.

Black Country Living Museum

Dudley, West Midlands DY1 4SQ
(0121) 557 9643
www.bclm.co.uk
A warm welcome awaits you at Britain's friendliest open-air museum. Wander around original shops and houses, ride on fair attractions, take a look down the underground coalmine.

Cadbury World
Bournville, West Midlands B30 2LU
0845 450 3599
www.cadburyworld.co.uk
Story of Cadbury's chocolate includes chocolate-making demonstration and attractions for all ages, with free samples, free parking, shop and restaurant. Phone to check availability and reserve admission.

Compton Verney

Stratford-upon-Avon CV35 9HZ
(01926) 645500
www.comptonverney.org.uk
Award-winning art gallery housed in a grade I listed Robert Adam mansion.

Etruria Industrial Museum
Staffordshire ST4 7AF
(01782) 233144
www.stoke.gov.uk/museum
Discover how they put the 'bone' in bone china at the last working steam-powered potters mill in Britain. Includes a Bone and Flint Mill and family-friendly interactive exhibition.

Hereford Museum and Art Gallery
Herefordshire HR4 9AU
(01432) 260692
www.herefordshire.gov.uk/leisure/museums_
galleries/2869.asp
In the museum, aspects of Herefordshire history and life - in the Gallery, regularly changing exhibitions of paintings, photography and crafts.

Ledbury Heritage Centre
Herefordshire, HR8 1DN
(01432) 260692
www.herefordshire.gov.uk/leisure/museums_
galleries/2861.asp
*The story of Ledbury's past displayed in a timber-framed
building in the picturesque lane leading to the church.*

Royal Air Force Museum Cosford
Shifnal, Shropshire TF11 8UP
(01902) 376200
www.rafmuseum.org
*FREE Admission. The award winning museum houses one of
the largest aviation collections in the
United Kingdom.*

Rugby Art Gallery and Museum
Warwickshire CV21 3BZ
(01788) 533201
www.ragm.org.uk
*Contemporary art & craft exhibitions; museum
showcasing the Tripontium Collection of Roman
artefacts & Rugby's Social History; the Rugby Collection
of 20th century & contemporary British art (annually);
fun activities for children/families.*

Thinktank-Birmingham Science Museum
West Midlands B4 7XG
(0121) 202 2222
www.thinktank.ac
*Thinktank is Birmingham's science museum where the
emphasis is firmly on hands on exhibits and interactive fun.*

Wolverhampton Art Gallery
West Midlands WV1 1DU
(01902) 552055
www.wolverhamptonart.org.uk
*Explore 300 years of art in this newly refurbished city
centre gallery.*

Worcester City Art Gallery & Museum
Worcestershire WR1 1DT
(01905) 25371
www.worcestercitymuseums.org.uk
*The art gallery & museum runs a programme of
exhibitions/events for all the family. Explore the
fascinating displays, exhibitions, cafe, shop and
Worcestershire Soldier Galleries.*

Family Fun

Aerial Extreme Trentham
Staffordshire ST4 8AX
0845 652 1736
www.aerialextreme.co.uk/index.php/courses/
trentham-estate
*Our tree based adventure ropes course, set within the
tranquil grounds of Trentham Estate is a truly spectacular
journey.*

Enginuity
Telford, Shropshire TF8 7DG
(01952) 433424
www.ironbridge.org.uk
*At Enginuity you can turn the wheels of your imagination,
test your horse power and discover how good ideas are
turned in to real things.*

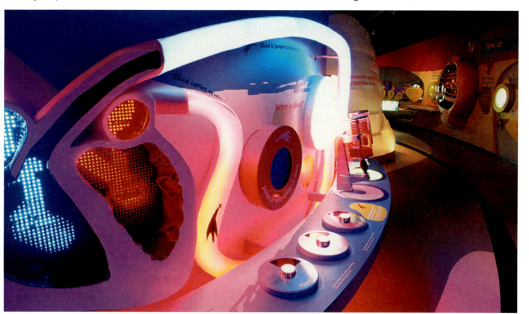

155

Heritage

Coventry Cathedral - St Michael's
West Midlands CV1 5AB
(024) 7652 1257
www.coventrycathedral.org.uk
Glorious 20th century Cathedral, with stunning 1950's art & architecture, rising above the stark ruins of the medieval Cathedral destroyed by German air raids in 1940.

Darby Houses (Ironbridge)
Telford, Shropshire TF8 7EW
(01952) 433424
www.ironbridge.org.uk
In the Darby houses, Dale House and Rosehill House, you can delve in to the everyday life of Quaker families.

Eastnor Castle
Ledbury, Herefordshire HR8 1RL
(01531) 633160
www.eastnorcastle.com
Fairytale Georgian Castle dramatically situated in the Malvern Hills.

Goodrich Castle
Ross-on-Wye, Herefordshire HR9 6HY
(01600) 890538
www.english-heritage.org.uk/goodrich
Come and relive the turbulent history of Goodrich Castle with our free audio and then climb to the battlements for breathtaking views over the Wye Valley.

Hanbury Hall
Droitwich Spa, Worcestershire WR9 7EA
(01527) 821214
www.nationaltrust.org.uk/hanburyhall
Early 18th century house, garden & park owned by the Vernon family for nearly 300 years.

Hereford Cathedral
Herefordshire HR1 2NG
(01432) 374202
www.herefordcathedral.org
Hereford Cathedral contains some of the finest examples of architecture from Norman times to the present day.

Iron Bridge and Toll House
Telford, Shropshire TF8 7DG
(01952) 433424
www.ironbridge.org.uk
You can peer through its railings and conjure a vision of sailing vessels heading downstream towards Bristol and the markets of the world.

Kenilworth Castle and Elizabethan Garden
Warwickshire CV8 1NE
(01926) 852078
www.english-heritage.org.uk/kenilworth
One of the most spectacular castle ruins in England.

Lichfield Cathedral
Staffordshire WS13 7LD
(01543) 306100
www.lichfield-cathedral.org
A medieval Cathedral with 3 spires in the heart of an historic City set in its own serene Close.

Much Wenlock Priory
Shropshire TF13 6HS
(01952) 727466
www.english-heritage.org.uk/wenlockpriory
Wenlock Priory, with it's stunning clipped topiary, has a pastoral setting on the edge of lovely Much Wenlock

National Memorial Arboretum
Lichfield, Staffordshire DE13 7AR
(01283) 792333
www.thenma.org.uk
150 acres of trees and memorials, planted as a living tribute to those who have served, died or suffered in the service of their Country.

Packwood House
Solihull, Warwickshire B94 6AT
0844 800 1895
www.nationaltrust.org.uk/main/w-packwoodhouse
Restored tudor house, park and garden with notable topiary.

Ragley Hall
Stratford-upon-Avon, Warwickshire B49 5NJ
(01789) 762090
www.ragleyhall.com
Ragley Hall is set in 27 acres of beautiful formal gardens

Severn Valley Railway
Bewdley, Worcestershire DY12 1BG
(01299) 403816
www.svr.co.uk
Steam-hauled trains running along the beautiful Severn Valley from Kidderminster - Bridgnorth.

Stokesay Castle
Craven Arms, Shropshire SY7 9AH
(01588) 672544
www.english-heritage.org.uk/stokesaycastle
Stokesay Castle, nestles in peaceful South Shropshire countryside near the Welsh Border. It is one of more than a dozen English Heritage properties in the county.

Tamworth Castle
Staffordshire B79 7NA
(01827) 709629
www.tamworthcastle.co.uk
The number one Heritage attraction located in the town. Explore over 900 years of history in the magnificent Motte and Bailey Castle.

The Almonry Museum and Heritage Centre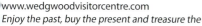
Evesham, Worcestershire WR11 4BG
(01386) 446944
www.almonryevesham.org
The 14th century house has 12 rooms of exhibits from 2000 years of Evesham history and pleasant gardens to the rear.

Warwick Castle
Warwickshire CV34 4QU
0871 265 2000
www.warwick-castle.co.uk
Imagine a totally electrifying, full day out at Britain's ultimate castle.

Wedgwood Visitor Centre
Stoke-on-Trent, Staffordshire ST12 9ER
(01782) 282986
www.wedgwoodvisitorcentre.com
Enjoy the past, buy the present and treasure the experience. The Wedgwood Visitor Centre offers a unique chance to immerse yourself in the heritage of Britain's greatest ceramics company.

Worcester Cathedral
Worcestershire WR1 2LA
(01905) 732900
www.worcestercathedral.co.uk
Worcester Cathedral is one of England's most magnificent and inspiring buildings, a place of prayer and worship for 14 centuries.

Wroxeter Roman City
Shrewsbury, Shropshire SY5 6PH
(01743) 761330
www.english-heritage.org.uk/wroxeter
Wroxeter Roman City, or Viroconium, to give it its Roman title, is thought to have been one of the largest Roman cities in the UK with over 200 acres of land, 2 miles of walls and a population of approximately 5,000.

Nature & Wildlife

Birmingham Botanical Gardens and Glasshouses
Edgbaston, West Midlands B15 3TR
(0121) 454 1860
www.birminghambotanicalgardens.org.uk
15 acres of ornamental gardens and glasshouses.

Cannock Chase
Staffordshire WS15 2UQ
(01543) 877666
www.visitcannockchase.co.uk
Central England's woodland jewel, packed with things to see and do.

Dudley Zoological Gardens
West Midlands DY1 4QB
(01384) 215313
www.dudleyzoo.org.uk
From lions and tigers to snakes and spiders there's something for all ages. Animal feeding, encounters, face painting, land train and fair rides.

Heart Park
Fillongley, Warwickshire CV7 8DX
(01676) 540333
www.heartpark.co.uk
"We believe that the heart of our Park is the beach and lake. But for those of you who'd like to try out a few 'different' activities - we've got a great assortment for you to try."

Hergest Croft Gardens
Kington, Herefordshire HR5 3EG
(01544) 230160
www.hergest.co.uk
The gardens extend over 50 acres, with more than 4000 rare shrubs and trees. With over 60 champion trees and shrubs it is one of the finest collections in the British Isles.

Park Hall - The Countryside Experience
Oswestry, Shropshire SY11 4AS
(01691) 671123
www.parkhallfarm.co.uk
With 40,000 square feet of indoor attractions, regular hands-on animal activities, lots of outdoor play and driving activities there is never a dull moment.

Ryton Pools Country Parks
Coventry, Warwickshire CV8 3BH
(024) 7630 5592
www.warwickshire.gov.uk/parks
The 100 acres of Ryton Pools Country Park are just waiting to be explored. The many different habitats are home to a wide range of birds and other wildlife.

West Midland Safari and Leisure Park
Bewdley, Worcestershire DY12 1LF
(01299) 402114
www.wmsp.co.uk
Fantastic family entertainment for the summer season.

John Smith's Midlands Grand National
March 15, Uttoxeter Racecourse
Biggest fixture in Uttoxeter's calendar.
www.uttoxeter-racecourse.co.uk

Shakespeare Birthday Celebrations
April 26-27, Stratford
In 2014, the birthday celebrations will mark the 450th anniversary of Shakespeare's birth. The town's streets overflow with pageantry, music and drama and over the three day birthday period you can enjoy a packed programme of special celebratory activities - great days out at Shakespeare's historic houses, literary and music events and amazing theatre.
www.shakespearesbirthday.org.uk

Stratford Literary Festival
April 26-May 4, Stratford
A selection of events and workshops running throughout the week featuring an array of writers and performers, so there is plenty to keep everyone entertained, whether you are a budding writer or poet, are keen to meet favourite authors and celebrities, or want to be involved in workshops and creating original pieces of work.
www.stratfordliteraryfestival.co.uk

The Telegraph Hay Festival
May 22-June 1, Hay-onWye
An annual literature festival held in Hay-on -Wye
www.hayfestival.com

Staffordshire County Show
May 28-29, Stafford
Agricultural show with all the usual country show attractions.
www.staffscountyshowground.co.uk

English Haydn Festival
June, Bridgnorth
An array of the music of Joseph Haydn and his contemporaries, performed in St. Leonards Church, Bridgnorth.
www.englishhaydn.com

RAF Cosford Air Show
June 8, Shifnal
The main focus will be the 75th Anniversary of RAF Cosford and this will be celebrated both in the air and on the ground. Other themes include 75 years since the Spitfire entered RAF Service and 40 years of service from the Jaguar aircraft.
www.cosfordairshow.co.uk

Three Counties Show
June 13-15, Malvern
Three jam-packed days of family entertainment and fun, all in celebration of the great British farming world and countryside.
www.threecounties.co.uk

Ludlow Festival
June, dates TBC, Ludlow
Annual Festival of the Arts. The Shakespeare production and Last Night Finale are both staged at Ludlow Castle.
www.ludlowfestival.co.uk

Lichfield Festival
July, dates TBC, Lichfield
Acclaimed arts festival with national and international artists and performers.
www.lichfieldfestival.org

Stratford River Festival
July, dates TBC, Stratford
The highly successful Stratford-upon-Avon River Festival brings the waterways of Stratford alive, with boatloads of family fun, on the first weekend of July.
www.stratfordriverfestival.co.uk

Godiva Festival
July, Coventry
The Godiva Festival is the UK's biggest free family festival held over a weekend in the War Memorial Park, Coventry. The event showcases some of the finest local, national and International artists, live comedy, family entertainment, Godiva Carnival, and lots more.
www.godivafestival.com

Wenlock Olympian Games
July, dates TBC, Much Wenlock
The games that inspired the modern Olympic Movement.
www.wenlock-olympian-society.org.uk

Birmingham International Jazz and Blues Festival
July 18-27, Birmingham
Musicians and fans come to the city from every corner of the UK as well as from further afield and significantly, almost all of the events are free to the public.
www.visitbirmingham.com

Shrewsbury Flower Show
August (mid), Shrewsbury
The world's longest running horticultural whow in Shrewsbury's beautiful 29-acre Quarry Park.
www.shrewsburyflowershow.org.uk

V Festival
August 16-17, Weston Park
Legendary rock and pop festival.
www.vfestival.com

Shrewsbury Folk Festival
August 22-25, Shrewsbury
Shrewsbury Folk Festival has a reputation for delivering the very finest acts from the UK and around the world.
www.shrewsburyfolkfestival.co.uk

Festival of Motoring
August, Stoneleigh
This major event takes place at Stoneleigh Park in Warwickshire. In addition to hundreds of fantastic cars to look at, there will be the traditional historic vehicle 'run' through delightful Warwickshire countryside, car gymkhanas and auto tests.
www.festival-of-motoring.co.uk

Abbots Bromley Horn Dance
September, Abbots Bromley
Ancient ritual dating back to 1226. Six deer-men, a fool, hobby horse, bowman and Maid Marian perform to music provided by a melodian player.
www.abbotsbromley.com

Ludlow Food Festival
September, Ludlow
Featuring more than 160 top quality independent food and drink producers inside Ludlow Castle.
www.foodfestival.co.uk

Artsfest
September, Birmingham
Artsfest is one of the UK's biggest free arts festival and showcases work across the performing arts, visual arts and digital arts genres to promote emerging and established talent.
visitbirmingham.com

Heritage Open Days
September, Coventry
Heritage Open Days celebrate England's architecture and culture by allowing visitors free access to interesting properties that are either not usually open or would normally charge an entrance fee. Heritage Open Days also include tours, events and activities that focus on local architecture and culture.
www.coventry.gov.uk/hod

Moseley Folk Festival
September, Birmingham
The Moseley Folk Festival offers an inner city Shangri-la bringing together people from all ages and backgrounds to witness folk legends playing alongside their contemporaries.
www.visitbirmingham.com

Stone Food & Drink Festival
October, Stone
Staffordshire's biggest celebration of all things gastronomic.
www.stonefooddrink.org.uk

Birmingham Book Festival
October, Birmingham
Celebrating the city's literature scene, the Birmingham Book Festival takes places every year with its trademark mix of literature events, talks and workshops.
www.visitbirmingham.com

Supersonic
October, Birmingham
The Festival is a combination of art, music and film along with other crafts.
www.visitbirmingham.com

Frankfurt Christmas Market & Craft Fair
November-December, Birmingham
The largest authentic German market outside Germany and Austria and the centrepiece of the city's festive event calendar.
www.visitbirmingham.com

159

Tourist Information Centres

When you arrive at your destination, visit an Official Partner Tourist Information Centre for quality assured help with accommodation and information about local attractions and events, or email your request before you go. To find a Tourist Information Centre visit www.visitengland.com

Bewdley	Load Street	0845 6077819	bewdleytic@wyreforestdc.gov.uk
Birmingham Central Library	Chamberlain Square	0844 888 3883/ 0121 202 5115	visit@marketingbirmingham.com
Bridgnorth	The Library	01746 763257	bridgnorth.tourism@shropshire.gov.uk
Church Stretton	Church Street	01694 723133	churchstretton.scf@shropshire.gov.uk
Coventry Cathedral	St Michael's Tower	024 7622 5616	tic@coventry.gov.uk
Hereford	1 King Street	01432 268430	reception@visitherefordshire.co.uk
Ironbridge	Museum of The Gorge	01952 433424/ 01952 435900	tic@ironbridge.org.uk
Leek	1 Market Place	01538 483741	tourism.services@staffsmoorlands.gov.uk
Lichfield	Lichfield Garrick	01543 412112	info@visitlichfield.com
Ludlow	Castle Street	01584 875053	ludlow.tourism@shropshire.gov.uk
Malvern	21 Church Street	01684 892289	info@visitthemalverns.org
Oswestry (Mile End)	Mile End	01691 662488	oswestrytourism@shropshire.gov.uk
Ross-on-Wye	Market House	01989 562768/ 01432 260675	visitorcentreross@herefordshire.gov.uk
Rugby	Rugby Art Gallery Museum & Library	01788 533217	visitor.centre@rugby.gov.uk
Shrewsbury	Barker Street	01743 281200	visitorinformation@shropshire.gov.uk
Solihull	Central Library	0121 704 6130	artscomplex@solihull.gov.uk
Stafford	Stafford Gatehouse Theatre	01785 619619	tic@staffordbc.gov.uk
Stoke-on-Trent	Victoria Hall, Bagnall Street	01782 236000	stoke.tic@stoke.gov.uk
Stratford-upon-Avon	Bridge Foot	01789 264293	tic@discover-stratford.com
Tamworth	Philip Dix Centre	01827 709581	tic@tamworth.gov.uk
Warwick	The Court House	01926 492212	info@visitwarwick.co.uk
Worcester	The Guildhall	01905 726311/ 01905 722561	touristinfo@visitworcester.com

Regional Contacts and Information

Marketing Birmingham
Tel: 0844 888 3883
Web: www.visitbirmingham.com

Visit Coventry & Warwickshire
Tel: (024) 7622 5616
Web: www.visitcoventryandwarwickshire.co.uk

Visit Herefordshire
Tel: (01432) 268430
Web: www.visitherefordshire.co.uk

Shakespeare Country
Tel: 0871 978 0800
Web: www.shakespeare-country.co.uk

Shropshire Tourism
Tel: (01743) 261919
Web: www.shropshiretourism.co.uk

Destination Staffordshire
Tel: (01785) 277397
Web: www.enjoystaffordshire.com

Stoke-on-Trent
Tel: (01782) 236000
Web: www.visitstoke.co.uk

Destination Worcestershire
Tel: 0845 641 1540
Web: www.visitworcestershire.org

Entries appear alphabetically by town name in each county. A key to symbols appears on page 7

RUGELEY, Staffordshire   Map ref 4B3
SatNav WS15 2TX

Silver Trees Holiday Park - Static Vans

Stafford Brook Road, Penkridge Bank, Rugeley, Cannock Chase, Staffordshire WS15 2TX
T: (01889) 582185 **F:** (01889) 582373 **E:** info@silvertreesholidaypark.co.uk
W: www.silvertreesholidaypark.co.uk

(9)   £277.00-£588.00

Holiday homes on quiet woodland park, suitable for couples and families enjoying wildlife, walks and cycling on Cannock Chase. Area of Outstanding Natural Beauty. View deer from your caravan! David Bellamy Gold Award for Wildlife Conservation. **Directions:** From A51 or A34 follow brown tourist signs for Silver Trees Holiday Park, the park is located between Rugeley and Penkridge on Cannock Chase. **Open:** March to January.

Payment: 💷 **Leisure:** 🚲 ♨ 🎣 🏊 **Property:** 📺 🛏

ASTON CANTLOW, Warwickshire   Map ref 2B1
SatNav B95 6JP

Island Meadow Caravan Park

The Mill House, Aston Cantlow, Henley in Arden, Warwickshire B95 6JP
T: (01789) 488273 **E:** holiday@islandmeadowcaravanpark.co.uk
W: www.islandmeadowcaravanpark.co.uk

🚐 (24)   £23.00
🚎 (24)   £23.00
⛺ (10)   £15.00-£20.00
🏠 (5)   £395.00-£460.00
24 touring pitches

A small secluded park in rural Warwickshire, close to the historic and picturesque village of Aston Cantlow and just six miles from Stratford. Ideal for visiting Warwick, Birmingham and the Cotswolds. We hold the David Bellamy Gold award. **Directions:** Aston Cantlow village lies within the triangle formed by Stratford-upon-Avon, Henley-in-Arden and Alcester. The park is South west of the village. **Open:** March to October.

Payment: 💷 € ☼ **Leisure:** 🎵 **Children:** 🛝 **Catering:** 🍴 **Park:** 🐕 📺 🛏 🚿 **Touring:** 🔌 🚰 🚽 🎵

Looking for something else?

The official and most comprehensive guide to independently inspected, star rated accommodation.

B&Bs and Hotels - B&Bs, Hotels, farmhouses, inns, serviced apartments, campus and hostel accommodation in England.

Self Catering - Self-catering holiday homes, approved caravan holiday homes, boat accommodation and holiday cottage agencies in England.

Camping, Touring and Holiday Parks - Touring parks, camping holidays and holiday parks and villages in Britain.

Now available in all good bookshops and online at **www.hudsons.co.uk/shop**

Visit our 2014 guide websites...

- Detailed information
- Up-to-date availability
- Book your accommodation online

Includes over 20,000 places to stay, all of them star rated.

Win amazing prizes, every month...

Enter our monthly competition at
www.visitor-guides.co.uk/prizes

STRATFORD-UPON-AVON, *Warwickshire*   Map ref 2B1   SatNav CV37 9SR

Dodwell Park

Evesham Road (B439), Dodwell, Stratford-upon-Avon CV37 9SR
T: (01789) 204957 **E:** enquiries@dodwellpark.co.uk
W: www.dodwellpark.co.uk

(50)	£18.00-£26.00
(50)	£18.00-£26.00
(50)	£17.00-£25.00

50 touring pitches

Small, family-run touring park 2 miles SW of Stratford-upon-Avon. Country walks to River Avon and Luddington village. Ideal for visiting Warwick Castle, Shakespeare properties and Cotswolds. Brochure on request. Rallies welcome. Over 50 years as a family business! **Directions:** Leaving Stratford-Upon-Avon take the B439 signposted 'B349 Bidford' (also signposted Racecourse) for 2 miles, we are on left (after going over a large hill). **Open:** All year.

Site: ▲🅿 Payment: 💷 ☼ Leisure: 🚲 ♪ ➤ Children: 🐎 Catering: 🍴 Park: 🐕 🎯 Touring: 💧 ♻ 🔌

EVESHAM, *Worcestershire*   Map ref 2B1   SatNav WR11 7PR

Ranch Caravan Park

Honeybourne, Evesham, Worcestershire, Evesham WR11 7PR
T: (01386) 830744 **F:** (01386) 833503 **E:** enquiries@ranch.co.uk
W: www.ranch.co.uk **£ BOOK ONLINE**

(100)	£25.00-£29.00
(20)	£25.00-£29.00
(4)	£345.00-£495.00

120 touring pitches

An established family-run holiday park located in Honeybourne, 6 miles from Evesham. Level pitches in a landscaped setting. Ideally situated for visiting the Cotswolds and Shakespeare Country. Overnight holding area available. **Directions:** From A46 Evesham bypass take B4035 to Badsey and Bretforton. Caravan park signposted from Bretforton. **Open:** March to November.

Site: 🏠 ▲🅿 Payment: 💷 ☼ Leisure: 🎣 ⚲ Children: 🐎 🎡 Catering: ✗ 🍴 Park: 🐕 🚽 🔲 📖 🎯 Touring: 💧 ♻ 🔌 🎵

Yorkshire

With the North York Moors, Yorkshire Dales and the Pennines within its borders, the largest county in the UK can also lay claim to being the greenest. There is a plethora of stunning locations and amazing sights to be found, and it's no wonder the area is popular with walkers, cyclists and tourists. Add cities like York, Leeds, Hull and Sheffield, and you have a region steeped in history. And if you enjoy breathtaking coastal views, then Yorkshire doesn't disappoint.

Highlights

Leeds

Leeds offers everything you would expect from one of the UK's leading cities, from great shopping to listed buildings and green spaces.

North York Moors

The North York Moors National Park is a landscape of stunning moorland, spectacular coast, ancient woodland and historic sites. It also has one of the largest expanses of heather moorland in the UK.

Saltaire

Saltaire in West Yorkshire is a well-preserved industrial village of the second half of the 19th century, and the buildings offer a vivid impression of Victorian philanthropic paternalism.

Sheffield

Sheffield is also a city bursting with ideas and energy, having transformed the world with Stainless Steel production back in 1913.

Studley Royal Park

A striking landscape was created around the ruins of the Cistercian Fountains Abbey and Fountains Hall Castle in Yorkshire in the 18th and 19th centuries.

York

The city of York is renowned for its splendid cathedral, has been a meeting place throughout Roman, Viking and Medieval ages. Meanwhile, Harrogate and the surrounding district is one of the most spectacular areas in England.

Yorkshire coast

The coastline is spectacular, varied, and interesting. It can be rocky and wild in places but is enhanced by numerous fishing villages and resorts like Scarborough, Filey and Whitby.

Yorkshire Dales

The Yorkshire Dales is home to outstanding scenery, a rich cultural heritage and breathtakingly peaceful atmosphere.

Editor's Picks

Watch out for the whales

Whitby is the finest place for whale watching on the Yorkshire coast and early autumn evenings are the best time.

Learn about the railways

The National Railway Museum in York is the largest in the world, offering three giant halls packed full of incredible trains and interactive fun.

Enjoy the surroundings

Yorkshire's three National Parks offer more than 3,200 square kilometres of beautiful landscapes and seascapes – all just waiting to be explored.

Spot the gull

The cliffs of the coast are a haven for all manner of sealife and perfect for bird watching. RSPB Bempton Cliffs is a family favourite, and easily the best place in England to see, hear and smell seabirds.

Take in the sea air

From miles of award-winning sandy beaches to hidden coastal coves, the Yorkshire Coast has over 100 miles of stunning coastline.

Things to do

Attractions with this sign participate in the Places of Interest Quality Assurance Scheme.

Attractions with this sign participate in the Visitor Attraction Quality Assurance Scheme.

Both schemes recognise high standards in all aspects of the visitor experience (see page 7)

Entertainment & Culture

Clifton Park Museum

Rotherham, South Yorkshire S65 2AA
(01709) 336633
www.rotherham.gov.uk/graphics/Learning/Museums/
EDSCliftonParkMuseum.htm
Local pottery, antiquities, natural and social history. Restored period kitchen. Major collection of Rockingham porcelain.

East Riding Rural Life Museum

Beverley, Yorkshire HU16 5TF
(01482) 392777
www.eastriding.gov.uk
Working early 19th century four-sailed windmill, plus Museum of East Riding Rural Life.

Eureka! The National Children's Museum

Halifax, West Yorkshire HX1 2NE
(01422) 330069
www.eureka.org.uk
Eureka! The National Children's Museum is a magical place where children play to learn and grown-ups learn to play.

Ferens Art Gallery

Hull, East Riding of Yorkshire HU1 3RA
(01482) 613902
www.hullcc.gov.uk/museums
Combines internationally renowned permanent collections with a thriving programme of temporary exhibitions.

National Coal Mining Museum for England
Wakefield, West Yorkshire WF4 4RH
(01924) 848806
www.ncm.org.uk
The National Coal Mining Museum offers an exciting and enjoyable insight into the working lives of miners through the ages.

National Media Museum
Bradford, West Yorkshire BD1 1NQ
0870 701 0200
www.nationalmediamuseum.org.uk
The museum is open Tuesday to Sunday (along with Bank and school holiday Mondays) from 10:00am until 6.00pm. Admission to the National Media Museum is free (charges apply for cinemas/IMAX).

National Railway Museum
York, North Yorkshire YO26 4XJ
0844 815 3139
www.nrm.org.uk
Awesome trains, interactive fun – and the world's largest railway museum is free.

Royal Armouries Museum
Leeds, West Yorkshire LS10 1LT
0870 034 4344
www.royalarmouries.org
Over 8,000 objects displayed in five galleries - War, Tournament, Oriental, Self Defence and Hunting. Among the treasures are Henry VIII's tournament armour and the world record breaking elephant armour. Regular jousting and horse shows.

Sheffield: Millennium Gallery
South Yorkshire S1 2PP
(0114) 278 2600
www.museums-sheffield.org.uk
The Millennium Gallery is one of modern Sheffield's landmark public spaces. Whether you're in town or just passing through, the Gallery always has something new to offer.

Treasure House and Art Gallery
Beverley, East Riding of Yorkshire HU17 8HE
(01482) 392790
www.eastriding.gov.uk/treasurehouse
Enthusiasts for East Riding history can access archive, library, art gallery and museum material. Exhibitions.

Xscape Castleford
Castleford, West Yorkshire WF10 4TA
(01977) 5230 2324
www.xscape.co.uk
The ultimate family entertainment awaits! Dine, bowl, snow, skate, climb, movies, shop, dance on ice.

Yorkshire Air Museum
York, North Yorkshire YO41 4AU
(01904) 608595
www.yorkshireairmuseum.co.uk
The Yorkshire Air Museum is based on a unique WWII Bomber Command Station with fascinating exhibits and attractive Memorial Gardens that have won 3 consecutive Yorkshire in Bloom awards.

Family Fun

Flamingo Land Theme Park and Zoo
Malton, North Yorkshire YO17 6UX
0871 911 8000
www.flamingoland.co.uk
One-price family funpark with over 100 attractions, 5 shows and Europe's largest privately-owned zoo.

Magna Science Adventure Centre
Rotherham, South Yorkshire S60 1DX
(01709) 720002
www.visitmagna.co.uk
Magna is the UK's 1st Science Adventure Centre set in the vast Templeborough steelworks in Rotherham. Fun is unavoidable here with giant interactives.

Heritage

Beverley Guildhall

East Riding of Yorkshire HU17 9XX
(01482) 392783
www.eastriding.gov.uk
Beverley Guildhall is a Grade 1 listed building, originally late medieval, remodelled in 17th and 18th century.

Brodsworth Hall and Gardens

Doncaster, South Yorkshire DN5 7XJ
(01302) 722598
www.english-heritage.org.uk/daysout/properties/brodsworth-hall-and-gardens
One of England's most complete surviving Victorian houses. Inside many of the original fixtures & fittings are still in place, although faded with time. Outside the 15 acres of woodland & gardens have been restored to their 1860's heyday.

Castle Howard

Malton, North Yorkshire YO60 7DA
(01653) 648444
www.castlehoward.co.uk
Magnificent 18th century historic house and Stable Courtyard within 1,000 acres of breathtaking gardens.

Harewood House

Leeds West Yorkshire LS17 9LG
(0113) 218 1010
www.harewood.org
Harewood House, Bird Garden, Grounds and Adventure Playground - The ideal day out for all the family.

JORVIK Viking Centre

York, North Yorkshire YO1 9WT
(01904) 615505
www.jorvik-viking-centre.co.uk
Travel back 1000 years on board your time machine through the backyards and houses to the bustling streets of Jorvik.

Lotherton Hall & Gardens
Leeds, West Yorkshire LS25 3EB
(0113) 264 5535
www.leeds.gov.uk/lothertonhall
Lotherton is an Edwardian country house set in beautiful grounds with a bird garden, red deer park and formal gardens.

Skipsea Castle
Hornsea, East Riding of Yorkshire
0870 333 1181
www.english-heritage.org.uk/daysout/properties/skipsea-castle/
The remaining earthworks of a motte-and-bailey castle dating from the Norman era.

Wilberforce House

Hull, East Riding of Yorkshire HU11NQ
(01482) 613902
www.hullcc.gov.uk/museums
Slavery exhibits, period rooms and furniture, Hull silver, costume, Wilberforce and abolition.

Yorkshire Sculpture Park
West Bretton, West Yorkshire WF4 4LG
(01924) 832631
www.ysp.co.uk
YSP is an extraordinary place that sets out to challenge, inspire, inform and delight.

Nature & Wildlife

RSPB Bempton Cliffs Reserve
Bridlington, East Riding of Yorkshire YO15 1JF
(01262) 851179
www.rspb.org.uk/reserves/guide/b/bemptoncliffs/index.aspx
Nature trail and spectacular cliff top walks.

RSPB Old Moor Nature Reserve
Barnsley, South Yorkshire S73 0YF
(01226) 751593
www.rspb.org.uk/reserves/guide/d/dearne-oldmoor/index.aspx
Whether you're feeling energetic or just fancy some time out visit Old Moor to get closer to the wildlife.

Sheffield Botanical Gardens
South Yorkshire S10 2LN
(0114) 267 1115
www.sbg.org.uk
Extensive gardens with over 5,500 species of plants, Grade II Listed garden pavillion.

The Deep
Hull, East Riding of Yorkshire HU1 4DP
(01482) 381000
www.thedeep.co.uk
Full with over 3500 fish and more than 40 sharks, it tells the story of the world's oceans using live animals and the latest hands on interactives.

The Walled Garden at Scampston
Malton, North Yorkshire YO17 8NG
(01944) 759111
www.scampston.co.uk
An exciting 4 acre contemporary garden, created by Piet Oudolf, with striking perennial meadow planting as well as traditional spring/autumn borders.

Wentworth Castle Gardens
Barnsley, South Yorkshire S75 3ET
(01226) 776040
www.wentworthcastle.org
This magnificent 600 acre Parkland estate features over 26 listed monuments as well as a 60-acre Garden.

Yorkshire Wildlife Park
Doncaster, South Yorkshire DN3 3NH
(01302) 535057
www.yorkshirewildlifepark.co.uk
A fabulous fun day and animal experience. Walk through 'Lemar Woods' and meet these mischievous primates, or come face to face with the wallabies in Wallaby Walk.

Outdoor Activities

York Boat Guided River Trips
North Yorkshire YO1 7DP
(01904) 628324
www.yorkboat.co.uk/buytickets-online.html
Sit back, relax and enjoy a drink from the bar as the sights of York city and country sail by onboard a 1 hour Guided River Trip with entertaining live commentary.

175

Events 2014

Diesel Gala Weekend
TBC, Haworth
Bringing together a collection of vintage diesel locomotives.
www.kwvr.co.uk

Malton Food Lovers Festival
May 24-25, Malton
Chance to fill up on glorious food and discover why Malton is considered 'Yorkshire's Food Town' with mountains of fresh produce.
www.maltonfoodfestival.co.uk

Swaledale Festival
May 24-June 7, Various locations
Varied programme of about 60 top-quality events, individually ticketed, realistically priced, and spread over two glorious weeks.
www.swaledale-festival.org.uk

Beverley Festival
June 20-22, Beverley Racecourse
This will be the 30th anniversary of this popular music festival.
www.beverleyfestival.com

Bradford Mela
June, Bradford
An annual celebration of the art, craft, culture and community, of Asian and global communities both traditional and modern.
www.bradfordmela.org.uk

Filey Town Festival
June 28-July 6, Filey
Concerts, craft fairs and street processions draw visitors to this picturesque North Yorkshire town.
www.fileytownfestival.com

Grassington Festival
June 13-28, Grassington
15 days of music and arts in the Yorkshire Dales.
www.grassington-festival.org.uk

Pontefract Liquorice Festival
July, Wakefield
The festival celebrates this unusual plant, the many wonderful products created from it and its historic association with the town.
www.experiencewakefield.co.uk

Scarborough Seafest
July, Scarborough
Seafest celebrates Scarborough's maritime heritage and brings together seafood kitchen cooking demonstrations, exhibitor displays and musical performances.
www.seafest.org.uk

York Early Music Festival
July 10-19, York
The 2013 festival will will focus on Rome, with music created under the patronage of medieval Popes, the renaissance polyphony of Palestrina, and the exuberant baroque of Handel in Italy.
www.ncem.co.uk

Ilkley Summer Festival
August, Ilkley
A wide selection of activities and events in and around this idyllic town.
www.summerfestival.ilkley.org

Leeds Festival
August 22-24, Wetherby
Top performers, including world renowned acts like Eminem.
www.leedsfestival.com

Ripon International Festival
September 6-20, Ripon
A festival packed with music events, solo dramas, intriguing theatre, magic, fantastic puppetry, literary celebrities, historical walks - and more!
www.riponinternationalfestival.com

Scarborough Jazz Festival
September 26-28, Scarborough
The festival is now firmly on both the national and international stage. Audiences and performers have acknowledged the consistently high quality of the artists and find the variety and range of the programme refreshing.
www.scarboroughjazzfestival.co.uk

St Leger Festival
September 10-13, Doncaster
Four days of great horse racing, culminating in the final Classic of the year.
www.doncaster-racecourse.co.uk

Autumn Steam Gala
October, Haworth
Spectacular, action-packed three-day weekend of intensive steam action.
www.kwvr.co.uk

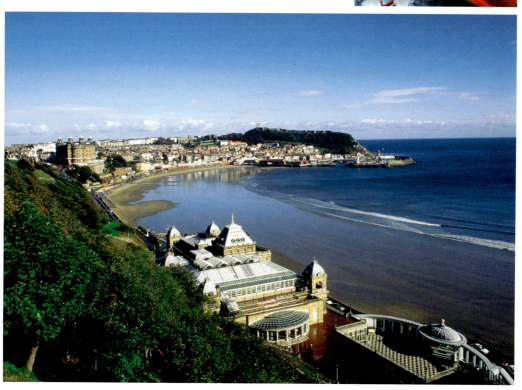

Tourist Information Centres

When you arrive at your destination, visit an Official Partner Tourist Information Centre for quality assured help with accommodation and information about local attractions and events, or email your request before you go. To find a Tourist Information Centre visit www.visitengland.com

Aysgarth Falls	Aysgarth Falls National Park Centre	01969 662910	aysgarth@yorkshiredales.org.uk
Beverley	34 Butcher Row	01482 391672	beverley.tic@eastriding.gov.uk
Bradford	Brittania House	01274 433678	bradford.vic@bradford.gov.uk
Bridlington	25 Prince Street	01262 673474	bridlington.tic@eastriding.gov.uk
Brigg	The Buttercross	01652 657053	brigg.tic@northlincs.gov.uk
Cleethorpes	Cleethorpes Library	01472 323111	cleetic@nelincs.gov.uk
Danby	National Park Centre, Danby Lodge	01439 772737	moorscentre@northyorkmoors.org.uk
Doncaster	Blue Building	01302 734309	tourist.information@doncaster.gov.uk
Filey	The Evron Centre	01723 383637	fileytic2@scarborough.gov.uk
Grassington	National Park Centre	01756 751690	grassington@yorkshiredales.gov.uk
Halifax	The Piece Hall	01422 368725	halifax@ytbtic.co.uk
Harrogate	Royal Baths	01423 537300	tic@harrogate.gov.uk
Hawes	Dales Countryside Museum	01969 666210	hawes@yorkshiredales.org.uk
Haworth	2/4 West Lane	01535 642329	haworth.vic@bradford.gov.uk
Hebden Bridge	Visitor Centre, New Road	01422 843831	hebdenbridge@ytbtic.co.uk
Helmsley	The Visitor Centre, Helmsley Castle	01439 770173	helmsley.tic@english-heritage.org.uk
Holmfirth	49-51 Huddersfield Road	01484 222444	holmfirth.tic@kirklees.gov.uk
Hornsea	Hornsea Museum	01964 536404	hornsea.tic@eastriding.gov.uk
Huddersfield	Huddersfield Library	01484 223200	huddersfield.information@kirklees.gov.uk
Hull	1 Paragon Street	01482 223559	tourist.information@hullcc.gov.uk
Humber Bridge	North Bank Viewing Area	01482 640852	humberbridge.tic@eastriding.gov.uk
Ilkley	Town Hall	01943 602319	ilkley.vic@bradford.gov.uk
Knaresborough	9 Castle Courtyard	01423 866886	kntic@harrogate.gov.uk
Leeds	The Arcade	0113 242 5242	tourinfo@leedsandpartners.com
Leeming Bar	The Yorkshire Maid	01677 424262	thelodgeatleemingbar@btconnect.com
Leyburn	The Dales Haven	01969 622317	

Malham	National Park Centre	01969 652380	malham@ytbtic.co.uk
Malton	Malton Library	01653 600048	maltontic@btconnect.com
Otley	Otley Library & Tourist Information	01943 462485	otleytic@leedslearning.net
Pateley Bridge	18 High Street	0845 389 0177	pbtic@harrogate.gov.uk
Pickering	Ropery House	01751 473791	pickeringtic@btconnect.com
Reeth	Hudson House, The Green	01748 884059	reeth@ytbtic.co.uk
Richmond	Friary Gardens	01748 828742	hilda@richmondtouristinformation.co.uk
Ripon	Minster Road	01765 604625	ripontic@harrogate.gov.uk
Rotherham	40 Bridgegate	01709 835904	tic@rotherham.gov.uk
Scarborough	Brunswick Shopping Centre	01723 383636	scarborough2@scarborough.gov.uk
Scarborough	Harbourside TIC	01723 383636	scarborough2@scarborough.gov.uk
Selby	Selby Library	0845 034 9540	selby@ytbtic.co.uk
Settle	Town Hall	01729 825192	settle@ytbtic.co.uk
Sheffield	Unit 1 Winter Gardens	0114 2211900	visitor@marketingsheffield.org
Skipton	Town Hall	01756 792809	skipton@ytbtic.co.uk
Sutton Bank	Sutton Bank Visitor Centre	01845 597426	suttonbank@northyorkmoors.org.uk
Todmorden	15 Burnley Road	01706 818181	todmorden@ytbtic.co.uk
Wakefield	9 The Bull Ring	0845 601 8353	tic@wakefield.gov.uk
Wetherby	Wetherby Library & Tourist Info. Centre	01937 582151	wetherbytic@leedslearning.net
Whitby	Langborne Road	01723 383637	whitbytic@scarborough.gov.uk
Withernsea	Withernsea Lighthouse Museum	01964 615683	withernsea.tic@eastriding.gov.uk
York	1 Museum Street	01904 550099	info@visityork.org

Regional Contacts and Information

For more information on accommodation, attractions, activities, events and holidays in Yorkshire, contact the regional tourism organisation. Their website has a wealth of information and produces many free publications to help you get the most out of your visit.

The following publication is available from the Yorkshire Tourist Board by logging on to www.yorkshire.com or calling Welcome to Yorkshire on 0113 322 3500.

This is Y Magazine

Yorkshire
Where to Stay

Entries appear alphabetically by town name in each county. A key to symbols appears on page 7

BRIDLINGTON, East Yorkshire   Map ref 5D3   SatNav YO16 6TG

North Bay Leisure Park

Lime Kiln Lane, Bridlington YO16 6TG
T: (01262) 673733 **F:** 01262 401851 **E:** enquiries@northbayleisurepark.com
W: www.northbayleisurepark.com

North Bay Leisure Limited is a caravan Holiday Home located in Bridlington. On the north side of the town, 300yds from the beach, 20 minutes' walk to the shops, town centre and the clifftop walks. Please contact us for prices. **Directions:** Please contact us for directions. **Open:** All Year.

Leisure: ▶ **Property:** 🐕 ▭ 🖥 **Children:** 🛝 **Catering:** ✗ 🛒

TUNSTALL, East Yorkshire   Map ref 4D1   SatNav HU12 0JF

Sand le Mere Holiday Village

Southfield Lane, Tunstall HU12 0JF
T: (01964) 670403 **E:** info@sand-le-mere.co.uk
W: www.sand-le-mere.co.uk

🚐		£12.00-£30.00
🚏	(59)	£12.00-£30.00
⛺	(50)	£12.00-£18.00
🛏	(6)	£235.00-£941.00
🏠	(50)	£80.00-£585.00
59 touring pitches		

£4 million recently spent on new park facilities, including new leisure complex with indoor heated pool, splashzone, waterslide and indoor & outdoor adventure play areas. Family entertainment available throughout the season. Fantastic park setting overlooking Tunstall beach, fresh water & beach fishing available. Close to Hull, historic York and the pretty town of Beverley. **Directions:** From Hull to Hedon take the B1362 at Withernsea, B1242 to Roos. Look for brown signs marked SLM. **Open:** 21st March – 14th November.

Site: 🏧 **Payment:** 💳 ☀ **Leisure:** 🚴 ♪ ▶ ∪ ⚲ ☂ **Children:** 🛝 ⚲ **Catering:** ✗ 🛒 **Park:** 🐕 ♫ ▭ 🖥 🏕 🏇 **Touring:** 🚽 ⟳ 🚿

FILEY, North Yorkshire   Map ref 5D3   SatNav YO14 0PU

Orchard Farm Holiday Village

Stonegate, Hunmanby, Filey YO14 0PU
T: (01723) 891582 **F:** (01723) 891582 **E:** info@orchardfarmholidayvillage.co.uk
W: www.orchardfarmholidayvillage.co.uk

🚐		£14.00-£22.00
🚏		£14.00-£22.00
⛺	(25)	£14.00-£22.00
🛏	(7)	£355.00-£889.00
60 touring pitches		

Family park in edge-of-village location with easy access to resorts of Filey, Scarborough and Bridlington. Amenities include children's play area, fishing lake and entertainment during peak season. **Directions:** From A165 from Scarborough take 1st right to Hunmanby under railway bridge 1st right. **Open:** March to October.

Site: 🏧 **Payment:** ☀ **Leisure:** ♪ ▶ ∪ ⚲ ☂ **Children:** 🛝 ⚲ **Catering:** 🛒 **Park:** 🐕 ♫ 🖥 🏕 🏇 **Touring:** 🚽 ⟳ 🚿

HARROGATE, North Yorkshire   Map ref 4B1   SatNav HG3 1JH

Rudding Holiday Park

Follifoot, Harrogate, North Yorkshire HG3 1JH
T: (01423) 870439 **E:** holiday-park@ruddingpark.com
W: www.ruddingholidaypark.co.uk **£ BOOK ONLINE**

🚐	£17.00-£40.00
🚏	£17.00-£40.00
⛺	£17.00-£40.00
141 touring pitches	

Award winning park for touring and camping with extensive facilities; outdoor pool, family pub, adventure playground and golf courses. Minutes from Harrogate and the motorway. Self-catering timber lodges also available. **Directions:** Situated 3 miles south of Harrogate, Rudding Park lies just off the A658 linking the A61 from Leeds to the A59 York Road. **Open:** March - January.

Site: 🏧 ⛺🅿 **Payment:** 💳 € ☀ **Leisure:** ♪ ▶ ∪ ⚲ ☂ **Children:** 🛝 ⚲ **Catering:** ✗ 🛒 **Park:** 🐕 ♫ ▭ 🖥 🏕 🏇 **Touring:** 🚽 ⟳ 🚿 ♪

HELMSLEY, North Yorkshire   Map ref 5C3   SatNav YO62 7RY

Wombleton Caravan Park

Moorfield Lane, Wombleton, Helmsley YO62 7RY
T: (01751) 431684 **E:** info@wombletoncaravanpark.co.uk
W: www.wombletoncaravanpark.co.uk **£ BOOK ONLINE**

🚐 (100)	£19.00-£23.00	
🚏 (6)	£19.00-£23.00	
⛺ (10)	£8.00-£23.00	
100 touring pitches		

A quiet park halfway between Helmsley and Kirkbymoorside, a flat level site with electric hook-ups, modern shower block/disabled facilities and a small shop. Touring and seasonal pitches, tents welcome. **Directions:** Off the A170 through Wombleton village, drive through the village turn left at the war memorial and left down the lane towards the airfield. **Open:** March to October.

Payment: ▣ ☼ **Leisure:** ∪ **Children:** 🛝 **Catering:** 🍴 **Park:** 🐕 🚽 🗐 📶 📡 **Touring:** 🔌 🔄 ♨ 🎵

SCARBOROUGH, North Yorkshire   Map ref 5D3   SatNav YO11 3NN

Cayton Village Caravan Park Ltd

Mill Lane, Cayton Bay, Scarborough YO11 3NN
T: (01723) 583171 **E:** info@caytontouring.co.uk
W: www.caytontouring.co.uk

🚐 (179)	£13.50-£35.00	
🚏 (76)	£15.50-£35.00	
⛺ (55)	£13.50-£28.00	
310 touring pitches		

Playground, recreation field, dog walk, shop, bus service from park entrance. Seasonal pitches, winter storage, caravan sales. Super sites, Hardstanding and grass pitches. Beach 0.5m, Scarborough 3m. Adjoining village with fish shop & pub. **Directions:** From A64 take B1261 to Filey. In Cayton turn left onto Mill Lane. From A165 turn inland at Cayton Bay roundabout onto Mill Lane. 0.5m on RHS. **Open:** 1st March to 31st October.

Site: ⛺📇 **Payment:** ▣ ☼ **Leisure:** 🎵 ➤ **Children:** 🛝 ⚙ **Catering:** 🍴 **Park:** 🐕 🚽 🗐 📡 **Touring:** 🔌 🔄 ♨ 🎵

SCARBOROUGH, North Yorkshire   Map ref 5D3   SatNav YO14 9PS

Crows Nest Caravan Park

Crows Nest Caravan Park, Gristhorpe, Filey YO14 9PS
T: (01723) 582206 **E:** enquiries@crowsnestcaravanpark.com
W: www.crowsnestcaravanpark.com **£ BOOK ONLINE**

🚐 (50)	£15.00-£35.00	
🚏 (50)	£15.00-£35.00	
⛺ (100)	£15.00-£30.00	
🏠 (40)	£250.00-£570.00	
50 touring pitches		

SPECIAL PROMOTIONS
See website for special offers.

Situated on the glorious Yorkshire coast between Scarborough and Filey. This family owned, award winning park is a perfect base. The facilities are of a very high standard, including heated-indoor swimming pool, children's play area and supermarket. Holidays and short breaks ideal for families and couples. We have a range of luxury holiday homes for hire. Tents and tourers are also welcome.

Directions: Just off the A165 between Scarborough (5 miles) and Filey (2 miles). Turn off at roundabout with Jet petrol station. Well signposted.

Open: March to October.

Site: 🏕 **Payment:** ▣ **Leisure:** 🎵 ➤ 🎱 🎣 **Property:** 🐕 🎵 🚽 🗐 📶 **Children:** 🛝 ⚙ **Catering:** 🍴

SCARBOROUGH, North Yorkshire   Map ref 5D3   SatNav YO11 3NU

Flower of May Holiday Parks

Flower of May Holiday Parks Ltd, Lebberston, North Yorkshire YO11 3NU
T: (01723) 584311 **F:** (01723) 585716 **E:** info@flowerofmay.com
W: www.flowerofmay.com **£ BOOK ONLINE**

🚐 (300)	£18.00-£24.00
🚏 (20)	£18.00-£24.00
⛺ (60)	£18.00-£24.00
🏠 (20)	£380.00-£690.00
300 touring pitches	

SPECIAL PROMOTIONS
Early booking offer and other offers available. Please refer to website.

Excellent family-run park. Luxury indoor pool, adventure playground, bar complex, mini-market, fish & chip shop, cafe and 9 hole golf course. Ideal for coast and country. Prices per pitch, per night, four people with car. Luxury hire caravans. Seasonal serviced pitches.

Directions: From A64 take the A165 Scarborough/Filey coast road. Well signposted at Lebberston.

Open: Easter to October.

Site: 🏪 ⛺🅿 **Payment:** 💳 **Leisure:** 🎣 ▸ 🔍 🎵 **Children:** 🧸 **Catering:** ✕ 🛒 **Park:** 🐾 🎵 📶
Touring: 🚾 🚙

SCARBOROUGH, North Yorkshire   Map ref 5D3   SatNav YO13 9BE

Jasmine Park

Cross Lane, Snainton, Scarborough YO13 9BE
T: (01723) 859240 **E:** enquiries@jasminepark.co.uk
W: www.jasminepark.co.uk **£ BOOK ONLINE**

🚐 (74)	£18.00-£30.00
🚏 (74)	£18.00-£30.00
⛺ (20)	£18.00-£30.00
🏠 (4)	£220.00-£445.00
94 touring pitches	

Family-owned, tranquil park in picturesque countryside setting between Scarborough (8 miles) and Pickering. Superbly maintained facilities including our fantastic children's play area. Yorkshire Coast Caravan Park of the Year 2010. Tents and tourers welcome. Seasonal pitches and storage available. Luxury caravans for hire.

Directions: Turn south off the A170 in Snainton opposite the junior school at traffic lights. Signposted.

Open: March to October.

Payment: 💳 ☀ **Leisure:** 🚴 🎣 ▸ ∪ **Children:** 🧸 ⛰ **Catering:** 🛒 **Park:** 🐾 🚫 📶 📦 📷
Touring: 🚰 🚾 🚙 🎵

SKIPTON, North Yorkshire   Map ref 4B1
SatNav BD23 4SD

HOLIDAY PARK

Crowtrees Park

Tosside, Skipton, North Yorkshire BD23 4SD
T: (01729) 840278 **F:** 01729 840863 **E:** enquiries@crowtreespark.co.uk
W: www.crowtreespark.co.uk

(163)   £249.00-£649.00

SPECIAL PROMOTIONS
Please contact us for
special offers.

Set in a secluded rural haven between the Yorkshire Dales National Park and the Forest of Bowland,
a designated "Area of Natural Beauty". Crowtrees is an ideal location for families and couples to
explore the unspoilt countryside. We are open seven days a week and visitors are welcome to view
the park and our range of luxury holiday homes and timber lodges.

Directions: Please contact us for directions.   **Open:** All Year.

Site: ⌂ **Payment:** 💳 **Leisure:** ♿ 🎵 ▶ ☾ 🎣 ❄ **Property:** 🐾 🎵 🖥 📱 **Children:** 🛝 ⛰ **Catering:** ✕ 🍴

SLINGSBY, North Yorkshire   Map ref 5C3
SatNav YO62 4AP

HOLIDAY, TOURING & CAMPING PARK

Robin Hood Caravan Park

Slingsby, York YO62 4AP
T: (01653) 628391 **F:** (01653) 628392 **E:** info@robinhoodcaravanpark.co.uk
W: www.robinhoodcaravanpark.co.uk **£ BOOK ONLINE**

(38)	£20.00-£28.00
(38)	£20.00-£28.00
(38)	£15.00-£25.00
(16)	£190.00-£510.00
38 touring pitches	

SPECIAL PROMOTIONS
Loyalty card available
for campers.

An award winning, privately owned park set in the heart of picturesque Ryedale. Peaceful and
tranquil, a perfect base for families and couples wishing to explore the stunning countryside of
North Yorkshire. Within easy reach of York, Castle Howard, Flamingoland and the coastal resorts of
Scarborough, Whitby and Filey. Overnight holding area available.

Directions: Situated on the edge of Slingsby   **Open:** March to October.
with access off the B1257 Malton to Helmsley
road.

Payment: 💳 ☀ **Leisure:** ♪ ☾ **Children:** 🛝 ⛰ **Catering:** 🍴 **Park:** 🐾 🖥 📱 🚿 **Touring:** 🚰 🔌 🚐

SOUTH OTTERINGTON, North Yorkshire   Map ref 5C3   SatNav DL7 9JB

Otterington Park

Station Road, South Otterington, Northallerton, North Yorkshire DL7 9JB
T: (01609) 780656 **E:** info@otteringtonpark.com
W: www.otteringtonpark.com **£ BOOK ONLINE**

(66)
(66)
66 touring pitches

Situated in the Vale of York, Otterington is an ideal base for visiting the Moors and Dales of Yorkshire, historic cities, market towns, leisure centres and tourist attractions. Camping pods £40, Overnight holding area available. Please contact us for prices.
Directions: Between Northallerton and Thirsk. Situated just off the C10 which links the A168 at Thornton-le-Moor and the A167 at South Otterington. **Open:** March to October.

Payment: **Leisure:** **Property:** **Children:**

STIRTON, North Yorkshire   Map ref 4B1   SatNav BD23 3LQ

Tarn House Caravan Park

Stirton, Nr Skipton, Yorkshire BD23 3LQ
T: (01756) 795309 **E:** reception@tarnhouse.net
W: www.partingtons.com **£ BOOK ONLINE**

£16.00-£20.50
£16.00-£20.50
(2) £260.00-£660.00
13 touring pitches

Family-run caravan park, situated in a rural location in the beautiful Yorkshire Dales. Bar on park and fantastic views. All touring pitches are now hard standing. New elsan point. Overnight holding area available.

Directions: 1.25 miles north west of Skipton.   **Open:** 1 March to 31 October.

Site: Payment: Leisure: Children: Catering: Park:
Touring:

WHITBY, North Yorkshire   Map ref 5D3   SatNav YO22 4QH

Flask Inn Holiday Home Park

Blacksmiths Hill, Robin Hood's Bay, Whitby, North Yorkshire YO22 4QH
T: (01947) 880592 **F:** (01947) 880592 **E:** info@flaskinn.com
W: www.flaskinn.com

(10) £290.00-£520.00

Small, family-run 5 star site for over 30 years, in the North York Moors. All our holiday homes have central heating and double glazing throughout. All have a double bedroom en suite, Freeview TV, DVD, full kitchen with fridge/freezer and microwave. All holiday homes have outside decking and seating. **Directions:** Situated in the North Yorkshire Moors on the A171, 7 miles to Whitby, 12 miles to Scarborough and 4 miles to Robin Hood's Bay. **Open:** March to November.

Site: Payment: Leisure: Property: Children: Catering:

Middlewood Farm Holiday Park

Middlewood Lane, Fylingthorpe, Whitby YO22 4UF
T: (01947) 880414 **F:** (01947) 880871 **E:** info@middlewoodfarm.com
W: www.middlewoodfarm.com

🚐 (21)	£16.00-£28.00
🚏 (21)	£16.00-£28.00
⛺ (100)	£12.00-£27.00
🏠 (30)	£175.00-£619.00

SPECIAL PROMOTIONS
Short Breaks available
early & late season,
from £120.00 (3 night
minimum).

Peaceful, 5 star award-winning family park. A walkers paradise with magnificent, panoramic coastal and moorland views! Level, sheltered, hardstandings, electric hook ups, luxury facilities (heated early and late season), private wash-cubicles, bath, childrens play area. 10 minutes walk to pub/shops/beach and Robin Hood's Bay. Superb holiday homes & gypsy cabins for hire. A friendly welcome awaits!

Directions: Follow A171 Scarborough/Whitby road, signposted from Fylingthorpe/Robin Hood's Bay junction. In Fylingthorpe turn onto Middlewood Lane. Park is 500 yds. Follow brown tourist signs.

Open: Holiday Hire: All Year. Tourers & Tents: March 1st to October 31st.

Payment: 💳 **Leisure:** ♿ ♪ ⛵ ∪ **Property:** 🐕 🖥 **Children:** 🎠 ⚑ **Catering:** 🛒

Northcliffe & Seaview Holiday Parks

Bottoms Lane, High Hawsker, Whitby, North Yorkshire YO22 4LL
T: (01947) 880477 **F:** 01947 880972 **E:** enquiries@northcliffe-seaview.com
W: www.northcliffe-seaview.com **£ BOOK ONLINE**

🏠 (62)	£1400.00-£1850.00
🏠 (3)	£275.00-£595.00

SPECIAL PROMOTIONS
Visit our website to
view our new caravans
for sale, check
availability & book your
holiday 24/7 and
register your email
address to receive our
'special offers' & late
availability emails.

Our award winning parks are situated on the beautiful Heritage Coast twixt Whitby & RHB. These conservation parks have fabulous countryside & coastal views with access to superb walks & cycle track. We sell & hire luxury caravans, have a 4 Star Gold Award cottage and an exclusive seasonal only touring park. Facilities include, Coast Café Bar, play parks, football pitches & lots more.

Directions: Located 3 miles south of Whitby on A171. Turn left onto the B1447 through Hawsker Village, turn left at the top of the hill onto the private road Bottoms Lane.

Open: March 1st until November 7th.

Site: 🏕 **Payment:** 💳 **Leisure:** ♿ ♪ ⛵ ∪ ⚲ ⚲ **Property:** ♪ 📺 🖥 **Children:** 🎠 ⚑ **Catering:** ✗ 🛒

WHITBY, North Yorkshire   Map ref 5D3   SatNav YO22 4JX

Whitby Holiday Park

Saltwick Bay, Whitby, North Yorkshire YO22 4JX
T: (01947) 602664 **F:** (01947) 820356 **E:** info@whitbyholidaypark.co.uk
W: www.whitbypark.co.uk

🚐 (18)
🚕 (18)
⛺ (18)
119 touring pitches

Family friendly spectacular cliff top location with views to Whitby Abbey. Beautiful sandy beaches great for seaside fun, walking and fossil hunting. Pretty peaceful villages and Whitby's bustling attractions nearby. Please contact us for prices. **Directions:** Approach Whitby directing you to Whitby Abbey. Follow green lane, t-junction, turn right, look out for brown signs (tourist) with caravan symbol. **Open:** March - January.

Payment: **Leisure:** **Property:** **Children:** **Catering:**

YORK, North Yorkshire   Map ref 4C1   SatNav YO61 1RY

Alders Caravan Park

Home Farm, Monk Green, Alne nr Easingwold, York YO61 1RY
T: (01347) 838722 **F:** (01347) 838722 **E:** enquiries@homefarmalne.co.uk
W: www.alderscaravanpark.co.uk

🚐 £19.50-£21.50
🚕 £19.50-£21.50
⛺ £19.50-£21.50
🛏 (2)   £37.00
87 touring pitches

A working farm in historic parkland where visitors may enjoy peace and tranquillity. York (on bus route), Moors, Dales and coast nearby. Tastefully landscaped, adjoins village cricket ground. Woodland walk. Overnight holding area available. **Directions:** From A19 exit at Alne sign, in 1.5 miles turn left at T-junction, 0.5 miles park on left in village centre. **Open:** March to October.

Site: **Payment:** **Leisure:** **Children:** **Catering:** **Park:** **Touring:**

YORK, North Yorkshire   Map ref 4C1   SatNav YO61 1ET

Goosewood Holiday Park

Sutton on the Forest, York, Easingwold YO61 1ET
T: (01347) 810829 **F:** (01347) 811498 **E:** enquiries@goosewood.co.uk
W: www.flowerofmay.com **£ BOOK ONLINE**

🚐 (90) £18.00-£24.00
🚕 (10) £18.00-£24.00
🛏 (6)   £340.00-£1249.00
⛺ (21) £340.00-£700.00
100 touring pitches

SPECIAL PROMOTIONS
Three night weekends. Early booking offers. Two person booking offers. Please call for details.

A quiet, peaceful park with fishing lake and children's updated adventure play area. New bar & indoor pool now open. Luxury holiday lodges and caravans, many with Hot Tubs. Coming soon - New luxury development for private owners with lake views. A perfect place to relax and amble through wooded walks. Ideal for visiting historic City of York and surrounding beauty spots of Yorkshire. A warm welcome.

Directions: North of York. Follow route to Strensall.   **Open:** March to 2nd January.

Payment: **Leisure:** **Children:** **Catering:** **Park:** **Touring:**

YORK, North Yorkshire Map ref 4C1

SatNav YO32 9ST

York Touring Caravan Site

Towthorpe Moor Lane, Towthorpe, York YO32 9ST
T: (01904) 499275 **F:** (01904) 499271 **E:** info@yorkcaravansite.co.uk
W: www.yorkcaravansite.co.uk

🚐 (20)	£16.00-£22.00	
🚎 (20)	£16.00-£22.00	
🅰 (10)	£16.00-£22.00	

40 touring pitches

Small family-run secluded park in countryside setting, 5 miles from York centre. Spacious pitches, luxury free showers and toilets. On-site golf driving range, 9 hole pay & play course and crazy golf. **Directions:** Travelling on the A64 towards Scarborough/Malton take the turn-off to the left signposted Strensall/Haxby. We are 1 mile down that road on the left. **Open:** All year.

Payment: 💷 ☼ **Leisure:** ♪ ♦ **Children:** 🛝 **Park:** 🐕 🚽 🗎 📶 **Touring:** 🔌 🚰

HAWORTH, West Yorkshire Map ref 4B1

SatNav BD22 9SS

Upwood Holiday Park

Black Moor Road, Oxenhope, Haworth BD22 9SS
T: (01535) 644242 **E:** info@upwoodpark.co.uk
W: www.upwoodpark.co.uk **£ BOOK ONLINE**

🚐 (60)	£9.50-£27.50	
🚎 (4)	£9.50-£27.50	
🅰 (15)	£9.50-£27.50	
🏠 (1)	£99.00-£395.00	
🛏 (3)	£99.00-£345.00	

75 touring pitches

A family-owned park, pleasantly situated close to the Yorkshire Dales National Park - an ideal base from which to explore the area by car or on foot. Large, modern toilet facilities, comfortable lounge bar serving snacks, games room with pool and arcade games and small shop for essential items. Overnight holding area available. Camping and mega pods available.

Directions: Come in from A629 turning at Flappit Pub towards Haworth.

Open: 1st March to 4th January.

Site: 🏧 **Payment:** 💷 € ☼ **Leisure:** ♿ ♪ ♦ ∪ 🎣 **Children:** 🛝 🎡 **Catering:** ✖ 🍴 **Park:** 🐕 🎵 🚽 🗎 📶 **Touring:** 🔌 🚰 🚰

HOLMFIRTH, West Yorkshire Map ref 4B1

SatNav HD9 7TD

Holme Valley Camping and Caravan Park

Thongsbridge, Holmfirth, West Yorkshire HD9 7TD
T: (01484) 665819 **F:** (01484) 663870 **E:** enquiries@holmevalleycamping.com
W: www.holmevalleycamping.com

🚐 (62)	£17.00-£21.00	
🚎 (62)	£13.50-£19.50	
🅰 (62)	£7.50-£21.50	

62 touring pitches

Picturesque setting in 'Summer Wine' country. Grass, concrete and gravel pitches. 16-amp hook-ups. Well-stocked food shop. Off-licence. Fishing in small lake and river. Children's play area. Five minutes walk from village. David Bellamy Gold Award. **Directions:** Turn into our lane off A6024, 1 mile north of Holmfirth, by bottle banks. Use either entrance. Follow lane to valley bottom, without turning left. **Open:** All year.

Site: 🅰📶 **Payment:** 💷 € ☼ **Leisure:** ♪ ♦ **Children:** 🛝 🎡 **Catering:** 🍴 **Park:** 🐕 🗎 📶 **Touring:** 🔌 🚰 🚰

North West

The North West is a region of contrast, from the cosmopolitan style and contemporary built environment of Manchester to the cultural credentials and architectural grandeur of Liverpool, from the Roman and medieval heritage of Chester to the rolling hills of Lancashire and the stunning scenery around the Lake District. Whether you are looking for urban or rural scenery, a relaxed or an energetic atmosphere, this region will not disappoint.

Highlights

Blackpool

Blackpool is Britain's most popular holiday destination, which comes as no surprise when you think about the resort's range of year-round attractions. But Blackpool is changing. There's a breathtaking new seafront plus world class events and spectacular lighting shows.

Chester

Visit Chester and Cheshire and you'll find a region bursting with character and variation. Quaint market towns and villages can be found dotted throughout the largely unspoilt rural landscape, while Chester provides top-class shopping, entertainment and dining opportunities.

Lake District

The largest of the UK's National Parks, this area contains 16 lakes, more than 150 high peaks, with four over 3000 feet, including England's highest mountain, Scafell Pike (3206 ft).

Liverpool

Liverpool was one of the largest ports in the world during the 18th and 19th centuries, and was a major port involved in the slave trade until its abolition in 1807.

Manchester

The city has over 90 museums and galleries, and its theatres offer a variety of performances from classic plays to spectacular musicals. Manchester is also a haven for shopping.

Scafell Pike

Scafell Pike is the highest mountain in England at 978 metres, and is located in the Lake District National Park. It is sometimes confused with the neighbouring Sca Fell, to which it is connected by the col of Mickledore.

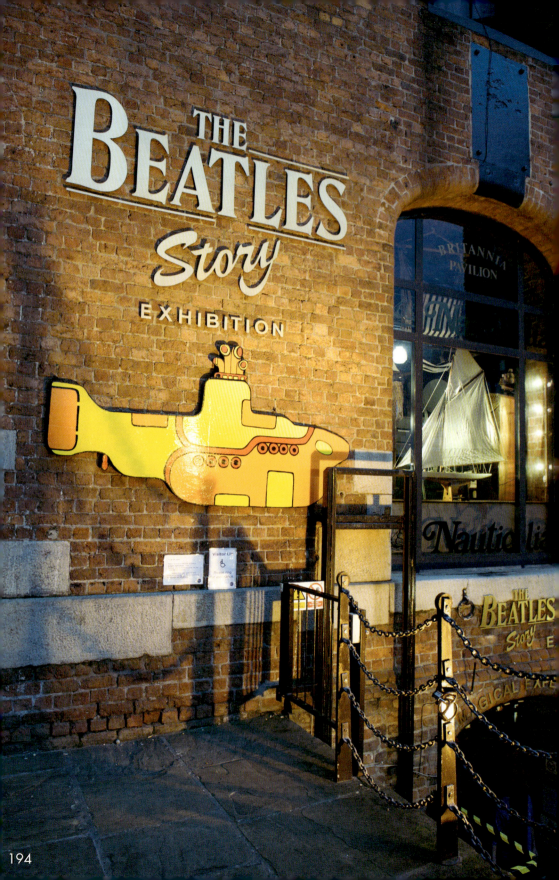

Editor's Picks

Visit a sporting venue

The North West has a great sporting tradition with football, cricket, golf and horse racing, and a trip to one of the area's main stadiums is a must for fans.

Cruise the Mersey

Mersey Ferries offer a 50-minute River Explorer cruise with commentary. Stop at Spaceport and experience the space themed attraction.

Don't get lost

The Lake District National Park runs map-reading skills days to improve visitors' navigation skills and organises hunting for treasure sessions for children.

Take to the water

With over 16 lakes and numerous tarns in the Lake District plus a stretch of coastline there's plenty of opportunity to go rowing, sailing, windsurfing, kayaking, fishing or simply splash about on the shore.

Discover the Beatles Story

Be transported on an incredible journey and see how four young lads from Liverpool were propelled to the dizzy heights of fame and fortune from their humble childhood beginnings.

Things to do

Attractions with this sign participate in the Places of Interest Quality Assurance Scheme.

Attractions with this sign participate in the Visitor Attraction Quality Assurance Scheme.

Both schemes recognise high standards in all aspects of the visitor experience (see page 7)

Entertainment & Culture

Beatles Story

Liverpool, Merseyside L3 4AD
(0151) 709 1963
www.beatlesstory.com
Located within Liverpool's historic Albert Dock, the Beatles Story is a unique visitor attraction that transports you on an enlightening and atmospheric journey into the life, times, culture and music of the Beatles.

Imperial War Museum North
Greater Manchester M17 1TZ
(0161) 836 4000
www.iwm.org.uk/north
Located at The Quays and offers dynamic display techniques to reflect on how people's lives are shaped by war. Free Admission.

Liverpool Football Club
Merseyside L4 0TH
(0151) 260 6677
www.liverpoolfc.tv
Meet an LFC Legend; get your photograph with one of our many trophies or indulge yourself in one of our award winning Experience Days.

Lowry

Salford, Greater Manchester M50 3AZ
08432 086000
www.thelowry.com
Salford's answer to the Sydney Opera House and the Guggenheim rolled into one. See LS Lowry's works and other outstanding exhibitions or take in a performance.

Manchester Art Gallery

Greater Manchester M2 3JL
(0161) 235 8888
www.manchestergalleries.org
Houses one of the country's finest art collections in spectacular Victorian and Contemporary surroundings. Also changing exhibitions and a programme of events and a host of free family friendly resources.

Manchester Museum

Greater Manchester M13 9PL
(0161) 275 2648
www.manchester.ac.uk/museum
Found on Oxford Road, on The University of Manchester campus (in a very impressive gothic-style building), highlights include Stan the T.rex, mummies, live animals such as frogs and snakes, object handling and a varied programme of events.

Manchester United Museum & Tour Centre
Greater Manchester M16 0RA
(0161) 868 8000
www.manutd.com
The official museum and tour offers every football fan a unique insight into Manchester United Football Club and a fantastic day out.

Museum of Lakeland Life
Kendal, Cumbria LA9 5AL
(015397) 22464
www.lakelandmuseum.org.uk
This award-winning museum takes you and your family back through time to tell the story of the Lake District and its inhabitants.

National Waterways Museum
Ellesmere Port, Cheshire CH65 4FW
(0151) 335 5017
www.nwm.org.uk/ellesmere
Unlock the wonders of our waterways.

People's History Museum
Greater Manchester M3 3ER
(0161) 838 9190
www.phm.org.uk
The new People's History Museum is now open

Ribchester Roman Museum
Preston, Lancashire PR3 3XS
(01254) 878261
www.ribchesterromanmuseum.org
Lancashire's only specialist Roman museum, located on the North bank of the beautiful River Ribble.

Tate Liverpool
Merseyside L3 4BB
(0151) 702 7400
www.tate.org.uk/liverpool
Tate Liverpool presents displays and international exhibitions of modern and contemporary art in beautiful light filled galleries.

The Gallery Liverpool
Merseyside L8 5RE
(0151) 709 2442
www.thegalleryliverpool.co.uk
Set in the heart of Liverpool's Independent Cultural District, the gallery occupies the entire upper floor of the industrial premises of John O'Keeffe and Son Ltd

The World of Beatrix Potter
Bowness, Cumbria LA23 3BX
(015394) 88444
www.hop-skip-jump.com
A magical indoor attraction that brings to life all 23 Beatrix Potter's Peter Rabbit tales

Walker Art Gallery
Liverpool, Merseyside L3 8EL
(0151) 478 4199
www.walkerartgallery.org.uk
Home to outstanding works by Rubens, Rembrandt, Poussin, Gainsborough and Hogarth, the Walker Art Gallery is one of the finest art galleries in Europe.

Whitworth Art Gallery
Manchester M15 6ER
(0161) 275 7450
www.whitworth.manchester.ac.uk
The Whitworth Art Gallery is home to an internationally-famous collection of British watercolours, textiles and wallpapers.

World Museum Liverpool
Merseyside L3 8EN
(0151) 478 4393
www.liverpoolmuseums.org.uk/wml
One of Britain's finest museums, with extensive collections from the Amazonian Rain Forest to the mysteries of outer space.

Family Fun

Catalyst Science Discovery Centre

Widnes, Cheshire WA8 0DF
(0151) 420 1121
www.catalyst.org.uk
Interactive science centre whose aim is to make science exciting and accessible to people of all ages and abilities.

Go Ape! Hire Wire Forest Adventure - Delamere
Northwich, Cheshire CW8 2JD
0845 643 9215
www.goape.co.uk
"Take to the trees and experience an exhilarating course of rope bridges, tarzan swings and zip slides...all set high above the forest floor."

Grizedale Forest Visitor Centre
Hawkshead, Cumbria LA22 0QJ
(01229) 860010
www.forestry.gov.uk/northwestengland
Grizedale Forest offers a range of activities for all ages through the year, from mountain biking to relaxing walks, Go-Ape to the sculpture trails.

Sandcastle Waterpark
Blackpool, Lancashire FY4 1BB
(01253) 343602
www.sandcastle-waterpark.co.uk
The UK's Largest Indoor Waterpark and with 18 slides and attractions.

Museum of Wigan Life
Greater Manchester WN1 1NU
(01942) 828128
www.wlct.org/culture/heritage/historyshop.htm
A magnificent Grade II listed building, designed by Alfred Waterhouse in 1878 as a public library for Wigan, and is now the hub of Wigan Heritage Services.

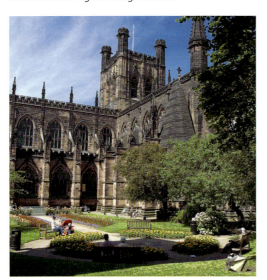

Heritage

Arley Hall & Gardens
Northwich, Cheshire CW9 6NA
(01565) 777353
www.arleyhallandgardens.com
Arley Hall's gardens are a wonderful example of the idea that the best gardens are living works of art.

Chester Cathedral

Cheshire CH1 2HU
(01244) 324756
www.chestercathedral.com
A must see for Chester, a beautiful cathedral with a fascinating history.

Croxteth Hall & Country Park

Liverpool, Merseyside L12 0HB
(0151) 233 6910
www.croxteth.co.uk
Stately home with 500 acres estate including visitor farm, Victorian walled garden and seasonal events.

East Lancashire Railway

Bury, Greater Manchester BL9 0EY
(0161) 764 7790
www.east-lancs-rly.co.uk
The beautifully restored East Lancashire Railway takes you on a captivating journey to discover the region's rich transport heritage.

Holker Hall & Gardens
Grange-over-Sands, Cumbria LA11 7PL
(015395) 58328
www.holker.co.uk
Home to Lord and Lady Cavendish, Victorian wing, glorious gardens, parkland and woodlands.

Jodrell Bank Discovery Centre
Macclesfield, Cheshire SK11 9DL
(01477) 571339
www.jodrellbank.manchester.ac.uk/visitorcentre
Come and take a trip to Mars...

Levens Hall & Gardens
Kendal, Cumbria LA8 0PD
(015395) 60321
www.levenshall.co.uk
Elizabethan mansion and world famous topiary gardens designed by M Beaumont in 1694, fountain garden and buttery, licenced restaurant and gift shop.

Mendips & 20 Forthlin Road [Beatles]
Liverpool, Merseyside
(0151) 427 7231
www.nationaltrust.org.uk/beatles
Take a tour inside the childhood homes of John Lennon and Paul McCartney, and the places where many of the earliest Beatles songs were composed and rehearsed.

Penrith Castle
Cumbria CA11 7HX
(01912) 691200
www.english-heritage.org.uk/daysout/properties/penrith-castle/
The mainly 15th Century remains of a castle begun by Bishop Strickland of Carlisle and developed by the Nevilles and Richard III.

Ravenglass & Eskdale Railway
Cumbria CA18 1SW
(01229) 717171
www.ravenglass-railway.co.uk
Heritage steam engines haul open-top and cosy covered carriages from the Lake District coastal village of Ravenglass to the foot of England's highest mountains.

Speke Hall, Gardens & Estate
Liverpool, Merseyside L24 1XD
(0151) 427 7231
www.nationaltrust.org.uk/main/w-spekehall
One of the most famous half timbered houses in Britain, dating from the 15th century.

Nature & Wildlife

Chester Zoo
Cheshire CH2 1EU
(01244) 380280
www.chesterzoo.org
With over 7,000 animals, including some of the most exotic and endangered species on the planet.

Farmer Ted's Farm Park
Ormskirk, Lancashire L39 7HW
(0151) 526 0002
www.farmerteds.com
A safe environment for families with children 0-12 yrs, with older children also welcome.

Hare Hill Gardens
Macclesfield, Cheshire SK10 4QB
(01625) 584412
www.nationaltrust.org.uk/main/w-harehill
A small but perfectly formed wooded and walled garden.

Knowsley Safari Park
Merseyside L34 4AN
(0151) 430 9009
www.knowsley.com/safari
Enjoy a 5 mile safari through 450 acres of historic parkland.

Old Holly Farm
Garstang, Lancashire PR3 1AA
(01524) 791200
www.oldhollyfarm.com
Appeals to visitors of all ages.

South Lakes Wild Animal Park
Dalton-in-Furness, Cumbria LA15 8JR
(01229) 466086
www.wildanimalpark.co.uk
The ultimate interactive animal experience. Get close to wildlife at Cumbria's top tourist attraction.

Wyre Estuary Country Park
Thornton Lancashire FY5 5LR
(01253) 857890
www.wyrebc.gov.uk/tourismplacestovisit.htm
Located in a Green Flag area and the centre catering for all ages with the ability to cater for all persons with a wide range of foods and drink.

Outdoor Activities

Ullswater Steamers
Cumbria CA11 0US
(01768) 482229
The 'Steamers' create the perfect opportunity to combine a cruise with some of the most famous and spectacular walks in the lake District.

Windermere Lake Cruises, Lakeside

Newby Bridge, Cumbria LA12 8AS
(015394) 43360
www.windermere-lakecruises.co.uk
Steamers and launches sail daily between Ambleside, Bowness and Lakeside. Additional summer routes. Timetabled services.

Manchester Histories Festival
March 21-30,
Various city centre locations
The ten-day MHF celebrates the heritage and history of Manchester across numerous city centre venues. The festival offers a fantastic opportunity to explore and learn this great city and is a great event for old and young alike.
www.manchesterhistoriesfestival.org.uk

FutureEverything
March,
Various city centre locations
FutureEverything is a collaborative festival which draws all kinds of artists together to present their visions of 'the future' to audiences. The festival uses art, digital culture, music and performance together to create something truly unique.
www.futureeverything.org

Global Village Market
Date TBC, Bolton
Bolton will be hosting two international food, gifts and crafts markets as Market Place (Europe) Limited, one of the UK's leading special event market companies, brings their Global Village Market to Bolton town centre for the third year running.
www.marketplaceeurope.co.uk

Wigan Food and Drink Festival
Date TBC, Wigan
Now in its sixth year, the Wigan Food and Drink Festival has evolved into one of the region's premier foodie feasts. Celebrating taste and tradition, the festival includes the CAMRA Wigan Beer Fest, Kitchen Theatre and over 20 food and drink events in local restaurants including celebrity chef events.
www.wlct.org./foodanddrink

Ramsbottom Chocolate Festival
April 12-13, Ramsbottom
Ramsbottom Chocolate Festival is the most talked about event in the North West. Alongside the two-day chocolate market showcasing high quality cocoa from award winning chocolatiers, expect interactive workshops and activities for adults/children, alfresco dining, chocolate rail ale tour, music, competitions, Giant Easter Egg display, our loveable mascot Charlie Chick and much more.
www. ramsbottomchocolatefestival.com

John Smith's Grand National
April 3-5, Aintree
The most famous horse race over jumps takes place over the challenging Aintree fences.
www.aintree.co.uk

Greater Manchester Marathon in Trafford
April 6, Trafford, Manchester
The second Greater Manchester Marathon has a new race village at Manchester United Football Club where the course also finishes. The improved course, entirely on main roads, is even flatter with only 55m of elevation gain. This is a great race for a first marathon, or if you're looking to set a new personal best time. www.greatermanchestermarathon.com

Liverpool Sound City
May 1-3, Liverpool
Liverpool Sound City is the largest international music, digital and film festival and conference in the UK, welcoming over 360 artists, in over 25 venues in Liverpool's city centre. www.liverpoolsoundcity.co.uk

Garstang Walking Festival
May, Garstang
A celebration of springtime in the stunning countryside of Garstang and the surrounding area. Guided walks and activities for all the family. www.visitlancashire.com

Saddleworth and District Whit Friday Brass Band Contest
June 13, Oldham
Last year well over a hundred brass bands participated in some 20 different contests at venues scattered around the moorland villages and towns on the western edge of the Pennines. All of the contests are open-air, many in delightful surroundings. whitfriday.brassbands.saddleworth.org

Electric Garden Progressive Rock Festival
May, Blackpool
The North West's newest progressive rock music festival is now in its second year. www.electricgardenfestival.com

Blackpool Dance Festival
May 22-30, Blackpool
The world's first and foremost festival of dancing. www.blackpooldancefestival.com

Wirral Folk on the Coast Festival
June 5-8, Wirral
All-on-one-site friendly festival at Whitby Sports & Social Club, with fine music real ale and good food being served plus many more visitor attractions. www.wirralfolkonthecoast.com

Great North Swim
TBC, Windermere
Europe's biggest open water swim series comes to the Lake District. www.greatswim.org

Horwich Festival of Racing
June 15, Bolton
Since it began in 2002, Horwich Festival of Racing has grown to become one of the most popular sporting events in the North West. The 2013 event features British standard cycling, running and road walking championships, a young person's swim and run plus street orienteering. www.horwichfestivalofracing.co.uk

Cheshire County Show
June 17-18, Knutsford
Agricultural event at Tabley Showground, near Knutsford, with many new attractions and thousands of animals, including livestock, horses, dogs and pigs. www.cheshirecountyshow.org.uk

Manchester International Festival
July, Various venues
Manchester International Festival, the world's first festival of original, new work and special events. www.mif.co.uk

RHS Flower Show Tatton Park
July 23-27, Tatton Park, Knutsford
A fantastic display of flora and fauna and all things garden related in stunning Cheshire countryside. www.rhs.org.uk

Audlem Festival of Transport
July, Audlem
This is a festival of transport and gathering of historic boats. www.audlem-aset.org

Coniston Water Festival
July, Coniston Water, Lake District
Features fun activities and events focused on the Coniston lake and the unique aspects of water-related culture and sport. www.conistonwaterfestival.org.uk

Grosvenor Park Open Air Theatre
July-August, Grosvenor Park, Chester
The greatest open air theatre outside of London returns for a summer of exciting performances. www.grosvenorparkopenairtheatre.co.uk

Lytham Proms Festival
August 1-3, Lytham & St Annes
Summer proms spectacular including performances from Russell Watson. www.visitlancashire.com

Clitheroe Food Festival
August, Clitheroe
Celebrating the very finest Lancashire food and drink produces. Includes chef demos, tastings and cookery workshops. www.visitlancashire.com

Birkenhead Festival of Transport
September, Birkenhead
Featuring classic cars, steam engines and other modes of vintage transport. www.bheadtransportfest.com

Blackpool Illuminations
Sept-Nov, Blackpool
This world famous display lights up Blackpool's promenade with over 1 million glittering lights. www.visitlancashire.com

Tourist Information Centres

When you arrive at your destination, visit an Official Partner Tourist Information Centre for quality assured help with accommodation and information about local attractions and events, or email your request before you go. To find a Tourist Information Centre visit www.visitengland.com

Accrington	Town Hall	01254 380293	information@leisureinhyndburn.co.uk
Altrincham	20 Stamford New Road	0161 912 5931	tourist.information@trafford.gov.uk
Ambleside	Central Buildings	015394 32582	tic@thehubofambleside.com
Barnoldswick	Post Office Buildings	01282 666704	tourist.info@pendle.gov.uk
Barrow-in-Furness	Forum 28	01229 876543	touristinfo@barrowbc.gov.uk
Blackburn	Blackburn Market	01254 688040	visit@blackburn.gov.uk
Bolton	Central Library Foyer	01204 334321	tourist.info@bolton.gov.uk
Bowness	Glebe Road	015394 42895	bownesstic@lake-district.gov.uk
Burnley	Parker Lane	01282 447210	tic@burnley.gov.uk
Bury	The Fusilier Museum	0161 253 5111	touristinformation@bury.gov.uk
Carlisle	Old Town Hall	01228 625600	tourism@carlisle.gov.uk
Chester	Town Hall	0845 647 7868	welcome@chestervic.co.uk
Cleveleys	Victoria Square	01253 853378	cleveleystic@wyrebc.gov.uk
Clitheroe	Platform Gallery, Station Road	01200 425566	tourism@ribblevalley.gov.uk
Congleton	Town Hall	01260 271095	congletontic@cheshireeast.gov.uk
Coniston	Ruskin Avenue	015394 41533	mail@conistontic.org

Discover Pendle Centre	Boundary Mill Stores	01282 856186	discoverpendle@pendle.gov.uk
Ellesmere Port	McArthur Glen Outlet Village	0151 356 5562	enquiries@cheshiredesigneroutlet.com
Garstang	1 Cherestanc Square	01995 602125	garstangtic@wyrebc.gov.uk
Kendal	25 Stramongate	01539 735891	info@kendaltic.co.uk
Keswick	Moot Hall	017687 72645	keswicktic@lakedistrict.gov.uk
Lancaster	The Storey	01524 582394	lancastervic@lancaster.gov.uk
Liverpool Albert Dock	Anchor Courtyard	0151 233 2008	jackie.crawford@liverpool.gov.uk
Liverpool John Lennon Airport	Arrivals Hall	0151 907 1058	information@liverpoolairport.com
Lytham St Annes	Town Hall	01253 725610	touristinformation@fylde.gov.uk
Macclesfield	Town Hall	01625 378123	karen.connon@cheshireeast.gov.uk
Manchester	45-50 Piccadilly Plaza	0871 222 8223	touristinformation@visit-manchester.com
Morecambe	Old Station Buildings	01524 582808	morecambevic@lancaster.gov.uk
Nantwich	Civic Hall	01270 537359	nantwichtic@cheshireeast.gov.uk
Northwich	1, The Arcade	01606 288828	infocentrenorthwich@cheshirewestandchester.gov.uk
Oldham	Oldham Library	0161 770 3064	tourist@oldham.gov.uk
Pendle Heritage Centre	Park Hill	01282 677150	pendleheritagecentre@htnw.co.uk
Penrith	Middlegate	01768 867466	pen.tic@eden.gov.uk
Preston	The Guildhall	01772 253731	tourism@preston.gov.uk
Rheged	Redhills	01768 860015	tic@rheged.com
Rochdale	Touchstones	01706 924928	tic@link4life.org
Saddleworth	Saddleworth Museum	01457 870336	saddleworthtic@oldham.gov.uk
Salford	The Lowry, Pier 8	0161 848 8601	tic@salford.gov.uk
Southport	112 Lord Street	01704 533333	info@visitsouthport.com
Stockport	Staircase House	0161 474 4444	tourist.information@stockport.gov.uk
Ulverston	Coronation Hall	01229 587120	ulverstontic@southlakeland.gov.uk
Windermere	Victoria Street	015394 46499	info@ticwindermere.co.uk

Regional Contacts and Information

There are various publications and guides about England's North West available from the following Tourist Boards or by logging on to www.visitenglandsnorthwest.com or calling 0845 600 6040:

Visit Chester and Cheshire
Chester Railway Station, 1st Floor, West Wing Offices, Station Road, Chester, CH1 3NT
Tel: (01244) 405600
Tel: 0844 647 7868 (accommodation booking)
Email: info@visitchesterandcheshire.co.uk
Web: www.visitchester.com

Cumbria Tourism
Windermere Road, Staveley, Kendal, LA8 9PL
Tel: (015398) 22222
Email: info@cumbriatourism.org
Web: www.golakes.co.uk

The Lancashire and Blackpool Tourist Board
St. George's House, St. George's Street, Chorley, PR7 2AA
Tel: (01257) 226600 (Brochure request)
Email: info@visitlancashire.com
Web: www.visitlancashire.com

Visit Manchester – The Tourist Board For Greater Manchester
Manchester Vic
Piccadilly Plaza, Portland Street
Manchester
M1 4BT
Tel: 0871 222 8223
Email: touristinformation@visitmanchester.com
Web: www.visitmanchester.com

The Mersey Partnership – The Tourist Board for Liverpool City Region
12 Princes Parade, Liverpool, L3 1BG
Tel: (0151) 233 2008 (information enquiries)
Tel: 0844 870 0123 (accommodation booking)
Email: info@visitliverpool.com
(accommodation enquiries)
Email: liverpoolvisitorcentre@liverpool.gov.uk
(information enquiries)
Web: www.visitliverpool.com

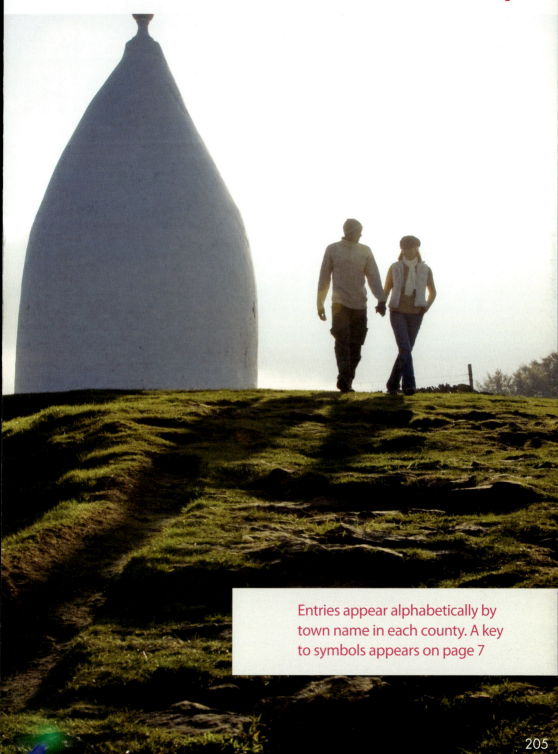

Entries appear alphabetically by town name in each county. A key to symbols appears on page 7

Wild Rose Park

Ormside, Appleby-in-Westmorland CA16 6EJ
T: (017683) 51077 **F:** (017683) 52551 **E:** reception@wildrose.co.uk
W: www.harrisonholidays.com **£ BOOK ONLINE**

£20.00-£40.00
£16.00-£33.50
(25) £265.00-£619.00
250 touring pitches

Friendly, family park in the lovely, unspoilt Eden Valley with mountain views. Within easy reach of the Lakes and the Dales. Spotless, super loos and private wash cubicles. Overnight holding area available. Wild Rose Park offers a five star treatment for your touring holidays, along with luxury holiday homes to rent for short and week long stays. A new bar & restaurant is open for the start of 2014 giving you the chance to taste the fantastic Cumbrian produce. We also have Wigwams & electric bike hire for the ultimate Eden camping experience.

Directions: Please contact us for Directions.   **Open:** All year.

Site: 🏕 ▲🅿 Payment: 💳 ☼ Leisure: 👶 ♪ ⚲ ♻ ♣ ⚵ ✈ Children: 🎠 ⚒ Catering: ✕ 🍴
Park: 🐕 ♫ 🖥 🏧 📷 Touring: 🚿 🚽 🚰 ♪

Looking for something else?

The official and most comprehensive guide to independently inspected, star rated accommodation.

B&Bs and Hotels - B&Bs, Hotels, farmhouses, inns, serviced apartments, campus and hostel accommodation in England.

Self Catering - Self-catering holiday homes, approved caravan holiday homes, boat accommodation and holiday cottage agencies in England.

Camping, Touring and Holiday Parks - Touring parks, camping holidays and holiday parks and villages in Britain.

Now available in all good bookshops and online at **www.hudsons.co.uk/shop**

BOUTH, Cumbria   Map ref 5A3

SatNav LA12 8JN

 (43)   £19.50-£25.50
(4)   £19.50-£25.50
(3)   £250.00-£620.00
39 touring pitches

SPECIAL PROMOTIONS
10% off 7 day tourer booking. Rebook within 28 days of holiday and receive 15% discount.

Black Beck Caravan Park

Bouth, Nr Ulverston, Cumbria LA12 8JN
T: (01229) 861274 **F:** (01229) 861041 **E:** reception@blackbeck.com
W: www.blackbeck.com **£ BOOK ONLINE**

Black Beck is situated within the Lake District National Park, nestled in the beautiful Rusland Valley between the southern tips of Lake Windermere and Coniston. Surrounded by spectacular woodland scenery. Jacuzzi and sauna. Overnight touring area with hardstanding pitches and overnight holding area available.

Directions: M6 jct 36. A590 towards Barrow, Newby Bridge. Pass steam railway, Next right to Bouth. Left at T-junction, 0.5 miles right after hump-backed bridge.

Open: 1st March to 15th November.

Payment: ⊡ ☼ **Leisure:** ᕗ ♪ ∪ **Children:** ⚘ ⚠ **Catering:** ⚒ **Park:** ⊟ 🐕 ▦ ▣ 📷 🎥 **Touring:** ☎ 🕭 🖀 ♫

GRANGE-OVER-SANDS, Cumbria   Map ref 5A3

SatNav LA11 6HR

(10)   £16.00-£18.00
(5)   £16.00-£18.00
(10)   £14.00-£18.00
(2)   £250.00-£450.00
20 touring pitches

Greaves Farm Caravan Park

c/o Nether Edge, Field Broughton, Grange-over-Sands, Cumbria LA11 6HR
T: (01539) 536587 **E:** info@greavesfarmcaravanpark.co.uk
W: www.greavesfarmcaravanpark.co.uk

Small, quiet park in rural location 2m north of Cartmel. Family owned and supervised. Convenient base for South Lakes, within easy reach of Windermere, Kendal and Furness Peninsula. 30 minutes from M6. Two luxury holiday caravans for hire. Spacious touring and camping park, hard-standings available, level grass pitches.

Directions: Exit 36 off M6. Follow A590 signed Barrow. 1 mile before Newby Bridge take left hand road signed Cartmel 4m. Continue 1.5m, Site is signed.

Open: March to October.

Payment: ☼ **Leisure:** ♪ ▶ ∪ **Children:** ⚘ **Park:** 🐕 ▣ 📷 **Touring:** ☎ 🕭 🖀

SatNav LA7 7NN

Waters Edge Caravan Park

Crooklands, Kendal, Cumbria LA7 7NN
T: (01539) 567708 **E:** info@watersedgecaravanpark.co.uk
W: www.watersedgecaravanpark.co.uk

🚐 (26)	£16.50-£23.80
🚍 (26)	£16.50-£23.80
⛺ (6)	£10.00-£27.50

26 touring pitches

Friendly site in open countryside. Lake District, Morecambe and Yorkshire Dales nearby. All hardstanding pitches. Lounge, bar, pool room and patio area. Shower block with laundry. Local pub/restaurant within 300yds. Overnight holding area available. **Directions:** Leave M6 at jct 36, take A65 toward Kirkby Lonsdale for approx 100 yds, then left on A65 toward Crooklands. Site approx 1 mile on the right. **Open:** 1st March to 14th November.

Site: 🏕 ⛺🅿 Payment: 💳 ☀ Leisure: ♪ ▶ ∪ 🔍 Children: 🛝 Catering: 🍴 Park: 🐕 🚭 📶 📷
Touring: 🚐 ♿ 🚿

SatNav CA12 4TE

Castlerigg Farm Camping & Caravan Site

Castlerigg, Keswick CA12 4TE
T: (01768) 772479 **E:** info@castleriggfarm.com
W: www.castleriggfarm.com

🚐	£19.00-£22.50
🚍	£19.00-£22.50
⛺ (80)	£2.40-£7.20

21 touring pitches

The rule of silence after 10.30pm is in keeping with the wonderful location of this family run site. Exceptional panoramic views of the surrounding fells and lakes. Camping prices: Adult £5.70-£7.20, Child £3.00-£4.00, Vehicles £2.40-£3.20. Please see our website for special offers. **Directions:** From A66 follow signs to A591 out of town towards Windermere. 1 mile near top of hill, turn right. Castlerigg Farm Camp Site on left. **Open:** March to November.

Payment: 💳 Leisure: ⚲ ♪ ▶ ∪ Children: 🛝 Catering: ✕ 🍴 Park: 🐕 🚭 📶 📷 Touring: 🚐 ♿ 🚿

SatNav CA12 4TE

Castlerigg Hall Caravan & Camping Park

Castlerigg Hall, Keswick, Cumbria CA12 4TE
T: (01768) 774499 **E:** info@castlerigg.co.uk
W: www.castlerigg.co.uk / www.foodatjiggers.co.uk

🚐 (65)	£19.75-£32.50
🚍 (65)	£19.00-£30.00
⛺ (120)	£17.00-£23.50
🛏 (4)	
🏠 (12)	£290.00-£540.00

Our elevated position commands wonderful panoramic views of the surrounding fells. Formerly a Lakeland hill farm, Castlerigg Hall has been sympathetically developed into a quality touring park. We now have a new restaurant; Food at Jiggers. **Directions:** Head out of Keswick on the A591 direction Windermere. At the top of the hill turn right at the brown tourist sign indicating Castlerigg Hall. **Open:** 12th March to 11th November.

Payment: 💳 Leisure: ♪ ▶ Property: 🐕 🚭 📶 📷 Children: 🛝 Catering: ✕

Book your accommodation online

Visit our new 2014 guide websites for detailed information, up-to-date availability and to book your accommodation online. Includes over 20,000 places to stay, all of them star rated.

www.visitor-guides.co.uk

KIRKBY LONSDALE, Cumbria Map ref 5B3 SatNav LA6 2SE

Woodclose Park

Chapel House Lane, High Casterton, Kirkby Lonsdale LA6 2SE
T: (01524) 271597 **F:** (01524) 272301 **E:** info@woodclosepark.com
W: www.woodclosepark.com **£ BOOK ONLINE**

(17) £13.50-£25.00
(14) £13.50-£24.50
(5) £14.00-£18.00
52 touring pitches

Enjoy England Bronze award winning park, set in the beautiful Lune valley between the Yorkshire Dales and the Lake District National Park. Tourers, camping, self catering Wigwams and holiday homes and lodges for sale. **Directions:** M6 jct 36, follow A65 for approx 6 miles. The park entrance can be found just past Kirkby Lonsdale on the left-hand side, up the hill. **Open:** 1st March - 31st October. Holiday Homes until 1st January.

Payment: **Leisure:** **Children:** **Catering:** **Park:** **Touring:**

PENRITH, Cumbria Map ref 5B2 SatNav CA11 0JB

Flusco Wood

Flusco, Penrith CA11 0JB
T: (01768) 480020 **E:** info@fluscowood.co.uk
W: www.fluscowood.co.uk

(26) £20.00-£23.00
(10) £20.00-£23.00
36 touring pitches

A high-standard, quiet woodland touring caravan park with fully serviced pitches and centrally heated amenity building. Short drive to many attractions and places of interest in the Lake District. Overnight holding area available. **Directions:** M6 jct 40, travel west on A66 towards Keswick. After about 4 miles turn right (signposted Flusco). Entrance along lane on the left. **Open:** Easter to November.

Payment: **Leisure:** **Children:** **Catering:** **Park:** **Touring:**

ULLSWATER, Cumbria Map ref 5A3 SatNav CA11 0JF

Waterfoot Caravan Park

Pooley Bridge, Penrith, Ullswater CA11 0JF
T: (017684) 86302 **F:** (017684) 86728 **E:** enquiries@waterfootpark.co.uk
W: www.waterfootpark.co.uk **£ BOOK ONLINE**

(34) £20.00-£32.00
(34) £20.00-£32.00
34 touring pitches

Set in the grounds of a Georgian mansion overlooking Ullswater. Waterfoot Park is a 5 star holiday park with excellent facilities which include reception, shop, licensed bar, games room and play area. David Bellamy Conservation Gold Award. **Directions:** M6 jct40, follow signs marked Ullswater Steamers. West on A66 1 mile. Left at roundabout A592 (Ullswater). Park located on right. Satnav not compatable. **Open:** 1st March to 14th November.

Site: **Payment:** **Leisure:** **Children:** **Catering:** **Park:** **Touring:**

WINDERMERE, Cumbria Map ref 5A3 SatNav LA23 3DL

Fallbarrow Park

Rayrigg Road, Bowness-on-Windermere, Windermere, Cumbria LA23 3DL
T: (01539) 569835 **E:** enquiries@southlakelandparks.co.uk
W: www.slholidays.co.uk/Fallbarrow **£ BOOK ONLINE**

(26) £18.50-£35.00
(26) £18.50-£35.00
(40) £318.00-£1059.00
(2) £552.00-£1379.00
(33) £232.00-£771.00
26 touring pitches

Fallbarrow is located in Bowness, on the shores of Lake Windermere. Boat launch facilities, picnic area, bar and deli. Use of swimming pool at White Cross Bay at an additional charge. **Open:** 1st March to 14th January.

Site: **Payment:** **Leisure:** **Property:** **Children:** **Catering:**

For **key to symbols** see page 7

WINDERMERE, Cumbria Map ref 5A3 SatNav LA12 8NR

Hill of Oaks Park

Tower Wood, Windermere LA12 8NR
T: (015395) 31578 **F:** (015395) 30431 **E:** enquiries@hillofoaks.co.uk
W: www.hillofoaks.co.uk **£ BOOK ONLINE**

🚗 (43) £18.00-£38.00
🚐 (43) £18.00-£38.00
🚎 (2) £295.00-£725.00
43 touring pitches

Hill of Oaks is a 5 star award-winning park, located on the shores of Windermere. The park has a play area and nature walks through the woodland. Five jetties, boat launching and access to watersport activities. Self-catering units for rent. **Directions:** M6 jct 36, west on A590 towards Barrow and Newby Bridge. At roundabout turn right, onto A592. Park is approx 3 miles on left-hand side. **Open:** 1st March to Mid November.

Site: **Payment:** **Leisure:** **Children:** **Catering:** **Park:** **Touring:**

WINDERMERE, Cumbria Map ref 5A3 SatNav LA23 1PA

Limefitt Park

Patterdale Road, Windermere, Cumbria LA23 1PA
T: (01539) 569835 **E:** enquiries@southlakelandparks.co.uk
W: www.slholidays.co.uk **£ BOOK ONLINE**

🚎 (8) £330.00-£978.00

Limefitt is spectacularly located in one of Lakeland's most beautiful valleys, capturing the very spirit of the Lake District National Park. Limefitt is a friendly place offering peace and tranquillity. For our latest deals and offers visit our website. **Open:** 1st March to 14th January.

Site: **Payment:** **Leisure:** **Property:** **Children:** **Catering:**

WINDERMERE, Cumbria Map ref 5A3 SatNav LA23 1LF

White Cross Bay Holiday Park and Marina

Ambleside Road, Windermere, Cumbria LA23 1LF
T: (01539) 569835 **E:** enquiries@southlakelandparks.co.uk
W: www.slholidays.co.uk/White-Cross-Bay **£ BOOK ONLINE**

🚎 (80) £374.00-£1201.00
🚐 (44) £244.00-£786.00

White Cross Bay sits directly on the shores of Lake Windermere, south of Ambleside. Fantastic facilities, including swimming pool, gym and sauna. Bar and restaurant on site. For our latest deals and offers visit our website. **Open:** 1st March to 14th January.

Site: **Payment:** **Leisure:** **Property:** **Children:** **Catering:**

Need more information?

Visit our new 2014 guide websites for detailed information, up-to-date availability and to book your accommodation online. Includes over 20,000 places to stay, all of them star rated.
www.visitor-guides.co.uk

OLDHAM, *Greater Manchester*   Map ref 4B1   SatNav OL3 5UN

Moorlands Caravan Park

Ripponden Road, Denshaw, Oldham OL3 5UN
T: (01457) 874348 **E:** moorlandscp@aol.com
W: www.moorlandscp.co.uk

Newly refurbished, 4 star park on the moors of Saddleworth. Ideal for walkers, horse riders, or just a family stay. Half a mile from the Pennine Way and Pennine Bridal Way. Short walk to pub and stunning views for Tents, caravans and camping pods. Limited Winter Availability. **Directions:** Junction 22 of the M62, 2 miles in the direction of Saddleworth. **Open:** All year.

🚐 (40)   £18.00-£21.00
🚏 (40)   £18.00-£21.00
⛺ (20)   £6.00
40 touring pitches

Site: **Payment:** ☼ **Leisure:** **Children:** **Park:** **Touring:**

ROCHDALE, *Greater Manchester*   Map ref 4B1   SatNav OL15 0AS

Hollingworth Lake Caravan Park

Roundhouse Farm, Hollingworth Lake, Littleborough OL15 0AT
T: (01706) 378661 **E:** mradammills2003@yahoo.co.uk

🚐 (30)   £10.00-£16.00
🚏 (10)   £10.00-£16.00
⛺ (10)   £8.00-£16.00
50 touring pitches

A popular, five-acre park adjacent to Hollingworth Lake. At the foot of the Pennines, within easy reach of many local attractions. Backpackers walking the Pennine Way are welcome at this family-run park. Hardstanding and grass areas. Excellent train service into Manchester Victoria. 20 minutes from Littleborough/Smithybridge. Overnight holding area available. Restaurant/cafe within 1m of site.

Directions: From M62. Jct 21 Milnrow. Follow Hollingworth Lake Country Park signs to the Fishermans Inn/The Wine Press. Take Rakewood Road then 2nd on right.   **Open:** All year.

Payment: ☼ **Leisure:** **Catering:** **Park:** **Touring:**

Newton Hall Holiday Park

Staining Road, Staining, Blackpool, Lancashire FY3 0AX
T: (01253) 882512 **F:** (01253) 893101 **E:** reception@newtonhall.net
W: www.partingtons.com **£ BOOK ONLINE**

(33)   £190.00-£650.00

SPECIAL PROMOTIONS
Rebook within 28 days
to receive 15%
discount,
3 nights minimum stay.

Family park, ideally situated in open countryside, 2.5 miles from Blackpool tower. Caravans, apartments & flats for hire. New club with regular live entertainment. Indoor swimming pool. Grunty's Fun Club - Children's entertainment every weekend & high season. Fishing pond. Indoor bowling. New enclosed ball game area. Winner of Lancashire & Blackpool Toursim Award 2008/09 & 2010/11.

Directions: M55 junction 4, 3rd exit. Right at 4th traffic lights past zoo. 3rd exit at roundabout. 1 mile on right Staining Rd. Park on right.

Open: 1st March to 15th November.

Site: 🏠 **Payment:** 💳 ☼ **Leisure:** 🎵 ▶ ⛳ 🎣 🎯 **Children:** 🛝 ⛰ **Catering:** ✗ 🛒 **Park:** 🎵 🖥 🔲 🛗 🐾 **Touring:** ⏰

Windy Harbour Holiday Park

Windy Harbour Road, Singleton, Poulton Le Fylde FY6 8NB
T: (01253) 883064 **E:** info@windyharbour.net
W: www.partingtons.com **£ BOOK ONLINE**

   £18.00-£27.50
   £18.00-£27.50
(11)   £190.00-£650.00
130 touring pitches

SPECIAL PROMOTIONS
10% discount on 7 day
touring holidays,
rebook holiday within
28 days to receive 15%
discount.

Situated on the banks of River Wyre in the beautiful Fylde countryside. Family-run park with many facilities including club with newly refurbished family room, indoor swimming pool, extensive outdoor play area, amusement arcade and shop. Grunty's Fun Club - Children's entertainment every weekend and high season. Very easy access from M55 motorway. Overnight holding area available.

Directions: From M6 onto M55 take jct 3 signposted Fleetwood (A585). At traffic lights go straight ahead onto Windy Harbour Road. The park is straight ahead.

Open: 1st March to 15th November.

Site: 🏠 **Payment:** 💳 ☼ **Leisure:** 🎵 ▶ ⛳ 🎣 🎯 **Children:** 🛝 ⛰ **Catering:** ✗ 🛒 **Park:** 🎵 🖥 🔲 🛗 🐾 **Touring:** 🚿 ⏰ 🔌 🎣

CLITHEROE, Lancashire   Map ref 4A1
SatNav BB7 4JJ

Todber Holiday Park
Burnley Road, Gisburn, Clitheroe BB7 4JJ
T: (01539) 569835 **E:** enquiries@southlakelandparks.co.uk
W: www.slholidays.co.uk/todber **£ BOOK ONLINE**

(7)   £256.00–£449.00

Todber overlooks Pendle Hill and the Ribble Valley. Todber is a short drive from the Yorkshire Dales, Skipton and Lancaster. There is a bar, children's play area and football field. **Directions:** Please contact for directions. **Open:** All year.

Site: **Payment:** **Leisure:** **Children:** **Catering:** **Park:**

FLEETWOOD, Lancashire   Map ref 4A1
SatNav FY7 8JX

Broadwater Caravan Park
Fleetwood Road, Fleetwood FY7 8JX
T: (01253) 872796 **F:** (01253) 877133 **E:** reception@broad-water.co.uk
W: www.partingtons.com **£ BOOK ONLINE**

(13)   £190.00–£650.00

SPECIAL PROMOTIONS
Re-book within 28 days to receive 15% discount, 3 night minimum stay.

Family run caravan park, ideally situated for Cleveleys, Blackpool and Fleetwood. Licensed club, children's room, pool, spa, sauna, playground and arcade. New Astroturf area for ball games. Bluetooth enabled music youth shelter on play park, Grunty's Fun Club - Children's entertainment every weekend & high season.

Directions: Please contact us for directions.   **Open:** March - November.

Site: **Payment:** **Leisure:** **Children:** **Park:** **Touring:**

Book your accommodation online

Visit our new 2014 guide websites for detailed information, up-to-date availability and to book your accommodation online. Includes over 20,000 places to stay, all of them star rated.

www.visitor-guides.co.uk

HEYSHAM, Lancashire   Map ref 5A3   SatNav LA3 2XA

★★★★
HOLIDAY PARK

🚐 (38)   £189.00-£572.00

Ocean Edge Leisure Park, Heysham
Moneyclose Lane, Heysham, Morecambe LA3 2XA
T: (01539) 569835 **E:** enquiries@southlakelandparks.co.uk
W: www.slholidays.co.uk/Ocean-Edge

Ocean Edge is close to the village of Heysham on the shores of Morecambe Bay overlooking the Irish Sea. Park facilities include a beer garden, cafe, indoor heated swimming pool and live entertainment. For our latest deals and offers, please visit our website. **Open:** 18th February to 3rd January.

Site: 🅿 **Payment:** 💷 ☼ **Leisure:** ♿ ♪ ⌖ ∪ ✎ ⚲ **Children:** 🛝 ⚠ **Catering:** ✗ 🍴 **Park:** 🐕 ♫ 🖥 📷 📱 ⌂ **Touring:** ⊙

LANCASTER, Lancashire   Map ref 5A3   SatNav LA2 9HH

★★★
TOURING &
CAMPING PARK

🚐 (36)   £16.00-£18.00
🚐 (4)   £16.00-£18.00
⛺ (8)   £8.00-£15.00
40 touring pitches

New Parkside Farm Caravan Park, Lancaster
Denny Beck, Caton Road, Lancaster LA2 9HH
T: (01524) 770723 **E:** enquiries@newparksidefarm.co.uk
W: www.newparksidefarm.co.uk

Peaceful, family-run park on a working farm on the edge of the Forest of Bowland. Extensive views of the Lune Valley and Ingleborough. Excellent base for exploring the Lakes, Dales and unspoilt coast and countryside of North Lancashire. **Directions:** Leave M6 at junction 34, A683 east towards Caton/Kirkby Lonsdale, caravan park entrance 1 mile from motorway junction on the right (signposted). **Open:** March to October.

Site: ⛺🅿 **Payment:** ☼ **Leisure:** ♪ **Children:** 🛝 **Park:** 🐕 ⌂ **Touring:** ♨ ⊙ 🚐

MORECAMBE, Lancashire   Map ref 5A3   SatNav LA3 3DF

★★★★
HOLIDAY PARK

🚐 (40)   £189.00-£600.00

Regent Leisure Park
Westgate, Morecambe, Lancashire LA3 3DF
T: (01539) 569835 **E:** enquiries@southlakelandparks.co.uk
W: www.slholidays.co.uk **£ BOOK ONLINE**

Regent is a few minutes from Morecambe and a 40 minute drive to the Lake District and Blackpool. Facilities include cabaret lounge, children's play area, indoor heated pool and live entertainment. **Open:** 1st March to 15th January.

Site: 🏠 ⛺🅿 **Payment:** 💷 **Leisure:** ⚲ ⌖ **Catering:** ✗ 🍴 **Park:** 🐕 ♫ 🖥 📱

MORECAMBE, Lancashire   Map ref 5A3   SatNav LA4 4TQ

★★★
HOLIDAY, TOURING
& CAMPING PARK

🚐 (56)   £17.00-£30.00
🚐 (56)   £17.00-£30.00
⛺   £14.00-£30.00
🚐 (15)   £160.00-£405.00
56 touring pitches

Venture Caravan Park
Langridge Way, Westgate, Morecambe LA4 4TQ
T: (01524) 412986 **E:** mark@venturecaravanpark.co.uk
W: www.venturecaravanpark.co.uk

Family-run park, 0.75 miles from the sea. Bar, entertainment, meals, heated enclosed swimming fun pool, shop & play areas. Tourers, tents & motorhomes welcome. Hire caravans also available. Separate park home section. **Open:** All year for tourers, tents & motorhomes.

Site: 🏠 **Payment:** 💷 ☼ **Leisure:** ♪ ⌖ ✎ ⚲ **Children:** 🛝 ⚠ **Catering:** ✗ 🍴 **Park:** 🐕 ♫ 🖥 📷 📱 ⌂ **Touring:** ♨ 🚐 ♪

ORMSKIRK, Lancashire   Map ref 4A1

SatNav L40 8HB

Hurlston Hall Country Caravan Park

Hurlston Lane, Scarisbrick, Ormskirk, Lancashire L40 8HB
T: (01704) 840400 **F:** (01704) 841400 **E:** info@hurlstonhall.co.uk
W: www.hurlstonhall.co.uk

(60)   £25.00

Picturesque, 60 pitch all electric touring park with 4.5 acre fishing lake, children's play area and golf club facilities on site. Excellent toilet block. No dogs. Please telephone to book a pitch. **Directions:** Hurlston Hall is situated on the A570, west of the historical market town of Ormskirk and ten minutes from the shops and attractions of Southport. **Open:** All Year.

Site: Payment: Leisure: Catering: Park: Touring:

PRESTON, Lancashire   Map ref 4A1

SatNav PR4 3HA

Mowbreck Holiday and Residential Park

Mowbreck Lane, Wesham, Preston, Lancashire PR4 3HA
T: (01772) 682494 **F:** 01772 672986 **E:** info@mowbreckpark.co.uk
W: www.mowbreckpark.co.uk

(4)   £252.00-£460.00

Enjoy the peace & quiet at Mowbreck, set in a delightful woodland location. Mowbreck is family owned and run to the highest standard. Luxury holiday home for hire, central heating, double-glazed, TV, microwave and 2 bedrooms. **Directions:** Turn off the M55 at Jct 3, follow the signs for Kirkham and Wesham. Turn left at St Joseph's Church into Mowbreck Lane. We are situated 1/2 mile down. **Open:** 1st February to 16th January.

Payment: Leisure: Property: Children:

AINSDALE, Merseyside   Map ref 4A1

SatNav PR8 3ST

Willowbank Holiday Home and Touring Park

Coastal Road, Ainsdale, Southport PR8 3ST
T: (01704) 571566 **E:** info@willowbankcp.co.uk
W: www.willowbankcp.co.uk

(87)   £14.50-£19.40
(87)   £14.50-£19.40
(228)
87 touring pitches

SPECIAL PROMOTIONS
Please see our web site for offers.

Willowbank Holiday Home & Touring Park offers an easily accessible location, convenient for Southport & Liverpool with well maintained modern facilities in a quiet and relaxed atmosphere. The park is open from 1st March to 31st January for holiday homes, touring caravans, motor homes and trailer tents. Last check in 9.00pm. Check out 12.00pm. No Commercial vehicles. Please note we do not let out holiday homes.

Directions: From M6 jct 26 for M58, from the M62 jct for M57. A5036 & A5207 leading to A565 towards Southport, RAF Woodvale, Coastal Rd.

Open: 1st March to 31st January.

Payment: Leisure: Children: Park: Touring:

North East

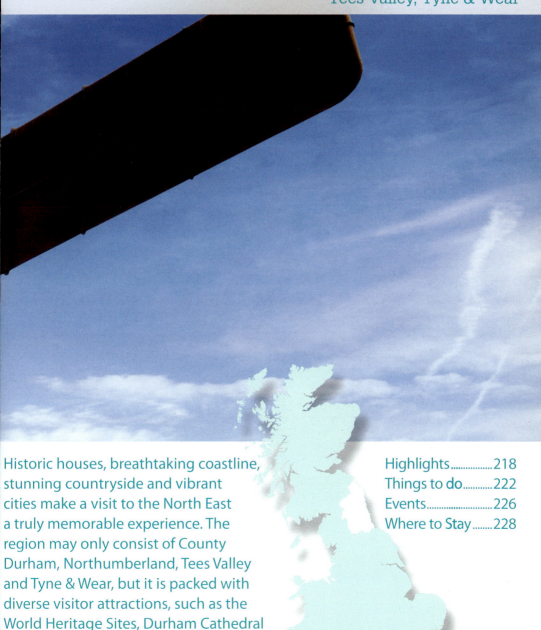

Historic houses, breathtaking coastline, stunning countryside and vibrant cities make a visit to the North East a truly memorable experience. The region may only consist of County Durham, Northumberland, Tees Valley and Tyne & Wear, but it is packed with diverse visitor attractions, such as the World Heritage Sites, Durham Cathedral and Hadrian's Wall. This is a magical place filled with ancient castles, golden sand beaches and rolling hills.

Highlights

County Durham

From ancient relics to railways, and from priceless art to archaeological finds, Durham's cultural treasures are waiting to be discovered.

Durham Castle and Cathedral

Built to house the relics of St Cuthbert and the Venerable Bede, Durham Cathedral is the largest example of Norman architecture in England. The castle housed the Durham prince-bishops.

Frontiers of the Roman Empire

Hadrian's Wall was built in 122 AD to defend the Roman Empire from 'barbarians'. The World Heritage Site was expanded to include all the frontiers of the Roman Empire, ranging from Antonine's Wall in the north to Trajan's Wall in eastern Europe.

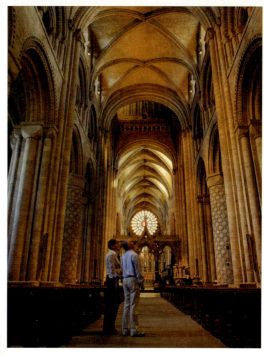

Newcastle/Gateshead

Newcastle/Gateshead is a destination of icons – from the seven spectacular bridges crossing the River Tyne to Antony Gormley's contemporary sculpture Angel of the North. In the heart of Newcastle city centre the Castle Keep hints at the region's thousands of years of heritage.

Northumberland

Northumberland National Park is the northernmost National Park in England, and is a magical place filled with ancient castles, rolling hills and rugged moorland.

Tees Valley

People tend to think of the Tees Valley as an urbanised region consisting of towns like Darlington, Hartlepool, Middlesbrough, Redcar and Stockton-on-Tees, but it also contains miles of stunning coastline, countryside and ancient woodland.

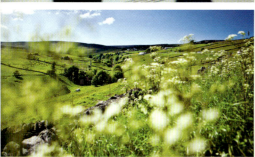

Editor's Picks

Marvel at Bamburgh Castle

Try standing on Bamburgh beach one sunny morning or sunset and view the site of the fortress towering over the dunes looking out defiantly towards the North Sea.

Step back in time

Discover Durham's fascinating history and heritage at award-winning attractions like the Beamish Museum.

Follow the code

Hadrian's Wall is a fragile environment and the archaeology is easily damaged, so the World Heritage Site urges visitors to follow its country code called 'Every Footstep Counts'.

Time to discover

At Discovery Museum find out about life in Newcastle and Tyneside, from the area's renowned maritime history to world-changing science and technology.

Things to do

 Attractions with this sign participate in the Places of Interest Quality Assurance Scheme.

 Attractions with this sign participate in the Visitor Attraction Quality Assurance Scheme.

Both schemes recognise high standards in all aspects of the visitor experience (see page 7)

Entertainment & Culture

Bailiffgate Museum

Alnwick, Northumberland NE66 1LX
(01665) 605847
www.bailiffgatemuseum.co.uk
Bailiffgate Museum brings to life the people and places of North Northumberland in exciting interactive style.

BALTIC Centre for Contemporary Art
Gateshead, Tyne and Wear NE8 3BA
(01914) 781810
www.balticmill.com
BALTIC is the biggest gallery of its kind in the world - presenting a dynamic, diverse and international programme of contemporary visual art.

Beamish Museum
County Durham DH9 0RG
(01913) 704000
www.beamish.org.uk
Beamish - The Living Museum of the North, is an open air museum vividly recreating life in the North East in the early 1800's and 1900's.

Discovery Museum

Newcastle-upon-Tyne, Tyne and Wear NE1 4JA
(01912) 326789
www.twmuseums.org.uk/discovery
Discovery Museum offers a wide variety of experiences for all the family to enjoy.

DLI Museum and Durham Art Gallery

Durham, County Durham DH1 5TU
(01913) 842214
www.durham.gov.uk/dli
Museum tells the 200-year story of Durham's famous regiment. Art Gallery has changing exhibition programme.

Great North Museum: Hancock

Newcastle-upon-Tyne,
Tyne and Wear NE2 4PT
(01912) 226765
www.greatnorthmuseum.org
See major new displays showing the wonder of the animal and plant kingdoms, spectacular objects from the Ancient Greeks and a planetarium and a life-size T-Rex.

Hartlepool Art Gallery

Hartlepool, Tees Valley TS24 7EQ
(01429) 869706
www.hartlepool.gov.uk/info/100009/leisure_and_culture/1506/hartlepool_art_gallery/1/3
Former church building also includes the TIC and a bell tower viewing platform looking over Hartlepool.

Hartlepool's Maritime Experience

Tees Valley TS24 0XZ
(01429) 860077
www.hartlepoolsmaritimeexperience.com
An authentic reconstruction of an 18th century seaport.

Hatton Gallery

Newcastle-upon-Tyne, Tyne and Wear NE1 7RU
(01912) 226059
www.twmuseums.org.uk/hatton
Temporary exhibitions of contemporary and historical art. Permanent display of Kurt Schwitters' Merzbarn.

Head of Steam Darlington Railway Museum

Tees Valley DL3 6ST
(01325) 460532
www.darlington.gov.uk/Culture/headofsteam/welcome.htm
Restored 1842 station housing a collection of exhibits relating to railways in the North East of England, including Stephenson's Locomotion, call for details of events.

Hexham Old Gaol

Northumberland NE46 3NH
(01434) 652349
www.tynedaleheritage.org
Tour the Old Gaol, 1330AD, by glass lift. Meet the gaoler, see a Reiver raid and try on costumes.

Killhope, The North of England Lead Mining Museum

Bishop Auckland, County Durham DL13 1AR
(01388) 537505
www.killhope.org.uk
The North East's Small Visitor Attraction of the Year and the most complete lead mining site in Great Britain.

Laing Art Gallery

Newcastle-upon-Tyne, Tyne and Wear NE1 8AG
(01912) 327734
www.twmuseums.org.uk/laing
The Laing Art Gallery is home to an important collection of 18th and 19th century painting, which is shown alongside temporary exhibitions of historic and contemporary art.

Locomotion: The National Railway Museum at Shildo

Shildon, County Durham DL4 1PQ
(01388) 777999
www.nrm.org.uk/locomotion
The first National Museum in the North East. Free admission. View over 60 vehicles, children's play area and interactive displays.

mima

Middlesbrough, Tees Valley TS1 2AZ
(01642) 726720
www.visitmima.com
mima, Middlesbrough Institute of Modern Art, is a £14.2m landmark new gallery in the heart of Middlesbrough. mima showcases an international programme of fine art and applied art from the 1900s to the present day.

Museum of Hartlepool

Hartlepool, Tees Valley TS24 0XZ
(01429) 860077
www.hartlepoolsmaritimeexperience.com
Hartlepool Museum, situated beside Hartlepool Historic Quay, includes local historical exhibits, PSS Wingfield Castle, exhibitions and the original lighthouse light.

Preston Hall Museum and Park

Stockton-on-Tees, Tees Valley TS18 3RH
(01642) 527375
www.stockton.gov.uk/museums
A Georgian country house set in beautiful parkland overlooking the River Tees. A Museum of social history with a recreated Victorian street and working craftsmen.

RNLI Grace Darling Museum

Bamburgh, Northumberland NE69 7AE
(01668) 214910
www.rnli.org.uk/gracedarling
A museum dedicated to Grace Darling and her family, as well as all those who Save Lives at Sea.

Segedunum Roman Fort, Baths and Museum

Wallsend, Tyne and Wear NE28 6HR
(01912) 369347
www.twmuseums.org.uk/segedunum
Segedunum Roman Fort is the gateway to Hadrian's Wall. Explore the excavated fort site, visit reconstructions of a Roman bath house, learn about the history of the area in the museum and enjoy the view from the 35 metre viewing tower.

The Bowes Museum

Barnard Castle, County Durham DL12 8NP
(01833) 690606
www.thebowesmuseum.org.uk
The Bowes Museum houses a collection of outstanding European fine and decorative arts and offers an acclaimed exhibition programme, alongside special events and children's activities.

Vindolanda (Chesterholm) Hadrian's Wall

Bardon Mill, Northumberland NE47 7JN
(01434) 344277
www.vindolanda.com
Visitors may inspect the remains of the Roman fort and settlement, see its extraordinary finds in the superb museum. Full-scale replicas of Roman buildings. Please ring to check winter opening times.

Family Fun

Centre for Life
Newcastle-upon-Tyne, Tyne and Wear NE1 4EP
(01912) 438210
www.life.org.uk
The Centre for Life is an award-winning science centre where imaginative exhibitions, interactive displays and special events promote greater understanding of science and provoke curiosity in the world around us.

Nature's World
Middlesbrough, Tees Valley TS5 7YN
(01642) 594895
www.naturesworld.org.uk
Nature's World now has a new Adventure Arena with assault course, climbing walls, pedal go-karts and tractors.

Heritage

Arbeia Roman Fort and Museum
South Shields, Tyne and Wear NE33 2BB
(01914) 561369
www.twmuseums.org.uk/arbeia
Arbeia is the best reconstruction of a Roman fort in Britain and offers visitors a unique insight into the every day life of the Roman army, from the soldier in his barrack room to the commander in his luxurious house.

Bamburgh Castle
Northumberland NE69 7DF
(01668) 214515
www.bamburghcastle.com
A spectacular castle with fantastic coastal views. The stunning Kings Hall and Keep house collections of armour, artwork, porcelain and furniture.

Belsay Hall, Castle and Gardens
Northumberland NE20 0DX
(01661) 881636
www.english-heritage.org.uk/belsay
With so much to see and do, a trip to Belsay is one of the best value family days out in North East England. Stunning gardens, beautiful acrchitecture and magnificent views all in one place.

Durham Castle
County Durham DH1 3RW
(01913) 343800
www.durhamcastle.com
Durham Castle is part of the Durham City World Heritage Site. Entrance by guided tour only. Opening can vary - please telephone 0191 334 3800 to check days open and guided tour times.

HMS Trincomalee
Hartlepool, Tees ValleyTS24 0XZ
(01429) 223193
www.hms-trincomalee.co.uk
HMS Trincomalee, built in 1817, is one of the oldest ship afloat in Europe. Come aboard for a unique experience of Navy life two centuries ago.

Housesteads Roman Fort
Haydon Bridge, Northumberland NE47 6NN
(01434) 344363
www.english-heritage.org.uk/daysout/properties/housesteads-roman-fort-hadrians-wall
The most complete example of a British Roman fort, Housesteads features magnificent ruins and stunning views of the countryside surrounding Hadrian's Wall.

Kielder Castle Forest Park Centre
Northumberland NE48 1ER
(01434) 250209
www.forestry.gov.uk/northeastengland
Features include forest shop, information centre, tearoom and exhibitions. Bike hire available.

Lindisfarne Priory
Holy Island, Northumberland TD15 2RX
(01289) 389200
www.english-heritage.org.uk/lindisfarnepriory
Take in panoramic views of the Northumbrian coast, unpack a picnic in the priory grounds, and take a break from the hustle and bustle of life.

National Glass Centre
Sunderland, Tyne and Wear SR6 0GL
(01915) 155555
www.nationalglasscentre.com
Enjoy an ever-changing programme of exhibitions, live glass blowing, and banqueting and a stunning restaurant overlooking the River Wear.

Raby Castle
Staindrop, County Durham DL2 3AH
(01833) 660202
www.rabycastle.com
Home of Lord Barnard's family since 1626, includes a 200 acre deer park, gardens, carriage collection, adventure playground, shop and tearoom.

Saltburn Smugglers Heritage Centre
Saltburn-by-the-Sea, Tees Valley TS12 1HF
(01287) 625252
www.redcar-cleveland.gov.uk/museums
Step back into Saltburn's past and experience the authentic sights, sounds and smells.

Warkworth Castle

Warkworth, Northumberland NE65 0UJ
(01665) 711423
www.english-heritage.org.uk/warkworthcastle
Set in a quaint Northumberland town, this hill-top fortress and hermitage offers a fantastic family day out.

Nature & Wildlife

Adventure Valley
Durham, County Durham DH1 5SG
(01913) 868291
www.adventurevalley.co.uk
Adventure Valley is Durham's newest day out! Split into six Play Zones (with three under cover), you'll find the very best in family fun come rain or shine.

Hall Hill Farm
Durham, County Durham DH7 0TA
(01388) 731333
www.hallhillfarm.co.uk
Award-winning farm attraction set in attractive countryside, see and touch the animals at close quarters.

High Force Waterfall
Middleton-in-Teesdale, County Durham DL12 0XH
(01833) 640209
www.rabycastle.com/high_force.htm
The most majestic of the waterfalls on the River Tees.

Hamsterley Forest
Bishop Auckland, County Durham DL13 3NL
(01388) 488312
www.forestry.gov.uk/northeastengland
A 5,000 acre mixed woodland open to the public all year.

Saltholme Wildlife Reserve and Discovery Park
Middlesbrough, Tees Valley TS2 1TU
(01642) 546625
www.rspb.org.uk/reserves/guide/s/saltholme
Saltholme is an amazing wildlife experience in the Tees Valley.

WWT Washington Wetland Centre
Washington, Tyne and Wear NE38 8LE
(01914) 165454
www.wwt.org.uk/visit/washington
45 hectares of wetland, woodland and wildlife reserve. Home to wildfowl, insects and flora with lake-side hides, wild bird feeding station, waterside cafe, picnic areas, sustainable garden, playground and events calendar.

Events 2014

Bishop Auckland Food Festival
April, Bishop Auckland
Be inspired by cookery demonstrations and entertained by performers.
www.bishopaucklandfoodfestival.co.uk

Evolution Festival
May, Newcastle
The North East's premier music event, taking place over a Bank Holiday.
www.evolutionfestival.co.uk

Haydon Bridge Beer Festival
July, Haydon Bridge
A celebration of the finest real ales and wines.
www.haydonbeerfestival.co.uk

Eat! Newcastle-Gateshead
July, Newcastle
For three days, the heart of Newcastle-Gateshead is turned into a taste bud-tempting array of foodie events. From cooking demos to cookery workshops, choice foods to chilli bonanzas, fish barbecues to street food festival.
www.newcastlegateshead.com/eat-home

Durham Folk Party
July, Durham
It is a celebration of folk song, music and dance which began in 1990 after the demise of the excellent Durham City Folk Festival and has developed into an important part of the music year of the city.
www.communigate.co.uk/ne/durhamfolkparty

Gateshead Summer Flower Show
July, Gateshead
The Gateshead Summer Flower Show is an annual horticultural event and competition.
www.gateshead.gov.uk

Billingham International Folklore Festival
August, Billingham
A festival of traditional and contemporary world dance, music and arts.
www.billinghamfestival.co.uk

Alnwick Beer Festival
September, Alnwick
If you enjoy real ale, or simply want to enjoy a fantastic social event, then make sure you pay this festival a visit.
www.alnwickbeerfestival.co.uk

Hexham Abbey Festival
September-October, Hexham
An exciting array of events to capture the imagination, bringing the very best world-class musicians and artists to Hexham.
www.hexhamabbey.org.uk

Wunderbar Festival
October-November, Newcastle
A week of activity, spontaneity, interaction, dialogue and play.
www.wunderbarfestival.co.uk

Tourist Information Centres

When you arrive at your destination, visit an Official Partner Tourist Information Centre for quality assured help with accommodation and information about local attractions and events, or email your request before you go. To find a Tourist Information Centre visit www.visitengland.com

Alnwick	2 The Shambles	01670 622152	alnwick.tic@northumberland.gov.uk
Amble	Queen Street Car Park	01665 712313	amble.tic@northumberland.gov.uk
Bellingham	Station Yard	01434 220616	bellinghamtic@btconnect.com
Berwick-upon-Tweed	106 Marygate	01670 622155	berwick.tic@northumberland.gov.uk
Bishop Auckland	Town Hall Ground Floor	03000 269524	bishopauckland.touristinfo@durham.gov.uk
Corbridge	Hill Street	01434 632815	corbridge.tic@northumberland.gov.uk
Craster	Craster Car Park	01665 576007	craster.tic@northumberland.gov.uk
Darlington	Central Library	01325 462034	crown.street.library@darlington.gov.uk
Durham	3 Millennium Place	03000 262626	visitor@thisisdurham.com
Gateshead	Central Library	0191 433 8420	libraries@gateshead.gov.uk
Guisborough	Priory Grounds	01287 633801	guisborough_tic@redcar-cleveland.gov.uk
Haltwhistle	Westgate	01434 322002	haltwhistle.tic@northumberland.gov.uk
Hartlepool	Hartlepool Art Gallery	01429 869706	hpooltic@hartlepool.gov.uk
Hexham	Wentworth Car Park	01434 652220	hexham.tic@northumberland.gov.uk
Middlesbrough	Albert Road	01642 729700	tic@middlesbrough.gov.uk
Morpeth	The Chantry	01670 623455	morpeth.tic@northumberland.gov.uk
Newcastle-upon-Tyne	8-9 Central Arcade	0191 277 8000	visitorinfo@ngi.org.uk
North Shields	Unit 18	0191 2005895	ticns@northtyneside.gov.uk
Once Brewed	Northumberland National Park Centre	01434 344396	tic.oncebrewed@nnpa.org.uk
Redcar	24 High Street	01642 471921	redcar_tic@redcar-cleveland.gov.uk
Saltburn by Sea	Saltburn Library	01287 622422	saltburn_library@redcar-cleveland.gov.uk
Seahouses	Seafield Car Park	01665 720884	seahouses.tic@northumberland.gov.uk
South Shields	South Shields Museum & Gallery	0191 454 6612	museum.tic@southtyneside.gov.uk
South Shields	(Amphiltheatre) Sea Road	0191 455 7411	foreshore.tic@southtyneside.gov.uk
Stockton-on-Tees	High Street	01642 528130	visitorinformation@stockton.gov.uk
Whitley Bay	York Road	0191 6435395	susan.clark@northtyneside.gov.uk
Wooler	Wooler TIC, The Cheviot Centre	01668 282123	wooler.tic@northumberland.gov.uk

Regional Contacts and Information

Log on to the North East England website at www.visitnortheastengland.com for further information on accommodation, attractions, events and special offers throughout the region. A range of free information is available to download from the website.

North East
Where to Stay

Entries appear alphabetically by town name in each county. A key to symbols appears on page 7

HAMSTERLEY COLLIERY, Co Durham Map ref 5C2 SatNav NE17 7RT

Byreside Caravan Site
Hamsterley Colliery, Newcastle upon Tyne NE17 7RT
T: (01207) 560280 **F:** (01207) 560280 **E:** byresidecaravansite@hotmail.co.uk
W: www.byresidecaravansite.co.uk

(31)	£15.00-£19.00	
(6)	£15.00-£19.00	
(6)	£15.00-£19.00	

31 touring pitches

A small, secluded family-run site on a working farm. Ideally situated for visiting Durham, Newcastle and Northumberland. Adjacent to Derwent Walk ideal for walkers and cyclists. **Directions:** From A1 at Swalwell follow A694 towards Consett. Turn left onto B6310 towards Medomsley. Turn right towards High Westwood. 0.5 miles on right hand side. **Open:** All year.

Payment: ☐ ☼ **Children:** ☜ **Catering:** ☎ **Park:** ♞ ♖ **Touring:** ♨ ☗ ☯

BAMBURGH, Northumberland Map ref 5C1 SatNav NE70 7EE

Waren Caravan and Camping Park
Waren Mill, Bamburgh, Northumberland NE70 7EE
T: (01668) 214366 **F:** (01668) 214224 **E:** waren@meadowhead.co.uk
W: www.meadowhead.co.uk **£ BOOK ONLINE**

(144)	£18.50-£25.00	
(144)	£18.50-£25.00	
(30)	£9.75-£22.00	
(27)	£260.00-£640.00	

144 touring pitches

SPECIAL PROMOTIONS
Please see website for special offers and details of our wigwams too!

Waren Caravan and Camping Park is nestled in coastal countryside with spectacular views to Holy Island and Bamburgh Castle. On site facilities include restaurant and bar, splash-pool, shop and children's play area. Our welcoming environment means you have all you need if you wish to stay on-site but we also make a great base from which to explore Northumberland's coast and castles.

Directions: Follow B1342 from A1 to Waren Mill towards Bamburgh. By Budle turn right, follow Meadowhead's Waren Caravan and Camping Park signs.

Open: 7th March to 1st November.

Site: ☗ **Payment:** ☐ € ☼ **Leisure:** ♪ ♜ ⚲ **Children:** ☜ ⛺ **Catering:** ✗ ☎ **Park:** ♞ ⛟ ▣ ⛊ ♖ **Touring:** ♨ ☗ ☯ ♪

Need more information?

Visit our new 2014 guide websites for detailed information, up-to-date availability and to book your accommodation online. Includes over 20,000 places to stay, all of them star rated.

www.visitor-guides.co.uk

HEXHAM, Northumberland   Map ref 5B2   SatNav NE46 2JP

TOURING & CAMPING PARK ★★★

Hexham Racecourse Caravan Site
High Yarridge, Yarridge Road, Hexham NE46 2JP
T: (01434) 606847 **F:** (01434) 605814 **E:** hexrace.caravan@btconnect.com
W: www.hexham-racecourse.co.uk

🚐 (50)   £14.00-£17.00
🚎 (30)   £14.00-£17.00
⛺ (10)   £10.00
50 touring pitches

Grass area, sloping in parts. Most pitches with electrical hook-up points. Separate area for tents. **Directions:** From Hexham take the B6305 Allendale Road for 3 miles turn left at T Junction, site 1.5 miles on the right. **Open:** May to September.

Site: ⛺🅿 **Payment:** 💷 ☼ **Leisure:** ► ♠ **Children:** 🐎 ⚠ **Park:** 🐕 🗐 📖 📷 **Touring:** ♻ 🕒 🔌

MORPETH, Northumberland   Map ref 5C2   SatNav NE65 9QH

HOLIDAY PARK ★★★

Felmoor Park
Eshottheugh, Felton, Morpeth, Northumberland NE65 9QH
T: (01670) 787790 **E:** info@felmoorpark.com
W: www.felmoorpark.com **£ BOOK ONLINE**

🚐 (8)
🚎 (8)
⛺ (18)
🏠 (22)   £500.00-£980.00
🏕 (10)   £500.00-£650.00
🚐 (5)   £150.00-£480.00
12 touring pitches

Felmoor Holiday Park is set in 40 acres of outstanding Northumberland woodland. We have luxury Log Cabins, Lodges and Static Holiday Homes. We also have a touring and camping area for guests use. Coming in 2014, accommodation in real Tipi' Wig Wams and Micro Lodges. Felmoor Park is central to visit all Northumberland's attractions. New Gym, Sauna, Swim Spa and Steam room. Full bar and cafe.

Directions: 6 miles North of Morpeth or 9 miles South of Alnwick on the East side of the A1.

Open: February 7th to January 7th.

Site: 🐾 ⛺🅿 **Payment:** 💷 ☼ **Leisure:** ⚲ ► ♠ **Children:** 🐎 ⚠ **Park:** 🐕 🖥 🗐

SEAHOUSES, Northumberland   Map ref 5C1   SatNav NE68 7SP

HOLIDAY & TOURING PARK ★★★★★   Gold AWARD

Seafield Caravan Park
Seafield Road, Seahouses NE68 7SP
T: (01665) 720628 **F:** (01665) 720088 **E:** info@seafieldpark.co.uk
W: www.seafieldpark.co.uk **£ BOOK ONLINE**

🚐 (18)   £25.00-£48.00
🚎 (18)   £25.00-£48.00
🚐 (44)   £245.00-£1035.00
18 touring pitches

Luxurious holiday homes and lodges for hire on Northumberland's 5* premier park. Fully serviced touring 'Super Pitches', booking recommended. Prices include use of Ocean Club facilities. Visit England Award for Excellence Silver Winner 2012. **Directions:** Take the B1340 from Alnwick for 14 miles, east towards the coast. **Open:** 9th Feb to 9th Jan.

Payment: 💷 ☼ **Leisure:** ⚲ ♪ ► ∪ ☆ **Children:** 🐎 ⚠ **Park:** 🐕 🖥 🗐 📷 **Touring:** ♻ 🔌

Scotland

Explore Scotland, famous for its historic castles, traditional Highland games and beautiful lochs, and discover the setting of world-famous movies, the place for stylish shopping and the perfect stage for new and exciting events. Whether you want to step onboard a Royal yacht in Leith, climb over 150 steps up St Rules Tower for views out across Fife or try your hand at keyhole surgery in Dundee, there are plenty of attractions in Scotland to fill the days, weeks and months of your trip.

Highlights

Aberdeen City & Shire

Discover a land where majestic landscapes meet the sea and the flourishing Granite City boasts beautiful architecture and cultural gems.

Aberdeen City and Shire is adored by the Royal Family, and is a region with a maritime heritage which offers lively events and a selection of thrilling activities.

The Victorian Heritage Trail is the perfect way to explore Royal Deeside and uncover the many royal connections within the area. The excellent Coastal Trail covers the breathtaking north east coastline, while the Castle Trail takes you around Aberdeen City and Shire's most famous historic buildings.

Argyll & The Isles

Argyll & The Isles is bursting with historic monuments, fascinating museums and galleries and lush gardens, all just waiting to be explored.

Spend a fascinating day in Inveraray, where you can visit the imposing Inveraray Castle, a Clan Campbell stronghold since the time of King Robert the Bruce.

Head to Benmore Botanic Garden, situated in a magnificent mountainside setting on the Cowal Peninsula, to wander round enchanting gardens which are steeped in history and surrounded by dramatic scenery.

You can hop aboard a ferry to explore the astonishingly beautiful mansion of Mount Stuart, or head to Rothesay Castle to marvel at its magnificent circular design and architecture on the Isle of Bute.

Ayrshire & Arran

With so many connections to Burns, Ayrshire & Arran boasts a wide range of related attractions.

The new Robert Burns Birthplace Museum was nominated for UK Museum of the Year in 2011 and is also home to the Burns Cottage, historic landmarks where he set his greatest work and the elegant Burns Monument and gardens that were created in his honour. For more Burns, check out the Irvine Vennel Gallery and Souter Johnnie's cottage. Continuing along the history theme, the magnificent Dean Castle and Country Park in Kilmarnock is a must-visit attraction.

For something a bit different, enjoy a day out with the animals at Heads of Ayr Farm Park, a wonderful family-friendly attraction that lets you see, touch and feed around 50 different exotic creatures from monkeys to meerkats.

Dumfries & Galloway

From streams to summits and forests to shores, the landscape in Dumfries & Galloway is naturally inspiring, influencing the region's history, culture and everyday life.

Discover how this region's beautiful scenery has filled artists and writers with the passion to create great works, and see how it is the perfect backdrop for exciting activities and an abundance of rare wildlife.

Dundee & Angus

Enjoy the best of both worlds in Dundee & Angus with city attractions, food and theatre alongside beautiful countryside, perfect for walking and uncovering historical connections.

Attractions include RRS Discovery, the ship which took Captain Scott on his remarkable voyage to Antarctica, and HMS Frigate Unicorn, a preserved warship which was first launched in 1824 and is the sixth oldest ship in the world. Sensation is the city's science centre which has unusual exhibits to interact with, and at Mills Observatory you can see incredible images of the moon and stars at the UK's only full-time observatory.

Fife

There are a wide selection of visitor attractions in Fife that range from unique and interesting museums to aquariums, a secret war bunker and animal parks.

Travel through the UK's longest underwater viewing tunnel, dive with sand tiger sharks, explore the seal sanctuary and witness the beautiful coral reefs at Deep Sea World, Scotland's national aquarium.

Did you know that Fife was home to Scotland's best-kept secret for over 40 years? Hidden beneath an innocent farmhouse in the East Neuk, discover Scotland's Secret Bunker, a 100ft underground bunker, the size of two football pitches, one on top of the other! Head down the 150m entrance tunnel through hermetically sealed, three-ton blast proof doors and uncover how the bunker would have been used in the event of a nuclear war.

Edinburgh & The Lothians

Edinburgh Castle is the city's defining feature and sits perched on an extinct volcano that overlooks the city. Inside the castle, some of which dates back to the 12th century, you will find treasures such as the Scottish Crown Jewels. The fascinating Scottish National War Museum is also within the walls, reflecting the castle's long military history.

One of the most unique ways to learn about the history of the city is on a visit to Camera Obscura and World of Illusions, a Victorian observatory on the Royal Mile. Enter a darkened rooftop chamber and marvel as a 19th century device resembling a periscope projects a white beam of light onto a concave table to reveal incredible moving images of the city and its inhabitants.

The Royal Yacht Britannia, which took the British Royal Family around the world, provides a glimpse into the private lives of royalty. Once onboard, you have the unique opportunity to see the state apartments and the engine room.

Glasgow & The Clyde Valley

There are not many cities in the world where you can enjoy world-class events, exciting, free attractions and stunning architecture alongside beautiful and serene parks and gardens.

The city's name of Glasgow is Gaelic for the 'dear green place'. Discover how green Glasgow is by exploring some of the city's parks and gardens.

Kelvingrove Park is one of Glasgow's best-loved parks due in part to its fine setting on the banks of the River Kelvin.

Take a walk around Glasgow's striking Botanic Gardens to see the amazing A-listed Kibble Palace, a ornate Victorian glasshouse built in 1873 and full of tropical plants from around the world.

Glasgow Green is home to the social history museum, the People's Palace, as well as another beautiful Victorian glasshouse, the Winter Gardens, and is host to a variety of exciting events including the World Pipe Band Championships.

Loch Lomond, The Trossachs & The Forth

Visit a famous castle, an amazing safari park, an exhilarating adventure course and more in Loch Lomond, The Trossachs & The Forth Valley.

Doune Castle near Stirling is a magnificent 14th century courtyard castle with an intriguing movie connection. Scenes from Monty Python and the Holy Grail were filmed at Doune and the castle's audio tour is narrated by Python member Terry Jones.

Callendar House in Falkirk is one of Scotland's finest baronial mansions and is where Mary Queen of Scots spent much of her early life. Watch costumed interpreters recreate daily routines from the past and sample authentic dishes in the Georgian Kitchen.

Tour Stirling Old Town Jail, condemned as Britain's worst jail in the 1840's due to overcrowding and disease. Meet the prison warden, the hangman and the convict determined to escape.

Perthshire

Perthshire is a place where you can explore majestic glens, championship golf courses and ancient forests. Spend an afternoon tumbling down swift currents on a white water raft before enjoying an evening of local cuisine in a first-class restaurant.

Find all that and much more in Perthshire with its captivating history, magnificent wildlife and stunning array of events and festivals.

Scottish Borders

Lose yourself amongst the spectacular scenery of the Scottish Borders and experience a wonderful array of things to see and do.

Take in the dramatic history and vibrant culture of the land of Sir Walter Scott at ruined castles and exciting festivals, uncover a wonderful arts and crafts scene, witness the Scottish Borders Common Ridings, enjoy delicious local produce and explore miles of rolling hills, leafy valleys and the beautiful Berwickshire coast.

The Highlands

The past is written all over the Highlands landscape which features famous battlefields, majestic monuments and intriguing ancient relics.

Glencoe is a place of great significance in Scottish history. You can learn all about the infamous massacre of 1692 at the Glencoe Visitor Centre and Glencoe Folk Museum.

The Glenfinnan Monument at the head of Loch Shiel is a tribute to the Jacobite clansmen and the history of the Jacobite Rebellion led by Bonnie Prince Charlie is told at the nearby visitor centre.

Culloden was the last battle fought on British soil and you can walk the battlefield, while in the visitor centre, you can get vivid detail of the Jacobites' 1746 defeat by government troops. Nearby Fort George was built by the government in the wake of Culloden and is one of the finest feats of 18th century military engineering. It took 20 years to complete and remains unaltered.

237

Editor's Picks

View the castles

Scotland's turbulent history has left a lasting mark on the landscape in shape of the many castles and fortresses that pepper the countryside.

Raise a glass

Discover Scotland's renowned Malt Whisky Trail and plan a three-day trip around unique and historic distilleries.

Rise early

Edinburgh Castle, home to the iconic Stone of Destiny, is a must see and is best toured first thing in the morning to beat the crowds.

Visit the battlefields

Experience over 5,000 years of Scotland's incredible history by visiting famous battlefields, Neolithic sites, Roman frontiers and hundreds more fascinating historical sites.

Join the homecoming party

In 2014 Scotland welcomes the world to join in the exciting Year of Homecoming. In addition to the Commonwealth Games and Ryder Cup, there's a year-long programme of events planned.

Things to do

Entertainment & Culture

British Golf Museum
St. Andrews, Fife KY16 9AB
(01334) 460046
www.britishgolfmuseum.co.uk
The British Golf Museum traces the history of golf, in both Britain and abroad, from the middle ages through to the present day.

Clydebuilt
(Scottish Maritime Museum Braehead)
Glasgow, Renfrewshire G51 4BN
(0141) 886 1013
www.scottishmaritimemuseum.org
The story of the River Clyde and the contribution it made to the development of West Central Scotland is brought vividly to life at Clydebuilt, the Scottish Maritime Museum at Braehead.

Gordon Highlanders Museum
Aberdeen AB15 7XH
(01224) 311200
www.gordonhighlanders.com
Regimental collection of the Gordon Highlanders housed in St Lukes, former home of artist Sir George Reid.

National Museum of Scotland
Edinburgh EH1 1JF
(0131) 225 7534
www.nms.ac.uk
All our collections have tales to tell. See treasures from the edges of history and trace Scotland's story from fascinating fossils to popular culture. For generations we've collected key exhibits from all over Scotland and beyond.

Riverside Museum
Glasgow G3 8DP
(0141) 287 2720
www.glasgow.gov.uk
A unique collection of transport and technology which reflects Glasgow's history as the second city of the British Empire.

The Queen's Gallery
Edinburgh EH8 8DX
(0131) 556 5100
www.royalcollection.org.uk
Built in the shell of the former Holyrood Free Church and Duchess of Gordon's School, the Gallery provides purpose-built, state-of-the-art facilities to enable a programme of changing exhibitions of the most delicate works of art.

Family Fun

Go Ape! High Wire Forest Adventure - Beecraigs
Linlithgow, West Lothian EH49 6PL
0845 643 9215
www.goape.co.uk
Take to the trees and experience an exhilarating course of rope bridges, tarzan swings and zip slides...all set high above the forest floor.

Our Dynamic Earth
Edinburgh EH8 8AS
(0131) 550 7800
www.dynamicearth.co.uk
Explore our planet's past present and future. You'll be shaken by volcanoes, fly over glaciers, feel the chill of polar ice, and even get caught in a tropical rainstorm.

New Lanark Visitor Centre
South Lanarkshire ML11 9DB
(01555) 661345
www.newlanark.org
Two hundred-year-old nominated World Heritage Site featuring a ride called the 'New Millennium Experience'.

Food & Drink

Isle of Arran Distillery Visitor Centre
North Ayrshire KA27 8HJ
(01770) 830264
www.arranwhisky.com
Five years ago, Isle of Arran Distillers started production of a unique single malt whisky to rank with Scotland's greatest.

Talisker Distillery
Isle of Skye, Highland IV47 8SR
(01478) 614306
www.whisky.com/distilleries/talisker_distillery.html
The only distillery on the Isle of Skye, set in an Area of Outstanding Natural Beauty. Guided tours, exhibition, shop.

Heritage

Balmoral Castle
Aberdeenshire AB35 5TB
(01339) 742534
www.balmoralcastle.com
The Scottish holiday home of the Royal Family.

Caerlaverock Castle

Dumfries And Galloway DG1 4RU
(01387) 770244
www.historic-scotland.gov.uk
Caerlaverock is an awe inspiring ruin with a long history of lordly residence and wartime siege.

Culzean Castle & Country Park
Maybole, South Ayrshire KA19 8LE
0844 493 2149
www.nts.org.uk
An 18th century castle perched on a rocky promontory with superb panoramic views over the Firth of Clyde.

Edinburgh Castle
Edinburgh EH1 2NG
(0131) 225 9846
www.edinburghcastle.gov.uk
Perched on an extinct volcano, Edinburgh Castle is a powerful Scottish symbol.

Paxton House and Country Park
Berwick-upon-Tweed,
Scottish Borders TD15 1SZ
(01289) 386291
www.paxtonhouse.com
An 18th century neo-palladian country house with Adam plasterwork, Chippendale and Trotter furniture.

The Official Loch Ness Monster Exhibition
Drumnadrochit, Highland IV63 6TU
(01456) 450573
www.loch-ness.scotland.com
An exhibition incorporating the latest in technology for visitor centres. Six room walkthrough is fully automated.

The Scotch Whisky Experience
Edinburgh EH1 2NE
(0131) 220 0441
www.scotchwhiskyexperience.co.uk
The mystery of whisky making revealed! Take a barrel ride through whisky history.

Nature & Wildlife

Logan Botanic Garden
Tranrae, Dumfries And Galloway DG9 9ND
(01776) 860231
www.rbge.org.uk
One of the National Botanic Gardens of Scotland, where many rare and exotic plants from temperate regions flourish outdoors. A plantsman's paradise.

Events 2014

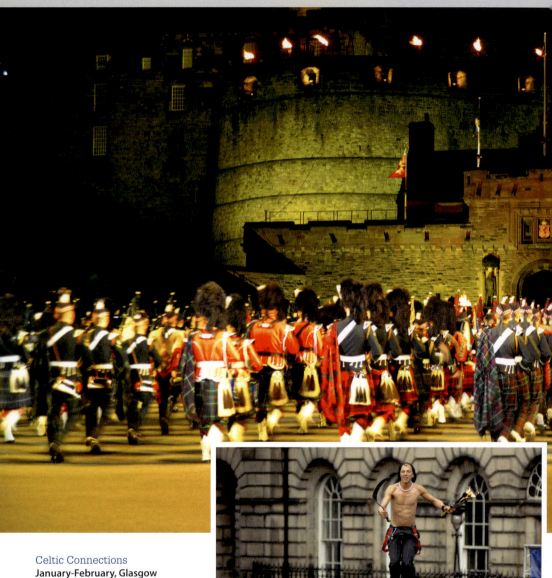

Celtic Connections
January-February, Glasgow
Glasgow's annual folk, roots
and world music festival, Celtic
Connections celebrates Celtic music
and its connections to cultures
across the globe.
www.celticconnections.com

Glasgow Film Festival
February, Glasgow
The festival has carved a reputation
for staging thought-provoking film
features.
www.glasgowfilm.org

Loch Ness Film Festival
May, Highlands
The Highlands host an intimate yet
expansive range of movies during
the Loch Ness Film Festival. Airing
everything from documentaries,
amateur shorts and features, the
grassroots event is a non-profit
organisation, with all funds raised
going to charitable causes.
www.lochnessfilmfestival.co.uk

Perth Festival of Arts
May 22-June 1, Perth
Quality abounds at this year's Perth
Festival of the Arts. Van Morrison,
Jools Holland, Sir James and Lady
Galway will headline the Festival. It
will also stage three operas, host a
world-class choir and a big Russian
Gala Concert.
www.perthfestival.co.uk

Common Ridings

June-July, various venues

11 towns across the Scottish Borders are filled with pageantry for the annual Common Riding festivals. These historical events mark the turbulent time between the 13th and 17th centuries when settlement boundaries were patrolled on horseback to protect against the Border Reivers, the raiders who pillaged the land on the either side of the Anglo-Scots border.
www.visitscotland.com

Lanimar Day

June, Lanark

Although the Lanimer celebrations consist of nearly a week long series of events Lanimer Day itself falls on the Thursday between the 6th and 12th June each year.
www.lanarklanimers.co.uk

Glasgow Merchant City Festival

July, Glasgow

Annual event featuring theatre, music, visual arts, comedy, dance, film, literature and fashion.
www.merchantcityfestival.com

Royal Edinburgh Military Tattoo

August 2-24, Edinburgh

This event highlights Scotland's reputation as a land of outstanding beauty as the Tattoo celebrates the Year of Natural Scotland.
www.edintattoo.co.uk

Edinburgh Festival Fringe

August 1-23, Edinburgh

One of the largest arts festival in the world and regarded as the cultural event of the year.
www.edfringe.com

Edinburgh International Festival

August 8-31, Edinburgh

Three spellbinding weeks of the very best in international opera, dance, music, theatre and the visual arts.
www.eif.co.uk

Crieff Highland Games

August 17, Crieff

The first Crieff Highland Gathering was in 1870 and has occurred every year since with the two exceptions of 1914-18 and 1939-49 when no gatherings took place.
www.crieff-highland-games.co.uk

Edinburgh Riding of the Marches

September 11, Edinburgh

The Edinburgh Riding of the Marches – men and women of horseback – set off on the edge of Edinburgh before heading into the city centre to be greeted by the Lord Provost.
www.edinburghridingthemarches.co.uk

Pitlochry Highland Games

September 14, Pitlochry

Pitlochry Highland Games has been hosting competitors and enthralling spectators since 1852
www.pitlochryhighlandgames.co.uk

Aberdeen Winter Festival

November-December, Aberdeen

Events include comedy, musicals, pantomime concerts and much more, taking place in several of Aberdeen's fantastic venues, such as the much-loved Lemon Tree and the Music Hall.
www.aberdeencity.gov.uk

Tourist Information Centres

When you arrive at your destination, visit a Visitor Information Centre for help with accommodation and information about local attractions and events. Alternatively call 0845 22 55 121 to receive information and book accommodation before you go.

Aberdeen	23 Union Street	01224 288828	aberdeen@visitscotland.com
Aberfeldy	The Square	01887 820276	aberfeldy@visitscotland.com
Aberfoyle	Main Street	01887 382352	aberfoyle@visitscotland.com
Alford	Railway Museum, Old Station Yard	019755 62052	alford@visitscotland.com
Anstruther	Scottish Fisheries Museum	01333 311073	anstruther@visitscotland.com
Arbroath	Fishmarket Quay	01241 872609	arbroath@visitscotland.com
Aviemore	Unit 7, Grampian Road	01479 810930	aviemore@visitscotland.com
Ayr	22 Sandgate	01292 290300	ayr@visitscotland.com
Ballater	Old Royal Station	013397 55306	ballater@visitscotland.com
Balloch	Balloch Road	01389 753533	balloch@visitscotland.com
Balloch (Park)	National Park Gateway Centre	01389 722600	info@lochlomond.visitscotland.com
Banchory	Bridge Street	01330 822000	banchory@visitscotland.com
Banff	Collie Lodge	01261 812419	banff@visitscotland.com
Blairgowrie	26 Wellmeadow	01250 876825	blairgowrie@visitscotland.com
Bo'ness	Bo'ness and Kinneil Railway Station	01506 826626	boness@visitscotland.com
Bowmore	The Square	01496 810254	islay@visitscotland.com
Braemar	The Mews	01339 741600	braemar@visitscotland.com
Brechin	Pictavia Visitor Centre	01356 623050	brechin@visitscotland.com
Brodick	The Pier	01770 303776	brodick@visitscotland.com
Callander	10 Ancaster Square	01877 330342	callander@visitscotland.com
Campbelltown	MacKinnon House	01586 552056	campbelltown@visitscotland.com
Castle Douglas	Market Hill	01556 502611	castledouglas@visitscotland.com
Castlebay	Pier Road	01871 810336	castlebay@visitscotland.com
Craignure	The Pier	01680 812377	mull@visitscotland.com
Crieff	Town Hall	01764 652578	crieff@visitscotland.com
Daviot Wood	Picnic Area	01463 791575	daviotwoods@visitscotland.com
Drumnadrochit	The Car Park	01456 459086	drumnadrochit@visitscotland.com
Dufftown	2 The Square	01340 820501	dufftown@visitscotand.com
Dumfries	64 Whitesands	01387 253862	dumfries@visitscotland.com
Dundee	Discovery Quay	01382 527527	dundee@visitscotland.com

Dunfermline	1 High Street	01383 720999	dumfermline@visitscotland.com
Dunkeld	The Cross	01350 727688	dunkeld@visitscotland.com
Dunoon	7 Alexandra Parade	01369 703785	dunoon@visitscotland.com
Durness	Durine	01971 511368	durnesstic@visitscotland.com
Edinburgh	3 Princes Street	0131 473 3898	info@visitscotland.com
Edinburgh Airport	Airport Tourist Information Desk	0131 344 3120	edinburgh.airport@visitscotland.com
Eyemouth	Auld Kirk	01890 750678	info@visitscotland.com
Falkirk	Lime Road	01324 620244	falkirk@visitscotland.com
Fort Augustus	Car Park	01320 366779	info@visitscotland.com
Fort William	15 High Street	01397 701801	info@visitscotland.com
Fraserburgh	3 Saltoun Square	01346 518315	fraserburgh@visitscotland.com
Glasgow	11 George Square	0141 204 4400	glasgow@visitscotland.com
Glasgow Airport	International Arrivals	0141 848 4440	glasgowairport@visitscotland.com
Grantown on Spey	54 High Street	01479 872773	grantown@visitscotland.com
Gretna Green	Unit 38, Gretna Gateway Outlet Village	01461 337834	gretnatic@visitscotland.com
Hawick	1 Tower Mill	01450 373993	info@visitscotland.com
Helensburgh	Clock Tower	01436 672642	helensburgh@visitscotland.com
Huntly	9a The Square	01466 792255	huntly@visitscotland.com
Inverary	Front Street	01499 302063	inverary@visitscotland.com
Inverness	Castle Wynd	01463 252401	inverness@visitscotland.com
Inverurie	18a High Street	01467 625800	inverurie@visitscotland.com
Jedburgh	Murray's Green	01835 863170	jedburgh@visitscotland.com
Kelso	Town House	01573 228055	kelso@visitscotland.com
Kirkaldy	The Merchant's House	01592 267775	kirkcaldy@visitscotland.com
Kirkcudbright	Harbour Square	01557 330494	kirkcudbright@visitscotland.com
Kirkwall	West Castle Street	01856 872856	kirkwall@visitorkney.com
Lanark	Horsemarket	01555 661661	lanark@visitscotland.com
Lerwick	Market Cross	01595 693434	info@visitshetland.com
Lochboisdale	Pier Road	01878 700286	lochboisdale@visitthebrides.com
Lochinver	Main Street	01571 844194	lochinver@visitscotland.com
Lochmaddy	Pier Road	01876 500321	lochmaddy@visitscotland.com
Melrose	Abbey House	01896 822283	melrose@visitscotland.com
Newton Stewart	Dashwood Square	01671 402431	newtownstewart@visitscotland.com
Newtongrange	Scottish Mining Museum	0131 663 4262	newtongrange@visitscotland.com
North Berwick	Quality Street	01620 892197	info@visitscotland.com
North Kessock	Picnic Site	01463 731836	northkessock@visitscotland.com
Oban	Argyll Square	01631 563122	oban@visitscotland.com
Peebles	23 High Street	01721 723159	peebles@visitscotland.com
Perth	Lower City Mills	01738 450600	perth@visitscotland.com
Pitlochry	22 Atholl Road	01796 472215	pitlochry@visitscotland.com
Portree	Bayfield House	01478 614906	portree@visitscotland.com
Rothesay	Isle of Bute Discovery Centre	01700 502151	rothesay@visitscotland.com
St Andrews	70 Market Street	01334 472021	standrews@visitscotland.com
Stirling	Old Town Jail	01786 475019	stirling@visitscotland.com
Stonehaven	66 Allardice Street	01569 762806	stonehaven@visitscotland.com
Stornoway	26 Cromwell Street	01851 703088	stornoway@visitscotland.com
Stranraer	28 Harbour Street	01776 702595	stranraer@visitscotland.com
Stromness	Ferry Terminal Building	01856 850716	stromness@visitscotland.com
Strontian	Strontian	01967 402382	strontian@visitscotland.com
Sumburgh Airport	Sumburgh Airport	01595 693434	info@visitshetland.com
Tarbert (Loch Fyne)	Harbour Street	01880 820132	tarbert@visitscotland.com
Tarbet (Loch Lomond)	Tarbet	01301 702260	tarbet@visitscotland.com
Thurso	Riverside	01847 893155	thurso@visitcotland.com
Tomintoul	The Square	01807 580285	tomintoul@visitscotland.com
Tyndrum	Main Street	01838 400246	tyndrum@visitscotland.com
Ullapool	20 Argyle Street	01854 612486	ullapool@visitscotland.com
Wick	McAllan's	01955 602547	info@visitscotland.com

Regional Contacts and Information

For more information on accommodation, attractions, activities, events and holidays in Scotland, contact the regional tourism organisation below. The website has a wealth of information and you can order or download publications.

The following is a selection of publications available online from VisitScotland.com or by calling the information and booking service on 0845 859 1006.

Touring Map of Scotland £4.99
An up-to-date touring map of Scotland. Full colour with comprehensive motorway and road information, the map details over 20 categories of tourist information and names over 1,500 things to do and places to visit in Scotland.

Touring Scotland Guide to quality assured accommodation and dining £8.99

Indulge in Scotland your luxury accommodation and fine dining guide £8.99

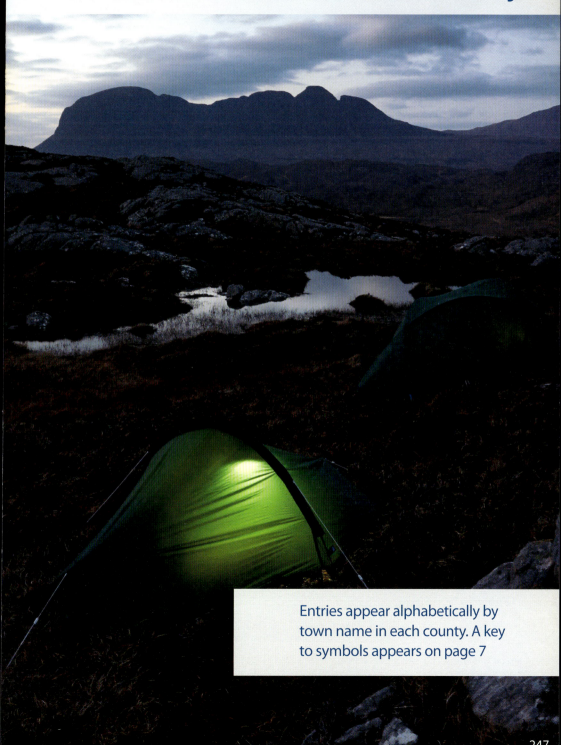

Scotland
Where to Stay

Entries appear alphabetically by town name in each county. A key to symbols appears on page 7

DUNBAR, East Lothian   Map ref 6D2

SatNav EH42 1TU

Belhaven Bay Caravan and Camping Park

Edinburgh Road, West Barns, Dunbar EH42 1TU

T: (01368) 865956 **F:** (01368) 865022 **E:** belhavenbay@meadowhead.co.uk
W: www.meadowhead.co.uk **£ BOOK ONLINE**

(43)	£15.50-£28.00
(43)	£15.50-£28.00
(32)	£9.75-£26.25
(6)	£280.00-£625.00

59 touring pitches

Belhaven Bay is situated on the stunning East Lothian Coastline and adjoins the John Muir Country Park: a haven for wildlife and an area of natural beauty. Visitors can also enjoy direct access to the beach. Facilities include free showers, laundry and kitchen facilities. Enjoy a relaxing break in one of our Thistle Award holiday homes for hire. There are also holiday homes for sale, so you can appreciate the beauty of Belhaven Bay all season long.

Directions: The Park is located in the small village of Belhaven, just 2 minutes off the A1 dual carriageway North of Dunbar.

Open: 7th March to 30th November.

Site: ▲🅿 Payment: 🖃 Leisure: ▶ Children: 🛝 ⚠ Park: 🐾 📺 🔲 🎒 🏠 Touring: 🔒 🕭 🔌 ♪

NORTH BERWICK, East Lothian   Map ref 6D2

SatNav EH39 5NJ

Tantallon Caravan and Camping Park

Tantallon Road, North Berwick EH39 5NJ

T: (01368) 865956 **E:** tantallon@meadowhead.co.uk
W: www.meadowhead.co.uk **£ BOOK ONLINE**

(108)	£18.50-£29.25
(108)	£18.50-£29.25
(65)	£9.00-£26.75
(10)	£299.00-£685.00

108 touring pitches

SPECIAL PROMOTIONS
Please see website for
up to date details.

Tantallon Caravan and Camping Park is situated in an idyllic location which offers spectacular views to the Bass Rock and Firth of Forth. Whether touring or staying in one of our Thistle Award holiday homes, you will be holidaying in an area of natural beauty which also offers plenty to do for all the family. North Berwick is a bustling seaside town with fine beaches and boutique shopping. East Lothian is a paradise for golfers. Facilities include free showers and fully equipped laundry and kitchen.

Directions: From North Berwick, A198 towards Dunbar. From the South, turn of at A1 north of Dunbar and follow signs for North Berwick and Tantallon Park.

Open: 7th March - 30th November.

Payment: ☼ Leisure: ♪ ▶ 🔍 Children: ⚠ Park: 🐾 📺 🔲 🎒 🏠 Touring: 🔒 🕭 🔌 ♪

DUNBAR, East Lothian   Map ref 6D2

SatNav EH42 1SA

Thurston Manor Leisure Park

Innerwick, Dunbar, East Lothian, Scotland EH42 1SA
T: (01368) 840643 **E:** holidays@thurstonmanor.co.uk
W: www.verdantleisure.co.uk **£ BOOK ONLINE**

	(59)	£12.00-£25.50
	(59)	£12.00-£25.50
	(58)	£7.00-£11.00
	(5)	£199.00-£872.00
	(31)	£146.00-£748.00

Nestling at the foot of the Lammermuir Hills in Scotland, near the stunning East Lothian coastlin. Thurston Manor offers you the chance to share special holidays & short breaks with family and friends that you will remember for a lifetime. **Open:** 16th February - 6th January.

Site: **Payment:** **Leisure:** **Children:** **Catering:** **Park:** **Touring:**

EDINBURGH, Edinburgh   Map ref 6C2

SatNav EH53 0HT

Linwater Caravan Park

West Clifton, East Calder, West Lothian EH53 0HT
T: (0131) 333 3326 **F:** (0131) 333 1952 **E:** linwater@supanet.com
W: www.linwater.co.uk

	(50)	£19.00-£22.00
	(50)	£19.00-£22.00
	(10)	£17.00-£20.00
	(4)	

60 touring pitches

A peaceful family-run park, west of Edinburgh. Excellent facilities and lovely walks to Country Park and Canal. Ideal for visiting Edinburgh from park and ride or touring. Try our timbertents, a warm and dry alternative to camping (Prices on request). **Directions:** Signposted from M9, junction 1 - Newbridge, or from Wilkieston on A71, along B7030. **Open:** Mid-March to end of October.

Payment: **Leisure:** **Children:** **Park:** **Touring:**

EDINBURGH, Edinburgh   Map ref 6C2

SatNav EH16 6TJ

Mortonhall Caravan and Camping Park

38 Mortonhall Gate, Frogston Road East, Edinburgh EH16 6TJ
T: (0131) 664 1533 **E:** mortonhall@meadowhead.co.uk
W: www.meadowhead.co.uk **£ BOOK ONLINE**

	(250)	£15.50-£33.50
	(250)	£15.50-£33.50
	(250)	£12.00-£28.75
	(20)	£250.00-£855.00

250 touring pitches

SPECIAL PROMOTIONS
Please see our website for all our current special offers and details of our wigwams!

Situated in a 200 acre country estate and only 4 miles from Edinburgh's city centre. Mortonhall has beautifully maintained and landscaped parkland, with views to the Pentland Hills. Only a short bus trip or drive, the capital's shopping, walking, arts, history and other leisure activities are all on our doorstep. Overnight holding area available.

Directions: From the north or south, exit the city bypass (A720) at Straiton or Lothianburn Junctions and follow the signs to Mortonhall. **Open:** All year.

Site: **Payment:** **Leisure:** **Children:** **Catering:** **Park:** **Touring:**

For **key to symbols** see page 7

Scottish
TOURIST BOARD
★★★★
HOLIDAY
PARK

Å (18)
⚑ (1)
⛺ (46)
43 touring pitches

Black Rock Caravan Park

Balconie Street, Evanton IV16 9UN
T: (01349) 830917 **E:** enquiries@blackrockscotland.co.uk
W: www.blackrockscotland.co.uk

We are a small, family run park located in the shelter of beautiful, wooded Glenglass with views of an impressive local landmark, the Fyrish Monument. Please contact us for prices.

Directions: 1 mile off the A9, 15 miles north east of Inverness.   **Open:** 1st April - 31st October.

Payment: ☼ **Leisure:** ♪ ∪ 🔍 **Children:** 🛝 ⛰ **Park:** 🐕 🚮 📺 🗄 🚿 ⛰ **Touring:** 🎪 ⛽ 🚐 ♪

Glen Nevis Caravan and Camping Park

Glen Nevis, Fort William PH33 6SX
T: (01397) 702191 **F:** (01397) 703904 **E:** holidays@glen-nevis.co.uk
W: www.glen-nevis.co.uk **£ BOOK ONLINE**

(250)	£11.00-£17.50
(250)	£11.00-£18.50
(300)	£7.50-£16.00
(12)	£370.00-£675.00
(22)	£295.00-£640.00

250 touring pitches

SPECIAL PROMOTIONS
Short Breaks available.

Our award-winning, touring caravan and camping park has a magnificent location in one of Scotland's most famous highland glens at the foot of mighty Ben Nevis, Britain's highest mountain. A range of walks, including the path up Ben Nevis, are right at your doorstep and there are stunning views in all directions. We are located near Fort William and are an ideal base to explore the Highlands.

Directions: Follow A82 North to Mini-Roundabout at N outskirts of Fort William - Second Exit for Glen Nevis - Park 2.5 Miles on right.

Open: Early March to end October.

Site: **Payment:** **Leisure:** **Children:** **Catering:** **Park:** **Touring:**

Linnhe Lochside Holidays

Corpach, Fort William PH33 7NL
T: (01397) 772376 **F:** (01397) 772376 **E:** relax@linnhe-lochside-holidays.co.uk
W: www.linnhe-lochside-holidays.co.uk

(65)	£14.25-£16.50
(65)	£14.25-£16.50
(15)	£10.75-£15.50
	£375.00-£899.00
(14)	£375.00-£899.00
(57)	£310.00-£550.00

80 touring pitches

SPECIAL PROMOTIONS
Discounts for senior citizen groups and for 2nd week. Quotes arranged for block booking, rallies etc.

Luxury chalets and caravans set in well tended gardens, with a fantastic view down the loch. A rural haven of peace and quiet, the park is just five miles away from Ben Nevis. Our handy shop has its own bakery. Free fishing from our shore and our own slipway. Overnight holding area available.

Directions: On A830 1.5 miles (3 km) west of Corpach village, 5 miles from Fort William.

Open: 15th December to 31st October.

Payment: **Leisure:** **Children:** **Catering:** **Park:** **Touring:**

COCKSBURNPATH, *Scottish Borders*   *Map ref 6D2*   SatNav TD13 5YP

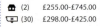

Pease Bay Leisure Park

Cockburnspath, Berwickshire TD13 5YP
T: (01368) 830206 **E:** holidays@peasebay.co.uk
W: www.peasebay.co.uk **£ BOOK ONLINE**

(2)	£255.00-£745.00	
(30)	£298.00-£425.00	

Beachfront holiday park on the Berwickshire coast, popular with families, surfers and outdoor enthusiasts alike. Relax to the sounds of the sea. The park is mid-way between Edinburgh and Berwick-upon-Tweed. **Directions:** Just off the A1, between Dunbar and Berwick. At the Cockburnspath roundabout take the Pease Bay exit and follow the road down to the bay. **Open:** 1st March - 31st January.

Site: **Payment:** **Leisure:** **Children:** **Catering:** **Park:**

CALLANDER, *Stirling*   *Map ref 6B1*   SatNav FK17 8LE

Gart Caravan Park

Stirling Road, Callander FK17 8LE
T: (01877) 330002 **E:** enquiries@theholidaypark.co.uk
W: www.theholidaypark.co.uk

(128)	£23.50-£27.50	
(128)	£23.50-£27.50	
128 touring pitches		

A peaceful and spacious park maintained to a very high standard with modern, heated shower block facilities. The ideal centre for cycling, walking and fishing or simply relaxing. Park wide Wi-Fi and hard standing pitches available. **Directions:** Leave jct 10 of the M9, west to Callander. **Open:** 1st April to 15th October.

Site: **Payment:** **Leisure:** **Children:** **Park:** **Touring:**

LINLITHGOW, *West Lothian*   *Map ref 6C2*   SatNav EH49 6PL

Beecraigs Caravan and Camping Site

Beecraigs Country Park, Nr Linlithgow, West Lothian EH49 6PL
T: (01506) 844516 **F:** (01506) 846256 **E:** mail@beecraigs.com
W: www.beecraigs.com

(36)	£18.21-£22.50	
(36)	£18.21-£22.50	
(20)	£15.00-£22.50	
56 touring pitches		

Situated near historic Linlithgow town & within the Beecraigs Country Park. Onsite facilities include electric hookups, modern toilet facilities with privacy cubicles, babychange & laundrette. MHD point. Pets are welcome. **Directions:** From M9, follow A803, then Beecraigs Country Park & Caravan Park signs. Park is 2 miles south of Linlithgow. From M8, follow B792 & Park signs. **Open:** All year.

Payment: **Leisure:** **Children:** **Catering:** **Park:** **Touring:**

Need more information?

Visit our new 2014 guide websites for detailed information, up-to-date availability and to book your accommodation online. Includes over 20,000 places to stay, all of them star rated.

www.visitor-guides.co.uk

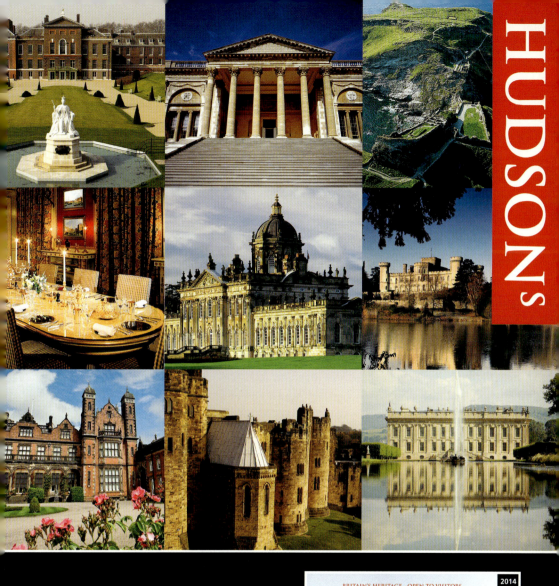

HUDSONs

ritain's definitive annual heritage guide.
Available from high street bookshops,
heritage shops and online at

www.hudsonsheritage.com/shop.aspx

Sponsors of Hudson's Heritage Awards

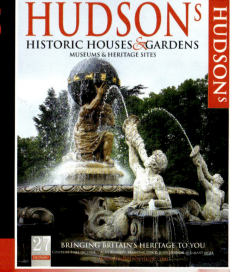

www.hudsonsheritage.com

Wales

So what do you need to know about Wales - the friendly green hilly country on the western side of Britain? Discover three National Parks; 1,200km of coastline; five Areas of Outstanding Natural Beauty; two languages; 11 million sheep and more castles per square mile than anywhere else in the world – 641 at the last count. If you want to experience the great outdoors, there's nowhere better than the Welsh countryside. Why not learn a few words of Welsh, and get to know the locals... 'Shwmae' – that's Welsh for hello.

Anglesey

Anglesey is the home of peace and quiet, a beautiful coastline and festivals – there are hundreds of them, including festivals for jazz, leisure, boats, beer and walking. It is also steeped in history with Beaumaris Castle being one of the finest examples of medieval architecture in the UK and was the last castle built in Wales by Edward I.

Cardiff

Set in the heart of the Welsh capital, the castle walls conceal plenty of history along with a newly opened interpretation centre. Events run throughout the year: midsummer evenings with Shakespeare, a Medieval Mêlée, Victorian Christmas as well as musical performances, lectures on art and architecture. There's so much more to see and do in Cardiff.

Carmarthenshire

The intriguing mythology of Merlin to the gritty wild-boy poetry of Dylan Thomas – that's Carmarthenshire. You'll find chic places to stay, stylish eateries, great local produce and welcoming country pubs. Think lush rural landscapes, crystalline coastlines and the rugged foothills of the Brecon Beacons National Park.

Ceredigion

One of the most beautiful sights in Ceredigion is Devil's Bridge spanning the Mynach River. Legend says it was built by the Devil in return for the soul of the first to cross it. Apparently the townspeople tricked him by sending a dog over. Cardigan Bay is home to one of only two resident groups of Bottlenose Dolphins in the UK.

Mid Wales and Brecon Beacons

If you like the unusual then you'll love Mid Wales. Take Hay-on-Wye for example. It has just four pubs yet can boast 18 bookshops – it's regarded as the second hand book capital of the world. And if you're not a book worm, there's always the Bog Snorkelling competition down the road at Llanwtryd Wells. The vast open hillsides of the Brecon Beacons are perfect for walking and pony trekking, particularly around the Black Mountains.

North Wales Borderlands

Pontcysyllte Aqueduct is just one of many water features in the North Wales Borderlands. Also known as 'the stream in the sky', it's the world's tallest canal boat crossing and recently became Wales' newest World Heritage Site. From the Alwen Trail to the heathery moors at Hiraethog, discover the wildlife of the Dee Estuary. You can also enjoy quiet riversides in Flintshire or forests and lakes of the Conwy Valley – there's more than enough space for an afternoon ramble.

Glamorgan

Home to the most southerly point in Wales, the Vale of Glamorgan is perfect for those who love the outdoor life and discovering towns and villages packed full of traditional charm and character. You can also take a sledge and ride the 'Big Dipper', one of the single highest dunes in Europe. Rolling towards the Ogmore/Porthcawl coast, Merthyr Mawr has a huge network of dunes that are great for exploring.

Lladudno & Colwyn Bay

Llandudno is a beautiful Victorian seaside resort at the foot of Great Orme. There's quite a mix of things to do here – for example, you can have an award-winning Victorian tea, visit 4,000-year-old mines, ride Britain's longest cable car, go to the mountain zoo or just stroll along the beach. And no visit to Llandudno is complete without a trip to the Victorian pier.

Pembrokeshire

Whoever dubbed part of Pembrokeshire 'Little England beyond Wales' didn't know what they were talking about. You'll find award winning beaches, national parks and breathtaking views. At 186 miles long, the Pembrokeshire Coastal Path offers sweeping cliff tops, secret coves, estuaries and wide sandy beaches.

Rhyl and Prestatyn

Rhyl and Prestatyn beach resorts have hotter, sunnier summers than most. There's not much to do here… unless you count watersports, fairgrounds, donkey rides, indoor beaches, castles, walking, cycling and the aquarium, that is. So don't feel bad for lazing on the beach.

Snowdonia Mountains and Coast

An exciting destination that includes the Snowdonia National Park, Llŷn Peninsula and Cambrian Coastline. A wide choice for all – castles, narrow-gauge railways, golf, cycling, walking, award winning beaches, country parks, World Heritage Site and Areas of Outstanding Natural Beauty.

South Wales Valleys

Think of green valleys. Think of warm welcomes. Think of castles, myths and magic. Think of a unique industrial heritage, male voice choirs and stunning scenery. Think the Welsh Valleys. Stand on top of a mountain in the morning, explore the bottom of a historic pit in the afternoon, and tap into the contemporary music scene in the evening. And you're still on day one. If you want a real Welsh experience then you must visit the Valleys.

Swansea

Wales' waterfront city enjoys a location that is hard to beat. It sits on the 5 mile sweep of Swansea Bay and most city centre attractions and shops are less than 10 minutes walk from the sea. At the west end of the bay is the pretty seaside village of Mumbles, complete with medieval castle, Victorian pier and four famous Welsh-Italian ice cream parlours. If you follow the coast you'll reach the UK's first Area of Outstanding Natural Beauty, the Gower Peninsula.

Editor's Picks

A high rope

Leave your walking boots unlaced and say goodbye to the beach. Instead visit a high rope centre dotted through Wales – they're a great family day out.

Don't leave without visiting a castle

There are over 600 castles, from Roman times to millionaires' follies of the 19th century, making Wales the castle capital of Europe.

Walk the coast

The Wales Coast Path is the world's first uninterrupted route along a national coast and stretches for 870 miles. Don't try it in one go!

Try mountain biking

Rugged natural trails criss-cross Wales in abundance. Adventure seekers prepared to go that extra mile can follow trails that escape into the wilderness.

Cymru Wales

Gweithgaredd Ardystiedig
Accredited Activity

Things to do

Attractions with this sign participate in the Visitor Attraction Quality Assurance Scheme (see page 7) which recognises high standards in all aspects of the vistor experience.

Entertainment & Culture

Big Pit National Coal Museum

Blaenavon, Torfaen NP4 9XP
(01495) 790311
www.museumwales.ac.uk/en/bigpit
Don a miners lamp and go 92m underground with a real miner and learn what life was like for the thousands of men who worked at the coal face.

Great Orme Tramway
Llandudno, Conwy LL30 2NB
(01492) 879306
www.greatormetramway.com
Take a ride on the 'San Francisco style' tramway - one of only tree still in existence in the world today.

Millennium Stadium
Cardiff CF10 1NS
(029) 2082 2228
www.millenniumstadium.com/tours/index.php
Take a tour. Run down the player's tunnel, and imagine yourself being greeted by 74,500 people eagerly awaiting the pain and the glory of rugby at its best.

Wales Millennium Centre

Cardiff CF10 5AL
(029) 2063 6464
www.wmc.org.uk
Cardiff's multi purpose arts centre, and home to The Welsh National Opera. The building is all glass and slate and looks very much like a Welsh armadillo

Family Fun

Centre For Alternative Technology
Machynlleth, Powys SY20 9AZ
(01654) 705950
www.cat.org.uk
Is one of the world's most renowned eco-centres, with interactive displays and practical examples of sustainable living, renewable energy and organic gardening.

The Dylan Thomas Centre
Swansea SA1 1RR
(01792) 463980
www.dylanthomas.com
Dylan Thomas is perhaps one of greatest poets of the 20th century, and the most famous literary figure to come from Wales.

Food & Drink

Penderyn Distillery
Aberdare Rhondda, Cynon, Taff CF44 0SX
(01685) 810651
www.welsh-whisky.co.uk
It's the only distillery in Wales and one of the smallest in the world. Take a tour of the visitor centre and distillery.

Heritage

Cardiff Castle
Cardiff CF10 3RB
(029) 2087 8100
www.cardiffcastle.com
Climb up to the top of the 12th century Norman keep for great views over the city.

Dolaucothi Gold Mines
Llanwrda, Carmarthenshire SA19 8US
(01588) 650177
www.nationaltrust.org.uk/main/w-dolaucothigoldmines
Try your hand at panning for gold, or take a guided underground tour through the Roman and underground workings and learn all about the history of the mine at the on-site exhibition and Interpretation Centre.

Harlech Castle
Harlech, Gwynedd LL46 2YH
(01766) 780552
www.cadw.wales.gov.uk/default
The castle's spectacular location atop a rocky crag assures you of a stunning photo opportunity.

Pontysycllte Aqueduct
Pontcysyllte, Wrexham
(01606) 723 800
www.waterscape.com
The highest cast-iron aqueduct in the world built to take a canal over the River Dee.

Powis Castle & Garden
Welshpool, Powys SY21 8RF
(01938) 551929
www.nationaltrust.org.uk/main/w-powiscastle_garden
A mecca for garden lovers. The impressive red medieval castle is framed by enormous clipped yew trees, and 18th century Italianate terraces with original lead statues, lush herbaceous borders and exotic plants cascading from the walls.

St Davids Cathedral
St. David's, Pembrokeshire SA62 6QW
(01437) 720691
www.stdavidscathedral.org.uk
Located in the smallest city in the UK, St Davids Cathedral is the burial place of Wales' patron saint St David (Dewi Sant) has been a church since the 6th century.

Vale of Rheidol Railway
Aberystwyth, Ceredigion SY23 1PG
(01970) 625819
www.rheidolrailway.co.uk
A narrow-gauge heritage railway that runs for just over 11 miles between Aberystwyth and Devil's Bridge.

Nature & Wildlife

Bodnant Gardens
Colwyn Bay, Conwy LL28 5RE
(01492) 650460
www.bodnantgarden.co.uk
Situated above the River Conwy with stunning views across Snowdonia, Bodnant Gardens is most well known for its laburnum arch, a 55m tunnel of golden blooms, most impressive in mid May-early June.

Ceredigion Coast Path
Cardigan Bay, Ceredigion
(01545) 572105
www.ceredigioncoastpath.org.uk
A 96km route between the Teifi and Dyfi estuaries, offers walkers the opportunity to discover towns and villages, and take in the spectacular coastal scenery. You might even spot dolphins, seals and porpoises.

Gigrin Farm
Powys LD6 5BL
(01597) 810243
www.gigrin.co.uk
Get up close and personal with the wild Red Kites - you'll be just 30 metres from the feeding ground. Feeding is every day at 3pm and 2pm in winter.

National Botanic Garden of Wales
Carmarthen, Carmarthenshire SA32 8HG
(01558) 668768
www.gardenofwales.org.uk
This was the first botanic garden in the UK, dedicated to conserving plant species. Set in 600 acres of 18th century parkland the centrepiece is its great glasshouse - the world's largest single span glass structure.

Events 2014

Bangor New Music Festival
March 12-15, Bangor
BNMF is an annual celebration of new and contemporary music. Artists to appear at the 2014 Festival include Madeleine Mitchell, Asaf Sirkis and Natasha Barrett.
www.bnmf.co.uk

Hay Festival
May 22-June 1, Hay-on-Wye
A literary festival with an international reputation. During the festival around 100,000 visitors will enjoy literature in all its forms and lots of music as well as plenty of celebrities.
www.hayfestival.com

Kaya Festival
May 25-26,
Vaynol Estate, Gwynedd
Overlooking the Snowdonia National Park in North Wales, Kaya is a festival of music, youth, diversity and culture.
www.kayafestival.co.uk

HowTheLightGetsIn
May 22-June 1, Hay-on-Wye
Hay-on-Wye is the internationally famous 'town of books', situated in a magical location on the edge of the Black Mountains. It's also the home of HowTheLightGetsIn, the world's first philosophy and music festival, now in its third year.
www.howthelightgetsin.org

International Ceramics Festival
June 28-30, Aberystwyth
This ever growing festival offers the chance to meet and study the work of distinguished, internationally known potters and ceramicists from Wales, the UK and around the world.
www.internationalceramicsfestival.org

All Wales Boat Show
May 30-June 1, Conwy
The All Wales Boat Show is the country's only major boat show and a celebratory festival of all water-based activities which will be all about the best of boating, watersports, outdoor activities and leisure in the region.
www.northwalesboatshow.com

Green Gathering
July 13-August 3, Chepstow
Promoting sustainable lifestyles by combining education with entertainment. With an eclectic range of music as well as many talks and discussions, crafts and activities for all the family.
www.greengathering.org.uk

National Eisteddfod
August 1-9, Vale of Glamorgan
One of the great festivals of the world, attracting over 160,000 visitors every year. An eclectic mixture of culture, music, visual arts and all kinds of activities.
www.eisteddfod.org.uk

Brecon Jazz Festival
August, Brecon Beacons
Held in the heart of the Brecon Beacons National park in mid-Wales, it plays host to a range of jazz musicians who travel from across the world.
www.breconjazz.com/en/

Green Man Festival
August 14-17, Crickhowell, Powys
A unique boutique festival which features three days of music as well as a full programme including art, literature, film, comedy, healing zones, ceilidhs, and Welsh language poetry.
www.greenman.net

Great British Cheese Festival
September, Cardiff Castle
Sniff and nibble on more than 450 different cheeses of all shapes, sizes and flavours at Britain's biggest cheese market.
www.greatbritishcheesefestival.co.uk

Abergavenny Food Festival
September,
Abergavenny, Monmouthshire
Celebrate the sociability that surrounds eating and drinking, whether with friends or strangers, and enjoy real Welsh hospitality with Abergavenny's own burgeoning food community
www.abergavennyfoodfestival.com

Gwleddd Conwy Feast
October, various venues
160 food stalls, farming for food marquee, cookery demonstrations, bands and the blinc digital festival.
www.gwleddconwyfeast.co.uk

Abertoir Film Festival
November, Aberystwyth
The national horror film festival which includes cult screenings and classics from around the world, as well as special guests, talks, masterclasses, live music and theatre events.
www.abertoir.co.uk

Tourist Information Centres

When you arrive at your destination, visit an Official Partner Tourist Information Centre for quality assured help with accommodation and information about local attractions and events, or email your request before you go. To find a Tourist Information Centre visit www.visitwales.co.uk

Aberaeron	The Quay	01545 570602	aberaerontic@ceredigion.gov.uk
Aberdulais Falls*	Aberdulais Tinworks and Waterfall	01639 636674	aberdulaistic@nationaltrust.org.uk
Aberdyfi*	The Wharf Gardens	01654 767321	tic.aberdyfi@eryri-npa.gov.uk
Abergevenny	Swan Meadow	01873 853254	abergavenny.ic@breconbeacons.org
Aberystwyth	Terrace Road	01970 612125	aberystwythtic@ceredigion.gov.uk
Anglesey	Station Site	01248 713177	anglesey@nwtic.com
Bala*	Pensarn Road	01678 521021	bala.tic@gwynedd.gov.uk
Barmouth	The Station	01341 280787	barmouth.tic@gwynedd.gov.uk
Beddgelert*	Canolfan Hebog	01766 890615	tic.beddgelert@eryri-npa.gov.uk
Bet ws y Coed	Royal Oak Stables	01690 710426	tic.byc@eryri-npa.gov.uk
Blaenavon*	Blaenavon World Heritage Centre	01495 742333	Blaenavon.tic@torfaen.gov.uk
Borth*	Cambrian Terrace	01970 871174	borthtic@ceredigion.gov.uk
Brecon	Cattle Market Car park	01874 622485	brectic@powys.gov.uk
Caerleon	5 High Street	01633 422656	caerleon.tic@newport.gov.uk
Caernarfon	Oriel Pendeitsh	01286 672232	caernarfon.tic@gwynedd.gov.uk
Caerphilly	The Twyn	029 2088 0011	tourism@caerphilly.gov.uk
Cardiff	The Old Library	029 2087 3573	visitor@cardiff.gov.uk
Cardiff Bay	Unit 1	029 2087 7927	visitorcentrecardiffbay@cardiff.gov.uk
Cardigan	Theatr Mwldan	01239 613230	cardigantic@ceredigion.gov.uk
Carmarthen	113 Lammas Street	01267 231557	carmarthentic@carmarthenshire.gov.uk

Chepstow	Castle Car Park	01291 623772	chepstow.tic@monmouthshire.gov.uk
Conwy	Castle Buildings	01492 592248	conwytic@conwy.gov.uk
Crickhowell	Crickhowell Resource & Information Centre (CRiC)	01873 812105	tic@visitcrickhowell.co.uk
Dogellau	Ty Meirion	01341 422888	tic.dolgellau@eryri-npa.gov.uk
Elan Valley*	Visitor Centre	01597 810898	elanrangers@dwrcymru.com
Fishguard	Town Hall	01437 776636	fishguard.tic@pembrokeshire.gov.uk
Harlech*	Llys y Graig	01766 780658	tic.harlech@eryri-npa.gov.uk
Haverfordwest	Old Bridge	01437 763110	haverfordwest.tic@pembrokeshire.gov.uk
Llanberis*	Electric Mountain Visitor Centre	01286 870765	llanberis.tic@gwynedd.gov.uk
Llandovery*	Heritage Centre	01550 720693	llandovery.ic@breconbeacons.org
Llandudno	Library Building	01492 577577	llandudnotic@conwy.gov.uk
Llangollen	Y Capel	01978 860828	llangollen@nwtic.com
Merthyr Tydfil	14a Glebeland Street	01685 727474	tic@merthyr.gov.uk
Milford Haven*	Suite 19 Cedar Court	01437 771818	milford.tic@pembrokeshire.gov.uk
Mold	Library & Museum	01352 759331	mold@nwtic.com
New Quay*	Church Street	01545 560865	newquaytic@ceredigion.gov.uk
Newport	Museum & Art Gallery	01633 842962	newport.tic@newport.gov.uk
Newport (Pembs)*	2 Bank Cottages	01239 820912	NewportTIC@Pembrokeshirecoast.org.uk
Oswestry Mile End	Mile End Services	01691 662488	oswestrytourism@shropshire.gov.uk
Pembroke*	Visitor Centre	01437 776499	pembroke.tic@pembrokeshire.gov.uk
Porthcawl*	Old Police Station	01656 786639	porthcawltic@bridgend.gov.uk
Porthmadog	High Street	01766 512981	porthmadog.tic@gwynedd.gov.uk
Pwllheli*	Min y Don	01758 613000	pwllheli.tic@gwynedd.gov.uk
Rhyl	The Village	01745 355068	rhyl.tic@denbighshire.gov.uk
Saundersfoot*	The Barbecue	01834 813672	saundersfoot.tic@pembrokeshire.gov.uk
St Davids	Visitor Centre	01437 720392	info@orielyparc.co.uk
Swansea	Plymouth Street	01792 468321	tourism@swansea.gov.uk
Tenby	Unit 2, The Gateway Complex	01834 842402	tenby.tic@pembrokeshire.gov.uk
Welshpool	Vicarage Gardens	01938 552043	ticwelshpool@btconnect.com
Wrexham	Lambpit Street	01978 292015	tic@wrexham.gov.uk

* seasonal opening

Regional Contacts and Information

For more information on accommodation, attractions, activities, events and holidays in Wales, contact the national tourism organisation below. The website has a wealth of information and you can order or download publications.

t: 08708 300306
www.visitwales.com and www.visitwales.co.uk

Wales

Where to Stay

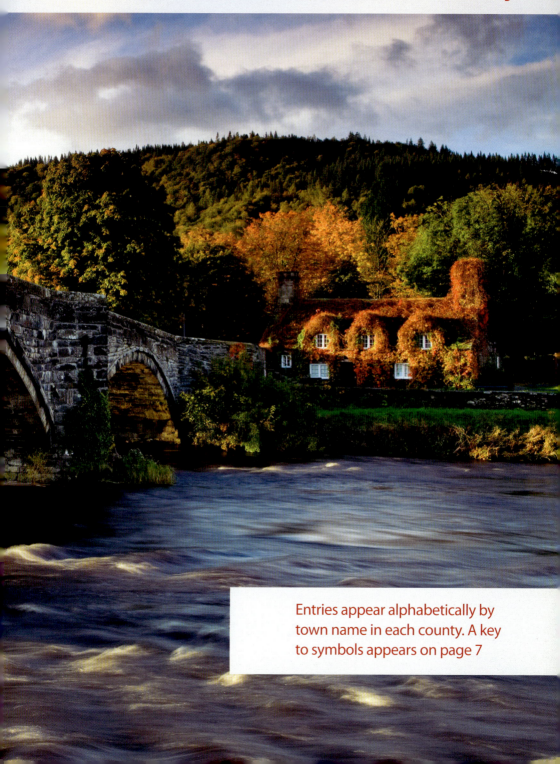

Entries appear alphabetically by town name in each county. A key to symbols appears on page 7

LLANDDULAS, Conwy Map ref 8B1 SatNav LL22 8HG

Bron-Y-Wendon Touring Caravan Park

Wern Road, Llanddulas, Colwyn Bay, North Wales LL22 8HG
T: (01492) 512903 **F:** (01492) 512903 **E:** stay@northwales-holidays.co.uk
W: www.northwales-holidays.co.uk

(120) £20.00-£25.00
(10) £20.00-£25.00
130 touring pitches

Award winning, highest grade Park, with pitches overlooking the sea & beach short walk away. Snowdonia, Llandudno, Anglesey & Chester all within easy reach, Wi-Fi, superpitches & wide range of activities nearby. Overnight holding area available. AA 5 Pennants. **Directions:** Leave the A55 at Llanddulas, junction 23, (A547) and follow the Tourist Information signs to the Park. **Open:** All year.

Payment: ▦ ☼ **Leisure:** ♪ ∪ ♣ **Children:** ✂ **Park:** ♖ ⊟ ⊟ ⊞ ⊡ **Touring:** ♔ ☗ ♧ ♪

PORTHMADOG, Gwynedd Map ref 8A1 SatNav LL49 9YD

Garreg Goch Caravan Park

Black Rock Sands, Morfa Bychan, Porthmadog LL49 9YD
T: (01766) 512210 **F:** (01766) 515820 **E:** info@garreggochcaravanpark.co.uk
W: www.garreggochpark.co.uk

(13) £16.00-£22.00
(13) £16.00-£22.00
(10) £255.00-£615.00
13 touring pitches

Near to famous Black Rock Sands and ideal for touring Snowdonia. **Directions:** In Porthmadog town centre, take the turning between the Post Office and Factory Outlet. Then take the third left after the Spar shop. **Open:** 1st March – 10th January.

Payment: ▦ **Leisure:** ♿ ♪ ♭ ∪ **Property:** ♖ ⊟ ⊟ ⊞ **Children:** ✂ ⛰ **Catering:** ⚊

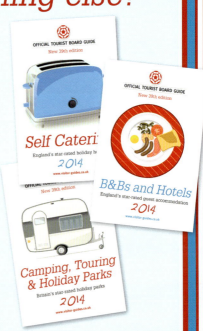

AMROTH, Pembrokeshire   Map ref 8A3

SatNav SA67 8PR

Amroth Bay Holidays

Amroth Bay Holidays, Amroth, South Pembrokeshire Coast SA67 8PR
T: (01834) 831259 **F:** (01834) 831702 **E:** amrothbay@aol.com
W: www.amrothbay.co.uk **£ BOOK ONLINE**

Your ideal holiday park set in a beautiful, peaceful and picturesque setting. 5 mins drive from beach. Winners in the Wales in Bloom 2013. Luxury caravans (some with C/H D/G) and cottages (4 star). Heated pool and playground. Couples discount available.
Directions: A40 from Carmarthen, A477 from St. Clears to Llanteg, turn left at the Colby Woodland Gardens sign in Llanteg, park 0.5 miles on right. **Open:** March to end October.

(13)   £300.00-£780.00

Payment: £ €   **Leisure:** ♪ ∪ ⚹   **Property:** ⋔ ▯   **Children:** ☃   **Catering:** ▤

FISHGUARD, Pembrokeshire   Map ref 8A2

SatNav SA65 9ET

Fishguard Bay Caravan & Camping Park

Garn Gelli, Fishguard, Pembrokeshire SA65 9ET
T: (01348) 811415 **F:** (01348) 811425 **E:** enquiries@fishguardbay.com
W: www.fishguardbay.com **£ BOOK ONLINE**

(20)   £19.00-£23.00
(20)   £19.00-£23.00
(30)   £11.00-£25.00
(12)   £270.00-£630.00
20 touring pitches

Enjoy your stay on this beautiful stretch of Pembrokeshire National Park coastline. Ideal centre for walking and touring. Quiet, family-run park. Beautiful location, and superb views towards Fishguard harbour. **Open:** 1st March to 10th January.

Site: ⛺▯   **Payment:** £ ☼   **Leisure:** ♪ ▸ ∪ ⚓   **Children:** ☃ ⚞   **Catering:** ▤ **Park:** ⋔ ▭ ▯
⛺ ⚘   **Touring:** ⚑ ⚐ ⚒

MANORBIER, Pembrokeshire   Map ref 8A3

SatNav SA70 7SN

Manorbier Country Park

Station Road, Manorbier, Tenby SA70 7SN
T: (01834) 871952 **F:** (01834) 871203 **E:** enquiries@countrypark.co.uk
W: www.countrypark.co.uk **£ BOOK ONLINE**

(45)   £18.00-£42.00
(5)   £18.00-£42.00
(4)   £16.00-£37.00
(25)   £137.00-£1130.00
50 touring pitches

SPECIAL PROMOTIONS
Short break bookings from £107.00 3-4 nights for 4 people.

The small park with the big heart. Indoor heated pool, tennis court, fully licensed bar & club, restaurant, live family entertainment, children's play areas, family entertainment centre, gym & solarium, sauna & steam room, big screen SKY Sports, laundrette and shop. What more could you want from your holiday? Overnight holding area available.

Directions: From Tenby follow A4139 to Pembroke, after Lydstep turn right for Manorbier Newton & Train Station, park located on left.   **Open:** March - November.

Site: ⛺   **Payment:** £   **Leisure:** ♿ ♪ ▸ ∪ ⚓ ≋ ⚹   **Property:** ⋔ ♫ ▭ ▯ ▤   **Children:** ☃ ⚞
Catering: ✕ ▤

Cymru
Wales

★★★★

 (26) £18.00-£23.00
(14) £12.50-£23.00
(72) £12.50-£17.00
(9) £260.00-£495.00
40 touring pitches

SPECIAL PROMOTIONS
Senior Citizens discount during low season (caravan field only).

Caerfai Bay Caravan & Tent Park
St. Davids, Haverfordwest, Pembrokeshire SA62 6QT
T: (01437) 720274 **F:** (01437) 720577 **E:** info@caerfaibay.co.uk
W: www.caerfaibay.co.uk

A quiet family-run park, situated within the Pembrokeshire Coast National Park. Caerfai Bay sandy bathing beach within 200 metres and St Davids within easy walking distance. Park situated at end of Caerfai road on the right. No dogs in tent fields during school summer holidays.

Directions: Haverfordwest to St Davids: A487. Turn left at Oriel Y Parc (OYP)/Visitor Centre, Caerfai signposted. From Fishguard: A487 to St Davids. Turn right at OYP.

Open: March to mid-November.

Payment: **Leisure:** **Children:** **Park:** **Touring:**

Cymru
Wales

★★★★

(60)
(10)
(40)
110 touring pitches

Anchorage Caravan Park
Bronllys, Brecon, Powys LD3 0LD
T: (01874) 711246 **F:** (01874) 711711
W: www.anchoragecp.co.uk

High standard, family-run park. Panoramic views of the Brecon Beacons National Park. Ideal for touring and walking mid and south Wales. Please contact us for prices. **Directions:** Midway between Brecon and Hay-On-Wye. In centre of Bronllys village. **Open:** All year.

Payment: **Leisure:** **Children:** **Catering:** **Park:** **Touring:**

Walkers and cyclists welcome

Look out for quality-assessed accommodation displaying the Walkers Welcome and Cyclists Welcome signs.

Participants in these schemes actively encourage and support walking and cycling. In addition to special meal arrangements and helpful information, they'll provide a water supply to wash off the mud, an area for drying wet clothing and footwear, maps and books to look up cycling and walking routes and even an emergency puncture-repair kit! Bikes can also be locked up securely undercover.

The standards for these schemes have been developed in partnership with the tourist boards in Northern Ireland, Scotland and Wales, so wherever you're travelling in the UK you'll receive the same welcome.

Map 1

Location
Maps

Every place name featured in the regional accommodation sections of this guide has a map reference to help you locate it on the maps which follow. For example, to find Colchester, Essex, which has 'Map ref 3B2', turn to Map 3 and refer to grid square B2.

All place names appearing in the regional sections are shown with orange circles on the maps. This enables you to find other places in your chosen area which may have suitable accommodation – the place index (at the back of this guide) gives page numbers.

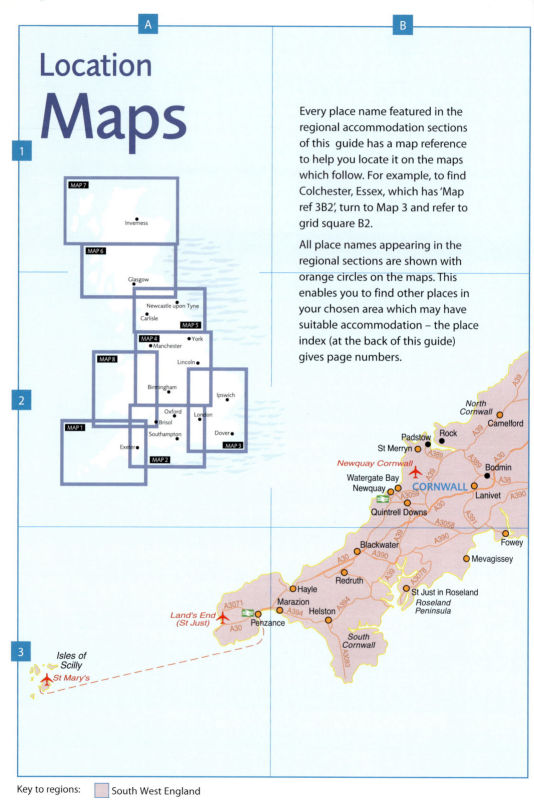

Key to regions: South West England

Map 1

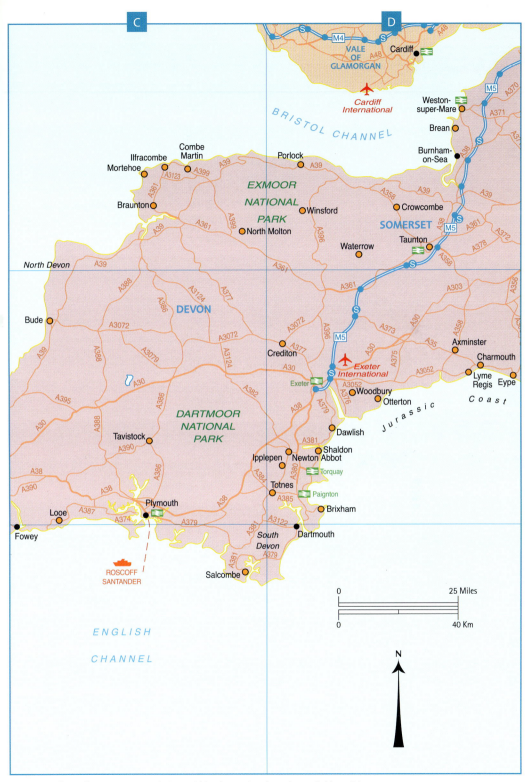

Orange circles indicate accommodation within the regional sections of this guide

Map 2

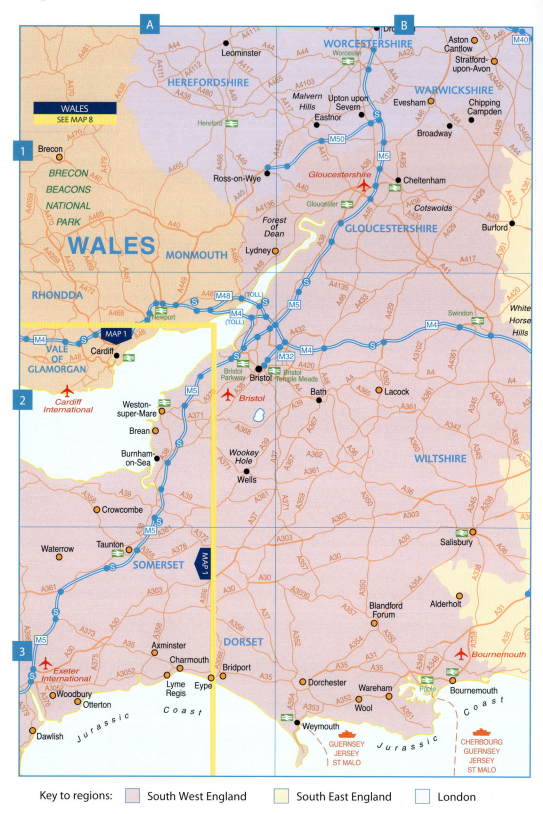

Key to regions: ▢ South West England ▢ South East England ▢ London

Map 2

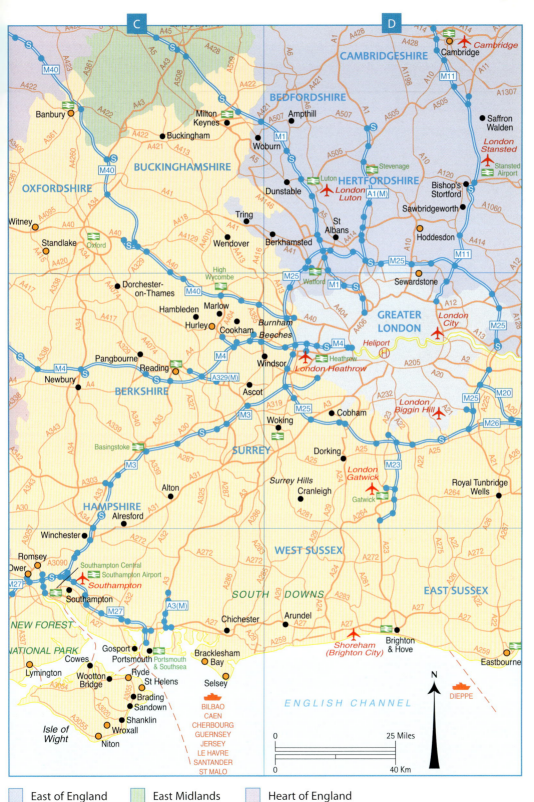

C   D

CAMBRIDGESHIRE

Cambridge — *Cambridge*

Saffron Walden

London Stansted — Stansted Airport

BEDFORDSHIRE

Banbury

Milton Keynes

Buckingham

Ampthill

Woburn

BUCKINGHAMSHIRE

M40

OXFORDSHIRE

Witney

Standlake

Oxford

Dunstable

Stevenage

Luton — *London Luton*

HERTFORDSHIRE

Bishop's Stortford

Sawbridgeworth

Tring

Wendover

Berkhamsted

St Albans

Hoddesdon

High Wycombe

Dorchester-on-Thames

Hambleden

Marlow

Hurley

Cookham

Burnham Beeches

Watford

GREATER LONDON

London City

Sewardstone

Pangbourne

Reading

Newbury

BERKSHIRE

Windsor

London Heathrow — Heathrow

Heliport

Ascot

Woking

Cobham

London Biggin Hill

SURREY

Basingstoke

Dorking

Alton

Alresford

HAMPSHIRE

Winchester

Romsey

Ower

Southampton Central — *Southampton* — Southampton Airport

Southampton

Cranleigh

Surrey Hills

London Gatwick — Gatwick

Royal Tunbridge Wells

WEST SUSSEX

SOUTH DOWNS

EAST SUSSEX

Chichester

Arundel

Shoreham (Brighton City)

Brighton & Hove

Eastbourne

NEW FOREST NATIONAL PARK

Cowes

Lymington

Gosport

Portsmouth

Portsmouth & Southsea

Wootton Bridge

Ryde

St Helens

Bracklesham Bay

Selsey

Brading

Sandown

Shanklin

Wroxall

Isle of Wight

Niton

BILBAO
CAEN
CHERBOURG
GUERNSEY
JERSEY
LE HAVRE
SANTANDER
ST MALO

ENGLISH CHANNEL

DIEPPE

N

0 — 25 Miles

0 — 40 Km

☐ East of England   ☐ East Midlands   ☐ Heart of England

Orange circles indicate accommodation within the regional sections of this guide

277

Map 3

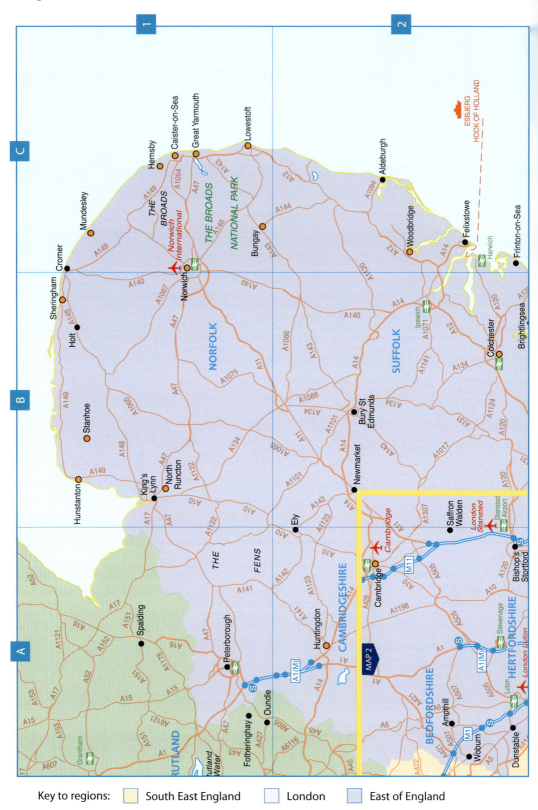

Key to regions: South East England   London   East of England

Map 3

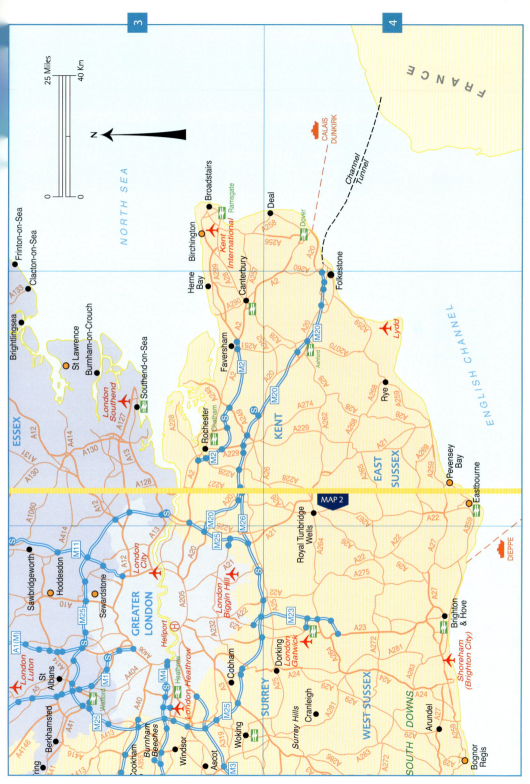

25 Miles
40 Km

N

3 | **4**

FRANCE

NORTH SEA

CALAIS
DUNKIRK

Channel Tunnel

Broadstairs
Ramsgate
Deal
Birchington
Kent International
Dover
A258
A256
A260
A20
Herne Bay
Canterbury
Folkestone
A299
A28
A257
A2
A290
A259
Lydd
A251
A2
Faversham
Ashford
A2070
M2
A28
A20
A268
Rye
A259
A228
M20
A259
Rochester
Chatham
A249
M20
A274
A262
A268
A229
A268
Eastbourne
M2
A229
A228
A229
EAST SUSSEX
A265
Pevensey Bay
A2
A228
A26
A259
Eastbourne
A128
A130
MAP 2
A267
A22
A259
ESSEX
A12
A414
A131
London Southend
Southend-on-Sea
St Lawrence
Burnham-on-Crouch
Brightlingsea
Frinton-on-Sea
Clacton-on-Sea
A133
Royal Tunbridge Wells
A264
A26
A22
A27
Eastbourne
DIEPPE
A1060
A414
M11
A12
London City
A13
A20
M25
M26
A21
A275
A27
Sawbridgeworth
Hoddesdon
Sewardstone
A10
M25
GREATER LONDON
A205
London Biggin Hill
A232
A22
A25
M23
London Gatwick
Brighton & Hove
A283
Shoreham (Brighton City)
A1(M)
London Luton
St Albans
M1
M25
Watford
Heathrow
London Heathrow
A406
A404
A3
Cobham
Dorking
A24
SURREY
A29
A281
A272
WEST SUSSEX
A24
SOUTH DOWNS
Arundel
A27
A259
Bognor Regis
Berkhamsted
A41
A4146
A416
A413
Cookham
Burnham Beeches
Windsor
Ascot
M3
Woking
Surrey Hills
Cranleigh
A281
A29
A286
A283
A272
A29
A24
A25
A3
A4
M4
A319
Heliport

ENGLISH CHANNEL

KENT

□ East Midlands

Orange circles indicate accommodation within the regional sections of this guide

279

Map 4

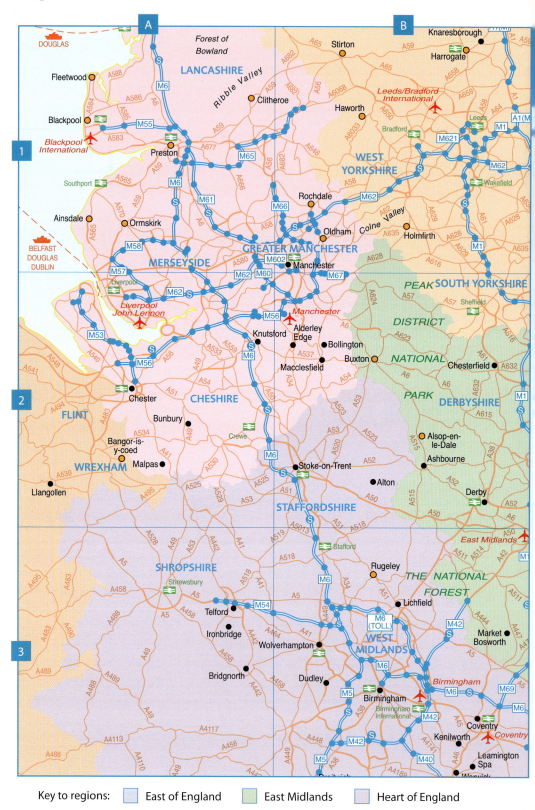

Key to regions: East of England   East Midlands   Heart of England

Map 4

Yorkshire · North West England · North East England

*Orange circles indicate accommodation within the regional sections of this guide

Map 5

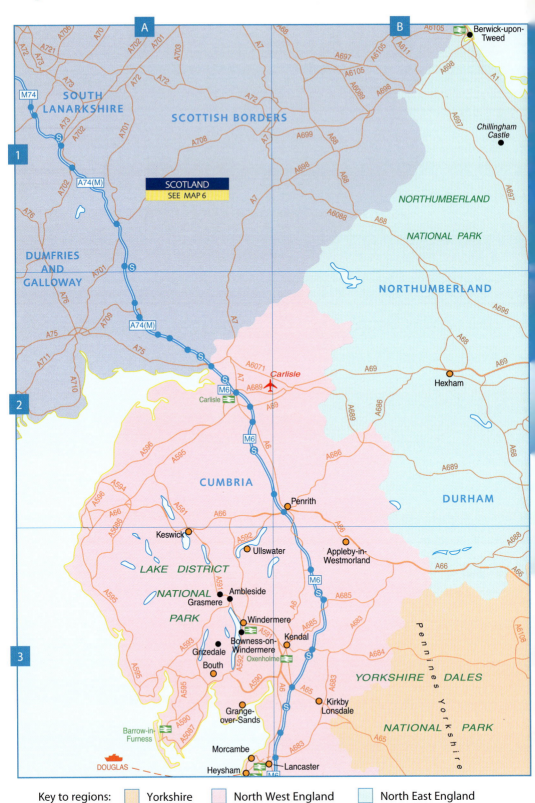

A6105 Berwick-upon-Tweed

SOUTH LANARKSHIRE

SCOTTISH BORDERS

SCOTLAND
SEE MAP 6

DUMFRIES AND GALLOWAY

NORTHUMBERLAND

NATIONAL PARK

Chillingham Castle

NORTHUMBERLAND

Carlisle

Hexham

CUMBRIA

DURHAM

Penrith

Keswick

Ullswater

Appleby-in-Westmorland

LAKE DISTRICT

NATIONAL

PARK

Ambleside

Grasmere

Windermere

Bowness-on-Windermere

Kendal

Grizedale

Oxenholme

Bouth

Kirkby Lonsdale

Grange-over-Sands

YORKSHIRE DALES

NATIONAL PARK

Barrow-in-Furness

Morcambe

DOUGLAS

Heysham

Lancaster

Key to regions: Yorkshire   North West England   North East England

Map 5

C D

Holy Island
(Lindisfarne)

Bamburgh
Seahouses

Alnwick

0   25 Miles
0   40 Km

N

Morpeth

Newcastle
International   North Tyneside

South Tyneside

AMSTERDAM
(Ijmuiden)

Newcastle-upon-Tyne

Gateshead   Sunderland

Hamsterley
Colliery   NORTH SEA

A19

Durham

A181

A1(M)

A689

A177   A19

Stockton-
on-Tees

Darlington   Middlesbrough

Durham
Tees Valley   Whitby

A174

A171

NORTH YORK MOORS

NATIONAL PARK   Yorkshire Coast

A172

A684

Scarborough

South Ottenington   Helmsley   Filey

A170   A1039

Thirsk

NORTH   Slingsby   A170

YORKSHIRE   A64

A1(M)   Yorkshire
Wolds

A61   A614

Orange circles indicate accommodation within the regional sections of this guide

Map 6

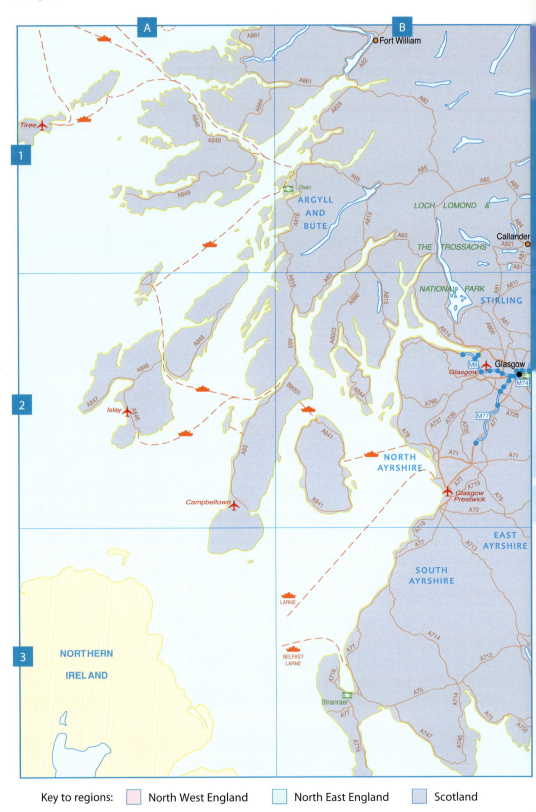

A861

B
● Fort William

A861

A82

A884

A848

Tiree ✈

A849

A849

A828

A85   A85   A85

A84

Oban   ARGYLL   LOCH LOMOND &

AND   THE TROSSACHS   Callander ○

BUTE   A83   A821   A81   A81

A816   A83   NATIONAL PARK   A811

A815   STIRLING

A846   A83   A8003   A814   A81   A809   A81

A846   A844   Glasgow   A726

Islay ✈   A841   M8   Glasgow   M74

A846   B8001   A760   A737   A736   A735   M77   A77

A83   North   A78   A71   A71

A841   AYRSHIRE   A71

Campbeltown ✈   A77   A719   A76

Glasgow   A70

Prestwick ✈

A719   A77   EAST

A713   AYRSHIRE

SOUTH

AYRSHIRE   A714

LARNE

A712

BELFAST   A77   A714   A75   A75

LARNE

NORTHERN   A718   A75   A755

IRELAND   Stranraer   A747   A746

A77   A716

1

2

3

Map 6

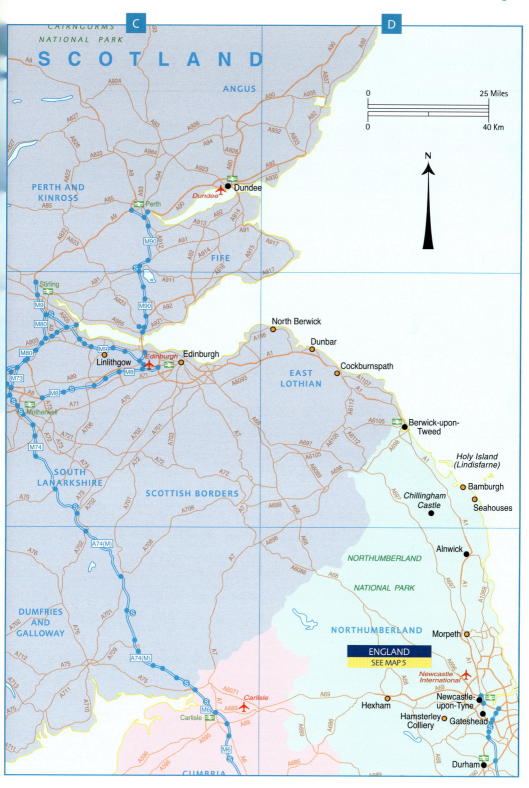

Orange circles indicate accommodation within the regional sections of this guide

Map 7

A

B

1

Isle of
Lewis

A857

A857

A858

Stornoway

A894

A837

A837

A859

2

WESTERN
ISLES

Harris

A859

A835

A837

A832

A830

A835

North
Uist

A867

Benbecula

A865

A865

A855

A850

A87

A863

Skye

A87

A832

A896

A896

A890

A832

HIGHLAND

Kyle of
Lochalsh

A890

3

South
Uist

A87

A887

A87

A87

Barra

A851

A830

A82

Key to regions: Scotland

286

Map 7

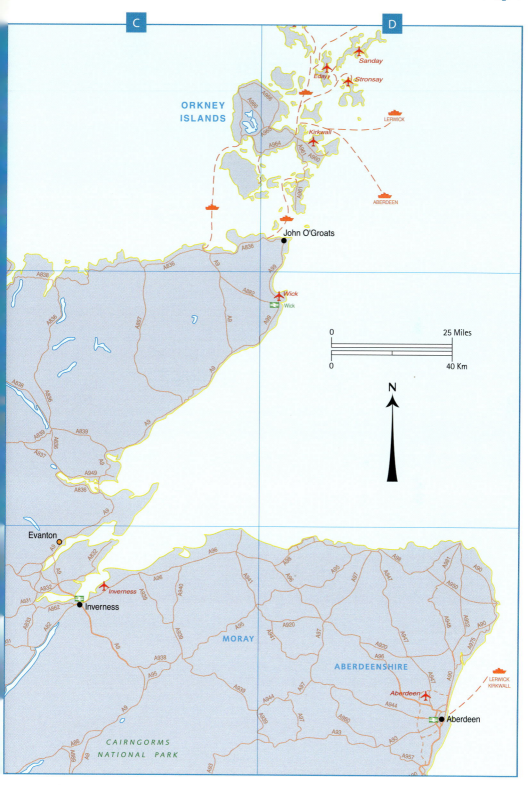

C

D

ORKNEY
ISLANDS

A986
A963
A966

Sanday
Eday
Stronsay

LERWICK

Kirkwall
A964
A961
A960

ABERDEEN

A961

John O'Groats

A836
A836
A9
A99

Wick
A882
Wick

A838
A9

A836
A896

A957

A9

A838
A896
A9

A839
A839

A836
A837
A836
A9

A949

A836

A9

Evanton
A9
A862
A832

0
25 Miles
0
40 Km

N

A835

A832
Inverness
A96
A96
A939
A9

A862
Inverness
A831
A833
A92
A9

A96
A96
A940
A939
A95
A938
A9

A95
A939
A9

A96
A941
A98
A96
A95
A97
A947
A98
A981
A90
A950
A948
A952
A90
A975
A90

A920
A97
A920
A947

MORAY

ABERDEENSHIRE

A947

LERWICK
KIRKWALL

A944
A97
Aberdeen
A947
A90
Aberdeen
A960
A944

A939
A944
A97
A93
A93
A957

CAIRNGORMS
NATIONAL PARK

A86
A889
A9

A93

A90

Map 8

Key to regions: ☐ Wales

Orange circles indicate accommodation within the regional sections of this guide

Map 9
London

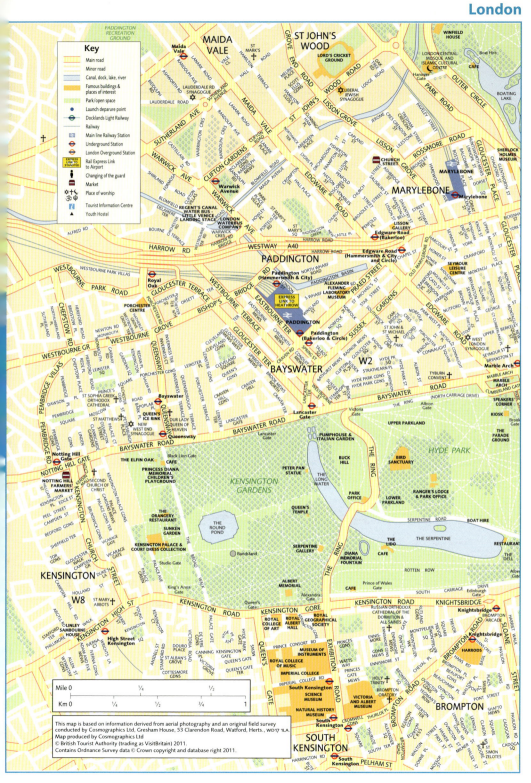

Map 10
London

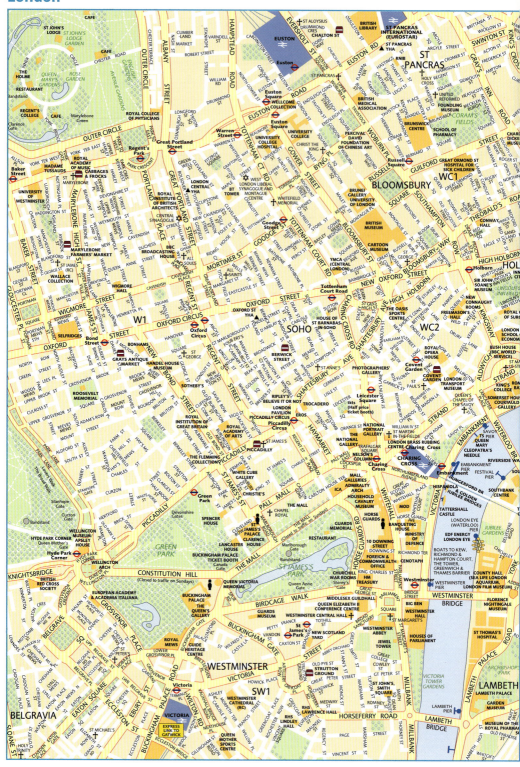

Map 11
London

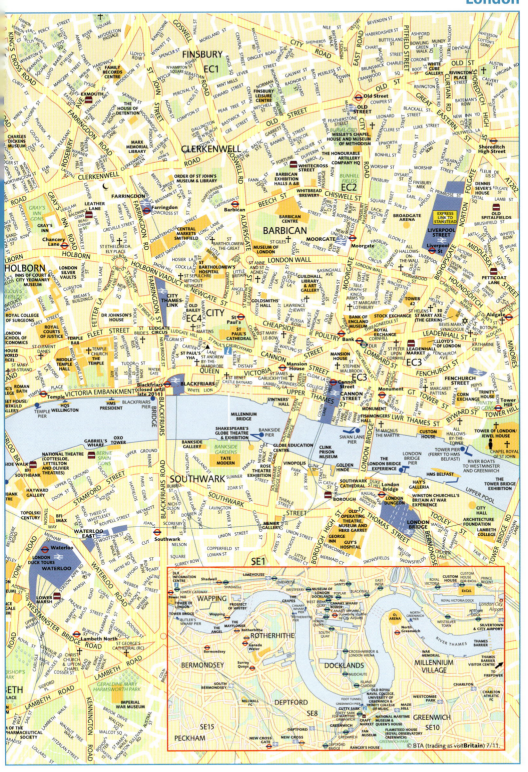

© BTA (trading as visitBritain) 7/11.

enjoyEngland.com
★★★★★
MOTORWAY
SERVICE AREA

Motorway Service Area Assessment Scheme

Something we all use and take for granted, but how good are they?

The star ratings cover over 250 different aspects of each operation, including cleanliness, the quality and range of catering and also the quality of the physical aspects, as well as the service. It does not cover prices or value for money.

OPERATOR: EXTRA

Baldock	★★★★
Beaconsfield	★★★★
Blackburn	★★★★
Cambridge	★★★
Cullompton	★★★
Peterborough	★★★★

OPERATOR: MOTO

Birch E	★★★
Birch W	★★★
Bridgwater	★★★
Burton in Kendal	★★★
Cherwell Valley	★★★★★
Chieveley	★★★
Doncaster N	★★★★
Donington Park	★★★★
Exeter	★★★
Ferrybridge	★★★
Frankley N	★★★
Frankley S	★★★
Heston E	★★★
Heston W	★★★
Hilton Park N	★★★
Hilton Park S	★★★
Knutsford N	★★★
Knutsford S	★★★
Lancaster N	★★★
Lancaster S	★★
Leigh Delamere E	★★★★
Leigh Delamere W	★★★★
Medway	★★★
Pease Pottage	★★★
Reading E	★★★★
Reading W	★★★
Severn View	★★
Southwaite N	★★★
Southwaite S	★★★

Stafford N	★★★★
Tamworth	★★★
Thurrock	★★★★
Toddington N	★★★★
Toddington S	★★★
Trowell N	★★★
Trowell S	★★★
Washington N	★★★
Washington S	★★★★
Wetherby	★★★★
Winchester N	★★★★
Winchester S	★★★
Woolley Edge N	★★★★
Woolley Edge S	★★★★

OPERATOR: ROADCHEF

Chester	★★
Clacket Lane E	★★★
Clacket Lane W	★★
Durham	★★★
Killington Lake	★★★
Maidstone	★★★
Northampton N	★★★
Northampton S	★★★
Norton Canes	★★★★
Rownhams N	★★
Rownhams S	★★★
Sandbach N	★★
Sandbach S	★★★
Sedgemoor S	★★
Stafford S	★★★
Strensham N	★★★★
Strensham S	★★★
Taunton Deane N	★★
Taunton Deane S	★★★
Tibshelf N	★★★
Tibshelf S	★★★
Watford Gap N	★★★
Watford Gap S	★★

OPERATOR: WELCOME BREAK

Birchanger Green	★★★★
Burtonwood	★★★
Charnock Richard W	★★★
Charnock Richard E	★★★
Corley E	★★★
Corley W	★★★
Fleet N	★★★★
Fleet S	★★★
Gordano	★★★★
Hartshead Moor E	★★★
Hartshead Moor W	★★★
Hopwood Park	★★★★
Keele N	★★★
Keele S	★★★
Leicester Forest East N	★★★
Leicester Forest East S	★★★
London Gateway	★★★★
Membury E	★★★
Membury W	★★★★
Michaelwood N	★★★
Michaelwood S	★★★
Newport Pagnell S	★★★
Newport Pagnell N	★★★
Oxford	★★★★
Sedgemoor N	★★★
South Mimms	★★★★
Telford	★★★
Warwick N	★★★
Warwick S	★★★★
Woodall N	★★
Woodall S	★★★

WESTMORLAND

Tebay N	★★★★
Tebay S	★★★★★

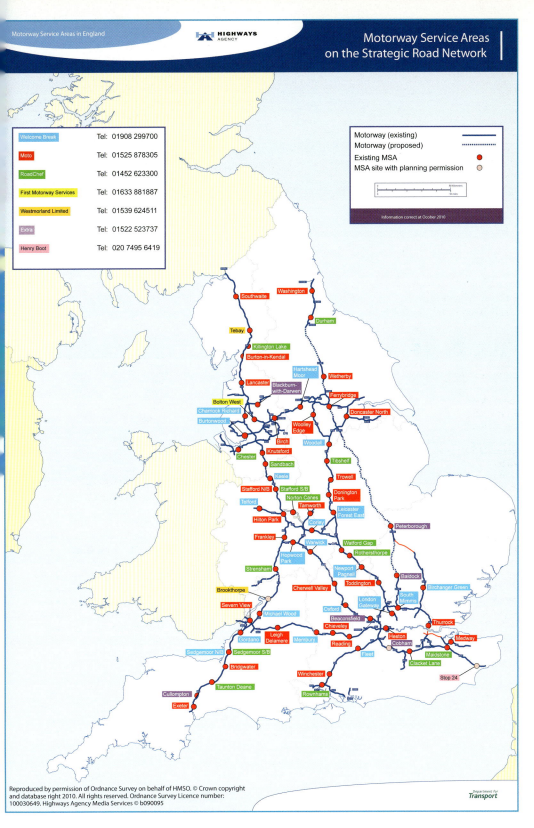

Welcome Break   Tel: 01908 299700

Moto   Tel: 01525 878305

RoadChef   Tel: 01452 623300

First Motorway Services   Tel: 01633 881887

Westmorland Limited   Tel: 01539 624511

Extra   Tel: 01522 523737

Henry Boot   Tel: 020 7495 6419

Motorway (existing)
Motorway (proposed)
Existing MSA
MSA site with planning permission

80 Kilometres
50 miles

Information correct at October 2010

Southwaite
Washington
Durham
Tebay
Killington Lake
Burton-in-Kendal
Hartshead Moor
Wetherby
Lancaster
Blackburn-with-Darwen
Ferrybridge
Bolton West
Charnock Richard
Doncaster North
Burtonwood
Woolley Edge
Birch
Woodall
Chester
Knutsford
Sandbach
Tibshelf
Keele
Trowell
Stafford N/B
Stafford S/B
Norton Canes
Donington Park
Telford
Tamworth
Leicester Forest East
Hilton Park
Corley
Frankley
Warwick
Watford Gap
Peterborough
Rothersthorpe
Hopwood Park
Strensham
Newport Pagnell
Baldock
Toddington
Birchanger Green
Brookthorpe
Cherwell Valley
South Mimms
Severn View
London Gateway
Michael Wood
Oxford
Beaconsfield
Thurrock
Gordano
Leigh Delamere
Chieveley
Heston
Medway
Membury
Cobham
Sedgemoor N/B
Reading
Sedgemoor S/B
Maidstone
Clacket Lane
Bridgwater
Fleet
Winchester
Cullompton
Taunton Deane
Rownhams
Stop 24.
Exeter

Department for
Transport

Here are just some of the most popular long distance routes on the 12,000 mile Sustrans National Cycle Network. To see the Network in it's entirety and to find routes near you, **visit www.sustrans.org.uk**

Sustrans is the UK's leading sustainable transport charity working on practical projects to enable people to choose to travel in ways which benefit their health and the environment.

68 National Cycle Network Route Number

Long Distance Routes

1. Coast & Castles Cycle Route
2. Pennine Cycleway - North Pennines
3. Hadrian's Cycleway
4. Sea to Sea
5. Pennine Cycleway - South Pennines & the Dales
6. Derby to York
7. Hull to Fakenham
8. East of England
9. South Midlands Cycle Route
10. Thames Valley Cycle Route
11. Garden of England
12. Downs & Weald Cycle Route
13. Devon Coast to Coast
14. The Cornish Way
15. The West Country Way
16. The Severn & Thames

Map reproduced from Ordnance Survey material with the permission of Ordnance Survey on behalf of the Controller of Her Majesty's Stationery Office © Crown copyright. Unauthorised reproduction infringes Crown copyright and may lead to prosecution or civil proceedings.
Licence number 100020852 (2009)

Further Information

Advice and information

Making a booking

When enquiring about accommodation, make sure you check prices, the quality rating and other important details. You will also need to state your requirements clearly and precisely, for example:

- Arrival and departure dates, with acceptable alternatives if appropriate;

- The accommodation you need;

- The number of people in your party and the ages of any children;

- Special requirements.

Booking by letter or email

Misunderstandings can easily happen over the telephone, so do request a written confirmation, together with details of any terms and conditions that apply to your booking.

Deposits and advance payments

In the case of caravan, camping and touring parks and holiday villages, the full charge often has to be paid in advance. This may be in two instalments – a deposit at the time of booking and the balance by, say, two weeks before the start of the booked period.

Cancellations

Legal contract

When you accept accommodation that is offered to you, by telephone or in writing, you enter into a legally binding contract with the proprietor. This means that if you cancel your booking, fail to take up the accommodation or leave early, you will probably forfeit your deposit and may expect to be charged the balance at the end of the period booked if the place cannot be re-let. You should be advised at the time of the booking of what charges would be made in the event of cancelling the accommodation or leaving early, which is usually written into the properties terms and conditions. If this is not mentioned you should ask the proprietor for any cancellation terms that apply before booking your accommodation to ensure any disputes are avoided. Where you have already paid the full amount before cancelling, the proprietor is likely to retain the money. However if the accommodation is re-let, the proprietor will make a refund to you which normally excludes the amount of the deposit.

Remember, if you book by telephone and are asked for your credit card number, you should check whether the proprietor intends to charge your credit card account should you later cancel your reservation. A proprietor should not be able to charge your credit card account with a cancellation fee without your consent unless you agreed to this at the time of your booking. However, to avoid later disputes, we suggest you check whether this is the intention before providing your details.

Insurance

A travel or holiday insurance policy will safeguard you if you have to cancel or change your holiday plans both abroad and in the UK. You can arrange a policy quite cheaply through your insurance company or travel agent.

Finding a park

Tourist signs similar to the one shown here are designed to help visitors find their park. They  clearly show whether the park is for tents or caravans or both.

Tourist information centres throughout Britain are able to give campers and caravanners information about parks in their areas. Some tourist information centres have camping and caravanning advisory services that provide details of park availability and often assist with park booking.

Electric hook-up points

Most parks now have electric hook-up points for caravans and tents. Voltage is generally 240v AC, 50 cycles. Parks may charge extra for this facility, and it is advisable to check rates when making a booking.

Avoiding peak season

In the summer months of June to September, parks in popular areas such as North Wales, Cumbria, the West Country or the New Forest in Hampshire may become full. Campers should aim to arrive at parks early in the day or, where possible, should book in advance. Some parks have overnight holding areas for visitors who arrive late. This helps to prevent disturbing other campers and caravanners late at night and means that fewer visitors are turned away. Caravans or tents are directed to a pitch the following morning.

Other caravan and camping places

If you enjoy making your own route through Britain's countryside, it may interest you to know that the Forestry Commission operates campsites in Britain's Forest Parks as well as in the New Forest. Some offer reduced charges for youth organisations on organised camping trips and all enquiries about them should be made well in advance of your intended stay to the Forestry Commission.

Travelling with pets

Dogs, cats, ferrets and some other pets can be brought into the UK from certain countries, provided they meet the requirements of the Pet Travel Scheme (PETS) they may not have to undertake six months' quarantine on arrival.

For full details, visit the PETS website at
w www.gov.uk/take-pet-abroad
or contact the PETS Helpline
t +44 (0)870 241 1710
e pettravel@ahvla.gsi.gov.uk
Ask for fact sheets which cover dogs and cats, ferrets or domestic rabbits and rodents.

There are no requirements for pets travelling directly between the UK and the Channel Islands. Pets entering Jersey or Guernsey from other countries need to be Pet Travel Scheme compliant and have a valid EU Pet Passport. For more information see www.jersey.com or www.visitguernsey.com.

What to expect at holiday, touring and camping parks

In addition to fulfilling its statutory obligations, including complying with the Regulatory Reform (Fire Safety) Order 2005, holding public liability insurance and ensuring that all caravan holiday homes/chalets for hire and the park and all buildings and facilities, fixtures, furnishings, fittings and decor are maintained in sound and clean condition and are fit for the purposes intended, the management is required to undertake the following:

Prior to booking

- To describe accurately in any advertisement, brochure, or other printed or electronic media, the facilities and services provided;
- To make clear to guests in print, electronic media and on the telephone exactly what is included in all prices quoted for accommodation, including taxes and any other surcharges. Details of charges for additional services/facilities should also be made clear, for example breakfast, leisure etc;
- To provide information on the suitability of the premises for guests of various ages, particularly for the elderly and the very young;
- To allow guests to view the accommodation prior to booking if requested.

At the time of booking

- To clearly describe the cancellation policy to guests i.e. by telephone, fax, internet/email as well as in any printed information given to guests;
- To adhere to and not to exceed prices quoted at the time of booking for accommodation and other services.

On arrival

- To welcome all guests courteously and without discrimination in relation to gender, sexual orientation, disability, race, religion or belief.

During the stay

- To maintain standards of guest care, cleanliness, and service appropriate to the style of operation;
- To deal promptly and courteously with all enquiries, requests, bookings and correspondence from guests;
- To ensure complaints received are investigated promptly and courteously to an outcome that is communicated to the guest.

On departure

- To give each guests, on request, details or payments due and a receipt, if required/requested.

General

- To give due consideration to the requirements of guests with special needs, and to make suitable provision where applicable;
- To ensure the accommodation, when advertised as open, is prepared for the arrival of guests at all times;
- To advise guests, at any time prior to their stay, of any changes made to their booking;
- To hold current public liability insurance and to comply with all relevant statutory obligations, including legislation applicable to health and safety, planning and fire;
- To allow assessment body representatives reasonable access to the operation, on request, to confirm that the Code of Conduct is being observed, or in order to investigate any complaint of a serious nature notified to them

What to expect at holiday villages

The operator/manager is required to undertake the following:

Prior to booking

- To describe accurately in any advertisement, brochure, or other printed or electronic media, the facilities and services provided;
- To make clear to guests in print, on the internet and on the telephone exactly what is included in all prices quoted for accommodation, including taxes, and any other surcharges. Details of charges for additional services/facilities should also be made clear, for example breakfast, leisure etc;
- To provide information on the suitability of the premises for guests of various ages, particularly for the elderly and the very young;
- To allow guests to view the accommodation prior to booking if requested.

At the time of booking

- To clearly describe the cancellation policy to guests by telephone, fax and internet/email, as well as in any printed information given to guests;
- To adhere to and not to exceed prices quoted at the time of booking for accommodation and other services;
- To advise guests at the time of booking, or subsequently in the event of any change in what has been booked;
- To make clear to guests, if the accommodation offered is in an unconnected annexe or similar, and to indicate the location of such accommodation and any difference in comfort and/or amenities from accommodation in the establishment.

On arrival

- To welcome all guests courteously and without discrimination in relation to gender, sexual orientation, disability, race, religion or belief.

During the stay

- To maintain standards of guest care, cleanliness, and service appropriate to the type of establishment;
- To deal promptly and courteously with all enquiries, requests, bookings and correspondence from guests;
- To ensure complaint handling procedures are in place and that complaints received are investigated promptly and courteously and that the outcome is communicated to the guest.

On departure

- To give each guests, on request, details or payments due and a receipt, if required/requested.

General

- To give due consideration to the requirements of guests with special needs, and to make suitable provision where applicable;
- To ensure the accommodation is prepared for the arrival of guests at all times when the operation is advertised as open to receive guests;
- To hold current public liability insurance and to comply with all relevant statutory obligations including legislation applicable to fire, health and safety, planning, food safety and all relevant statutory requirements;

- To allow assessment body representatives reasonable access to the establishment, on request, to confirm that the Code of Conduct is being observed or in order to investigate any complaint of a serious nature notified to them.

Comments and complaints

Information

The proprietors themselves supply the descriptions of their establishments and other information for the entries (except ratings). They have all signed a declaration that their information conforms to The Consumer Protection from Unfair Trading Regulations 2008. VisitBritain cannot guarantee the accuracy of information in this guide, and accepts no responsibility for any error or misrepresentation.

All liability for loss, disappointment, negligence or other damage caused by reliance on the information contained in this guide, or in the event of bankruptcy or liquidation or cessation of trade of any company, individual or firm mentioned, is hereby excluded. We strongly recommend that you carefully check prices and other details when you book your accommodation.

Problems

Of course, we hope you will not have cause for complaint, but problems do occur from time to time.

If you are dissatisfied with anything, make your complaint to the management immediately. Then the management can take action at once to investigate the matter and put things right. The longer you leave a complaint, the harder it is to deal with it effectively.

In certain circumstances, the assessment body may look into complaints. However, it has no statutory control over establishments or their methods of operating. The assessment body cannot become involved in legal or contractual matters or in seeking financial compensation.

If you do have problems that have not been resolved by the proprietor and which you would like to bring to our attention, please write to:

England
Quality in Tourism, Security House, Alexandra Way, Ashchurch, Tewkesbury, Gloucestershire GL20 8NB

Scotland
Quality and Standards, Ocean Point One, 94 Ocean Drive, Edinburgh EH6 6JH

Wales
VisitWales, Welsh Government, Rhodfa Padarn, Llanbadarn Fawr, Aberystwyth, Ceredigion SY23 3UR

Useful contacts

British Holiday & Home Parks Association

Chichester House, 6 Pullman Court,
Great Western Road, Gloucester GL1 3ND
t (01452) 526911 (enquiries and brochure requests)
w parkholidayengland.org.uk

Professional UK park owners are represented by the British Holiday and Home Parks Association. Over 3,000 parks are members, and each year welcome millions of visitors seeking quality surroundings in which to enjoy a good value stay.

Parks provide caravan holiday homes and lodges for hire and pitches for your own touring caravan, motor home or tent. On many, you can opt to buy your own holiday home.

A major strength of the UK's park industry is its diversity. Whatever your idea of holiday pleasure, there's sure to be a park which can provide it. If your preference is for a quiet, peaceful holiday in tranquil rural surroundings, you'll find many idyllic locations.

Alternatively, many parks are to be found at our most popular resorts – and reflect the holiday atmosphere with plenty of entertainment and leisure facilities. For more adventurous families, parks often provide excellent bases from which to enjoy outdoor activities.

Literature available from BH&HPA includes a guide to parks which have this year achieved the David Bellamy Conservation Award for environmental excellence.

The Camping and Caravanning Club

Greenfields House, Westwood Way,
Coventry CV4 8JH
t 0845 130 7631
t 0845 130 7633 (advance bookings)
w campingandcaravanningclub.co.uk

Discover the peace and quiet of over 100 award-winning club sites. Experience a different backdrop to your holiday every time you go away, with sites in the lakes and mountains, coastal and woodland glades or cultural and heritage locations.

The Club is proud of its prestigious pedigree and regularly achieves awards for spotless campsites, friendly service and caring for the environment – a guarantee that you will enjoy your holiday.

Non-members are welcome at the majority of our sites and we offer special deals for families, backpackers, overseas visitors and members aged 55 and over. Recoup your membership fee in just six nights and gain access to over 1,300 Certificated Sites around the country.

For more details, please refer to our entries listed at the back of this publication or if you require any more information on what The Friendly Club can offer you then telephone 0845 130 7632, or call to request your free guide to The Club.

The Caravan Club

East Grinstead House, East Grinstead,
West Sussex RH19 1UA
t (01342) 326944
w caravanclub.co.uk

The Caravan Club offers 200 sites in the UK and Ireland. These include city locations such as London, Edinburgh, York and Chester, plus sites near leading heritage attractions such as Longleat, Sandringham, Chatsworth and Blenheim Palace. A further 30 sites are in National Parks.

Virtually all pitches have an electric hook-up point. The toilet blocks and play areas are of the highest quality. Friendly, knowledgeable site wardens are on hand too.

Most Caravan Club Sites are graded four or five stars according to The British Graded Holiday Parks Scheme, run by the national tourist boards, so that you can be assured of quality at all times. Over 130 sites are open to non-members, but why not become a member and gain access to all sites, plus a further 2,500 certificated locations – rural sites for no more than five vans. Tent campers are welcome at over 60 sites.

Join The Club and you can save the cost of your subscription fee in just five nights with member discounts on site fees!

Forest Holidays

Bath Yard, Moira, Derbyshire DE12 6BA
t 0845 130 8223 (cabins)
t 0845 130 8224 (campsites)
w forestholidays.co.uk

Forest Holidays, a new partnership between the Forestry Commission and the Camping and Caravanning Club, have over 20 camping and caravan sites in stunning forest locations throughout Great Britain in addition to three cabin sites. Choose from locations such as the Scottish Highlands, the New Forest, Snowdonia National Park, the Forest of Dean, or the banks of Loch Lomond. Some sites are open all year and dogs are welcome at most. Advance bookings are accepted for many sites.

For a unique forest experience, call Forest Holidays for a brochure on 0845 130 8224 or visit our website.

The Motor Caravanners' Club Ltd

1st Floor, Woodfarm Estate, Marlbank Road, Welland, Malvern WR13 6NA
t (0) 1684 311677
e info@motorcaravanners.eu
w motorcaravanners.eu

The Motor Caravanners' Club is authorised to issue the Camping Card International (CCI). It also produces a monthly magazine, Motor Caravanner, for all members. Member of The Federation Internationale de Camping et de Caravanning (FICC).

The National Caravan Council

The National Caravan Council,
Catherine House, Victoria Road,
Aldershot, Hampshire
GU11 1SS
t (01252) 318251
w thecaravan.net

The National Caravan Council (NCC) is the trade body for the British caravan industry – not just touring caravans and motorhomes but also caravan holiday homes. It has in its membership parks, manufacturers, dealers and suppliers to the industry – all NCC member companies are committed continually to raise standards of technical and commercial excellence.

So, if you want to know where to buy a caravan, where to find a caravan holiday park or simply need advice on caravans and caravanning, see the website thecaravan.net where there is lots of helpful advice including:

* How to check whether the caravan, motorhome or caravan holiday home you are buying complies with European Standards and essential UK health and safety regulations (through the Certification scheme that the NCC operates).

* Where to find quality parks to visit on holiday.

* Where to find approved caravan and motorhome workshops for servicing and repair.

Caravan holidays are one of the most popular choices for holidaymakers in Britain – the NCC works closely with VisitBritain to promote caravan holidays in all their forms and parks that are part of the British Graded Quality Parks Scheme.

About the accommodation entries

Entries

All accommodation featured in this guide has been assessed or has applied for assessment under a quality assessment scheme.

Start your search for a place to stay by looking in the 'Where to Stay' sections of this guide where proprietors have paid to have their establishment featured in either a standard entry (includes photograph, description, facilities and prices) or an enhanced entry (photograph(s) and extended details).

Locations

Places to stay are listed by town, city or village, if a property is located in a small village, you may find it listed under a nearby town (providing it is within a seven-mile radius).

Within each region, counties run in alphabetical order. Place names are listed alphabetically within each county, and include interesting county information and a map reference.

Map references

These refer to the colour location maps at the back of the guide. The first figure shown is the map number, the following letter and figure indicate the grid reference on the map. Only place names that have a standard or enhanced entry feature appear on the maps. Some standard or enhanced entries were included in the scheme after the guide went to press, therefore they do not appear on the maps.

Telephone numbers

Booking telephone numbers are listed below the contact address for each entry. Area codes are shown in brackets.

Prices

The prices printed are to be used as a guide only; they were supplied to us by proprietors in summer 2013. Remember, changes may occur after the guide goes to press, therefore we strongly advise you to check prices before booking book your accommodation.

Prices are shown in pounds sterling, including VAT where applicable. Touring pitch prices are based on the minimum and maximum charges for one night for two persons, car and caravan or tent. (Some parks may charge separately for a car, caravan or tent and for each person and there may be an extra charge for caravan awnings.) Minimum and maximum prices for caravan holiday homes are given per week.

Prices often vary throughout the year and may be significantly lower outside of peak periods. You can get details of other bargain packages that may be available from the establishments themselves, regional tourism organisations or your local Tourist Information Centre (TIC). Your local travel agent may also have information and can help you make your booking.

Opening period

If an entry does not indicate an opening period, please check directly with the site.

Symbols

The at-a-glance symbols included at the end of each entry show many of the services and facilities available at each property. You will find the key to these symbols on page 7.

Smoking

In the UK and the Channel Islands, it is illegal to smoke in enclosed public spaces and places of work. Smoking may be allowed in self-contained short-term rental accommodation, such as holiday cottages, flats or caravans, if the owner chooses to allow it.

If you wish to smoke, we advise you to check the proprietors smoking policy before you book.

Pets

Many places accept guests with dogs, but we advise that you check this with the proprietor before booking, remember ask if there are any extra charges or rules about exactly where your pet is allowed. The acceptance of dogs is not always extended to cats and it is strongly advised that cat owners contact the property well in advance of your stay.

Some establishments do not accept pets at all. Pets are welcome by arrangement where you see this symbol 8. The quarantine laws have changed and now dogs, cats and ferrets are able to come into Britain and the Channel Islands from over 50 countries. For details of the Pet Travel Scheme (PETS) please turn to page 297.

Payment accepted

The types of payment accepted by an establishment are listed in the payment accepted section. If you plan to pay by card, check that the establishment will accept the particular type of card you own before booking. Some proprietors will charge you a higher rate if you pay by credit card rather than cash or cheque. The difference is to cover the charges paid by the proprietor to the credit card company.

When you book by telephone, you may be asked for your credit card number as confirmation. Remember, the proprietor may then charge your credit card account if you cancel your booking. See details of this under Cancellations on page 296.

Awaiting confirmation of rating

At the time of going to press some properties featured in this guide had not yet been assessed therefore their rating for this year could not be included. The term 'Rating Applied For' indicates this throughout your guide.

Looking for something else?

The official and most comprehensive guide to independently inspected, star rated accommodation.

B&Bs and Hotels - B&Bs, Hotels, farmhouses, inns, serviced apartments, campus and hostel accommodation in England.

Self Catering - Self-catering holiday homes, approved caravan holiday homes, boat accommodation and holiday cottage agencies in England.

Camping, Touring and Holiday Parks - Touring parks, camping holidays and holiday parks and villages in Britain.

Now available in all good bookshops and online at **www.hudsons.co.uk/shop**

Getting around

Travelling in London

London transport

London Underground has 12 lines, each with its own unique colour, so you can easily follow them on the Underground map. Most lines run through central London, and many serve parts of Greater London. Buses are a quick, convenient way to travel around London, providing plenty of sightseeing opportunities along the way. There are over 6,500 buses in London operating 700 routes every day. You will need to buy a ticket before you board the bus – available from machines at the bus stop.

London's National Rail system stretches all over London. Many lines start at the main London railway stations (Paddington, Victoria, Waterloo, Kings Cross) with links to the tube. Trains mainly serve areas outside central London, and travel overground.

Children usually travel free, or at reduced fare, on all public transport in London.

Oyster cards

Oyster cards can be used to pay fares on all London Underground, buses, Docklands Light Railway and trams, however are generally not valid for National Rail services in London.

Oyster cards are very easy to use, you just touch the card on sensors at stations or on buses and you are charged the lowest fare available for your journey. You buy credit for your journey and when it runs out you simply top up with more.

Oyster cards are available to adults only. Children below the age of 11 can accompany adults free of charge. Children between the ages of 11 and 15 should use the standard child travel card. You can purchase an Oyster card for a fee of £5, which is refundable on its return, at any underground station, one of 3,000 Oyster points around London displaying the London Underground sign (usually shops), or from www.visitbritainshop.com, or www.oyster.tfl.gov.uk/oyster

London congestion charge

The congestion charge is £10 daily charge to drive in central London at certain times. Check if the congestion charge is included in the cost of your car before booking. If your car's pick up point is in the congestion-charging zone, the company may pay the charge for the first day of your hire.

Low Emission Zone

The Low Emission Zone is an area covering most of Greater London, within which the most polluting diesel-engine vehicles are required to meet specific emissions standards. If your vehicle does not, you will be required to pay a daily charge.

Vehicles affected by the Low Emission Zone are older diesel-engine lorries, buses, coaches, large vans, minibuses and other heavy vehicles such as motor caravans and motorised horse boxes. This also includes vehicles registered outside of Great Britain. Cars and motorcycles are not affected by this scheme. For more information visit www.tfl.gov.uk

Rail and train travel

Britain's rail network covers all main cities and smaller regional towns. Trains on the network are operated by a few large companies running routes from London to stations all over Britain. Therefore smaller companies that run routes in regional areas. You can find up-to-the-minute information about routes, fares and train times on the National Rail Enquiries website (www.nationalrail.co.uk). For detailed information about routes and services, refer to the train operators' websites (see page 309).

Railway passes

BritRail offer a wide selection of passes and tickets giving you the freedom to travel on all National Rail services. Passes can also include sleeper services, city and attraction passes and boat tours. Passes can usually be purchased from travel agents outside Britain or by visiting the BritRail website (www.britrail.com).

Bus and coach travel

Public buses

Every city and town in Britain has a local bus service. These services are privatised and managed by separate companies. The largest bus companies in Britain are First (www.firstgroup.com/ukbus), Stagecoach (www.stagecoachbus.com) and Arriva (www.arrivabus.co.uk), and run buses in most UK towns. Outside London, buses usually travel to and from the town centre or to the busiest part of town. Most towns have a bus station, where you'll be able to find maps and information about routes. Bus route information may also be posted at bus stops.

Tickets and fares

The cost of a bus ticket normally depends on how far you're travelling. Return fares may be available on some buses, but you would usually need to buy a 'single' ticket for each individual journey.

You can also buy your ticket when boarding a bus by telling the driver where you are going. One-day and weekly travel cards are available in some towns, and these can be purchased from either the driver or from an information centre at the bus station. Tickets are valid for each separate journey rather than for a period of time, so if you get off the bus you'll need to buy a new ticket when getting on another.

Domestic flights

Flying is a time-saving alternative to road or rail when it comes to travelling around Britain. Domestic flights are fast and frequent and there are 33 airports across Britain that operate domestic routes. You will find airports marked on the maps at the front of this guide.

Domestic flight advice

Photo ID is required to travel on domestic flights. However it is advisable to bring your passport as not all airlines will accept other forms of photo identification. Please be aware of the high security measures at all airports in Britain which include include restrictions on items that may be carried in hand luggage. It is important that you check the restrictions in place with your airline prior to travel, as these can vary over time and don't forget to allow adequate time for check-in and boarding on arrival.

Cycling

Cycling is a great way to see some of England's iconic scenery and there are many networks of cycling routes available across England. The National Cycle Network offers over 10,000 miles of walking and cycling routes details for connecting towns and villages, countryside and coast across England. For more information and view these routes see page 294 or visit Sustrans at www.sustrans.co.uk.

Think green

If you'd rather leave your car behind and travel by 'green transport' to some of the attractions highlighted in this guide you'll be helping to reduce congestion and pollution as well as supporting conservation charities in their commitment to green travel.

The National Trust encourages visits made by non-car travellers and it offers admission discounts or a voucher for the tea room at a selection of its properties if you arrive on foot, cycle or public transport (you may need to produce a valid bus or train ticket if travelling by public transport.).

More information about The National Trust's work to encourage car-free days out can be found at www.nationaltrust.org.uk. (Refer to the section entitled 'Information for Visitors').

Book your accommodation online

Visit our new 2014 guide websites for detailed information, up-to-date availability and to book your accommodation online. Includes over 20,000 places to stay, all of them star rated.

www.visitor-guides.co.uk

By car and by train

Distance chart

The distances between towns on the chart below are given to the nearest mile, and are measured along routes based on the quickest travelling time, making maximum use of motorways or dual-carriageway roads. The chart is based upon information supplied by the Automobile Association.

To calculate the distance in kilometres multiply the mileage by 1.6

For example: Brighton to Dover 82 miles x 1.6 =131.2 kilometres

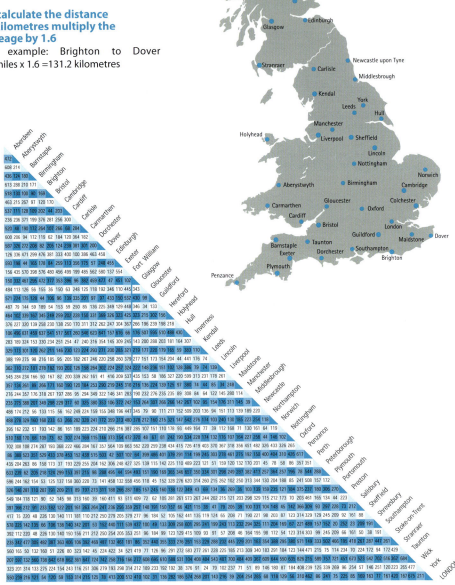

	Aberdeen	Aberystwyth	Barnstaple	Birmingham	Brighton	Bristol	Cambridge	Cardiff	Carlisle	Carmarthen	Dorchester	Dover	Edinburgh	Exeter	Fort William	Glasgow	Gloucester	Guildford	Hereford	Holyhead	Hull	Inverness	Kendal	Leeds	Lincoln	Liverpool	Maidstone	Manchester	Middlesbrough	Newcastle	Northampton	Norwich	Nottingham	Oxford	Penzance	Perth	Peterborough	Plymouth	Portsmouth	Preston	Salisbury	Sheffield	Shrewsbury	Southampton	Stoke-on-Trent	Stranraer	Taunton	Wick	York
Aberystwyth	472
Barnstaple	608	214
Birmingham	436	124	180
Brighton	613	288	210	171
Bristol	518	130	100	90	169
Cambridge	463	215	267	97	120	170
Cardiff	537	111	128	109	202	44	203
Carlisle	236	236	371	199	376	281	256	300
Carmarthen	520	48	190	172	264	107	266	68	284
Dorchester	600	206	94	172	119	62	184	120	364	182
Dover	587	326	272	208	82	205	124	239	381	301	200
Edinburgh	126	336	471	299	476	381	333	400	100	386	463	458
Exeter	593	198	44	165	178	84	259	113	356	175	57	248	455
Fort William	156	435	570	398	576	480	456	499	199	485	562	580	137	554
Glasgow	150	332	467	295	472	377	353	396	96	382	459	477	47	451	102
Gloucester	484	113	126	56	155	36	150	63	248	125	118	192	346	110	445	343
Guildford	571	224	175	128	44	106	96	139	335	201	97	97	433	150	532	430	99
Hereford	487	79	144	59	189	54	153	59	250	85	136	225	349	129	448	346	34	133
Holyhead	464	102	339	167	345	249	259	202	228	150	331	369	326	323	425	323	215	302	156
Hull	376	227	320	139	258	230	138	250	170	311	312	262	247	304	367	266	196	239	198	218
Inverness	106	496	631	459	637	541	517	561	260	546	623	641	157	616	66	176	507	595	510	488	430
Kendal	283	189	324	153	330	234	251	254	47	240	316	354	145	309	245	143	200	288	203	181	164	307
Leeds	329	173	301	120	262	211	146	230	123	224	293	271	200	285	321	219	177	220	179	165	59	383	110
Lincoln	388	199	275	98	216	185	95	205	182	267	246	220	258	260	379	277	151	173	154	204	44	441	176	74
Liverpool	362	110	272	101	278	182	193	202	126	158	264	302	224	257	324	222	148	236	151	102	128	386	79	74	139
Maidstone	545	284	234	166	50	167	82	200	339	262	161	41	416	209	537	435	153	58	186	327	220	599	313	231	178	261
Manchester	357	134	261	89	266	171	160	190	120	184	253	290	219	245	318	216	136	224	139	125	97	380	74	44	85	34	248
Middlesbrough	276	244	357	176	318	267	197	286	95	294	349	322	146	341	283	190	232	276	235	235	89	308	84	64	122	145	280	114
Newcastle	235	275	388	207	349	298	229	317	60	325	380	353	106	372	242	153	264	307	266	266	142	267	102	95	154	176	311	145	39
Northampton	486	174	212	56	133	115	56	162	249	224	159	155	348	196	447	345	79	90	111	217	152	509	203	136	94	151	113	139	189	220
Norwich	488	278	329	160	168	233	63	266	282	328	241	172	359	313	480	378	212	160	215	321	147	542	276	174	103	240	130	185	223	254	118
Nottingham	395	162	232	51	193	142	86	161	189	223	224	210	266	216	387	285	107	151	110	178	93	449	164	77	39	112	168	71	130	161	64	119
Oxford	510	160	170	68	109	73	82	107	274	169	115	146	373	154	472	370	48	67	81	242	190	534	228	174	132	176	107	164	227	258	44	146	102
Penzance	702	308	108	274	287	193	368	222	466	284	167	357	564	109	663	562	220	259	238	434	415	726	419	403	370	367	318	356	451	482	326	433	326	265
Perth	86	388	523	351	529	433	378	453	152	438	515	503	42	507	102	64	399	486	401	379	291	114	199	245	303	278	461	275	192	150	400	404	310	426	617
Peterborough	435	204	263	86	158	173	37	193	229	255	204	162	306	248	427	325	139	115	142	225	110	489	223	121	51	159	120	132	170	201	45	78	58	86	357	351
Plymouth	633	239	62	205	218	124	299	153	397	215	98	288	495	44	594	493	151	190	169	365	346	657	350	334	301	298	249	287	382	413	257	364	257	196	78	544	288
Portsmouth	596	244	162	154	53	125	137	158	360	220	73	141	458	132	558	456	118	45	152	328	276	620	314	260	215	262	102	250	313	344	130	204	188	85	241	508	157	172
Preston	326	146	281	110	287	191	209	211	89	197	273	311	188	266	287	185	157	245	160	138	122	349	43	69	134	36	269	35	103	139	159	235	121	184	375	237	180	306	270
Salisbury	549	184	118	121	90	52	145	98	313	160	39	160	411	93	511	409	72	62	105	281	261	573	267	244	202	215	121	203	298	329	115	212	173	70	203	461	165	134	44	223
Sheffield	397	166	272	91	233	182	122	201	161	263	264	247	236	256	359	257	148	191	150	157	66	421	115	38	47	79	205	39	100	131	104	148	45	142	366	309	93	297	228	73	212
Shrewsbury	417	75	220	48	226	130	140	111	181	110	212	250	279	205	379	277	96	184	52	105	162	441	135	119	124	65	208	71	190	221	98	203	87	123	314	329	129	245	209	92	161	88
Southampton	578	225	142	135	66	106	136	140	342	201	53	152	440	111	539	437	100	49	133	309	258	601	295	241	199	243	113	232	294	325	111	204	169	67	221	489	157	152	20	252	23	209	191
Stoke-on-Trent	392	112	220	48	226	130	140	150	156	211	212	250	254	205	353	251	96	184	99	123	129	415	109	93	91	57	208	46	164	195	98	172	54	123	314	303	99	245	209	66	161	50	38	191
Stranraer	235	342	477	305	482	387	363	406	106	392	469	487	132	461	181	86	352	440	355	333	276	261	153	229	288	232	445	229	201	163	354	388	295	380	571	149	333	502	466	195	418	267	287	447	261
Taunton	560	165	50	132	160	51	226	80	323	142	45	224	422	34	521	419	77	126	96	291	272	583	277	261	228	225	185	213	309	340	183	291	184	123	144	471	215	75	114	234	70	224	172	94	172	429
Wick	207	597	732	560	738	642	618	662	361	647	724	742	258	716	166	277	608	695	610	588	531	104	408	484	543	487	700	484	409	367	609	644	550	635	826	215	589	757	721	451	673	523	542	702	516	362	684
York	323	201	314	133	275	224	154	243	116	251	306	279	193	298	314	212	189	233	192	192	38	376	91	24	79	102	237	71	51	89	146	180	87	184	408	239	125	339	269	96	254	57	146	251	120	223	265	477
LONDON	550	239	216	121	54	120	59	153	314	215	125	78	413	200	512	410	102	31	136	282	186	574	268	201	143	216	39	204	254	285	68	118	129	56	310	462	86	241	75	225	85	169	163	77	161	420	167	675	211

National Rail
Britain's train companies working together

— Principal routes
— Other selected routes
⊗ Airport interchange
✈ Railair coach link with Heathrow Airport
⛴ Ferry interchange

LONDON TERMINALS

C	Charing Cross
E	Euston
F	Fenchurch Street
K	Kings Cross
L	Liverpool Street
M	Marylebone
P	Paddington
S	St Pancras Int.
V	Victoria
W	Waterloo

Channel Tunnel services to mainland Europe

National Rail Enquiries
08457 48 49 50
www.nationalrail.co.uk

Travel information

General travel information

Streetmap	www.streetmap.co.uk	
Transport Direct	www.transportdirect.info	
Transport for London	www.tfl.gov.uk	0843 222 1234
Travel Services	www.departures-arrivals.com	
Traveline	www.traveline.info	0871 200 2233

Bus & coach

Megabus	www.megabus.com	0900 160 0900
National Express	www.nationalexpress.com	08717 818 178
WA Shearings	www.shearings.com	0844 824 6351

Car & car hire

AA	www.theaa.com	0800 085 2721
Green Flag	www.greenflag.co.uk	0845 246 1557
RAC	www.rac.co.uk	0844 308 9177
Alamo	www.alamo.co.uk	0871 384 1086*
Avis	www.avis.co.uk	0844 581 0147*
Budget	www.budget.co.uk	0844 544 3407*
Easycar	www.easycar.com	
Enterprise	www.enterprise.com	0800 800 227*
Hertz	www.hertz.co.uk	0870 844 8844*
Holiday Autos	www.holidayautos.co.uk	0871 472 5229
National	www.nationalcar.co.uk	0871 384 1140
Thrifty	www.thrifty.co.uk	01494 751500

Air

Air Southwest	www.airsouthwest.com	0870 043 4553
Blue Islands (Channel Islands)	www.blueislands.com	08456 20 2122
BMI	www.flybmi.com	0844 848 4888
BMI Baby	www.bmibaby.com	0905 828 2828*
British Airways	www.ba.com	0844 493 0787
British International (Isles of Scilly to Penzance)	www.islesofscillyhelicopter.com	01736 363871*
CityJet	www.cityjet.com	0871 663 3777
Eastern Airways	www.easternairways.com	08703 669100
Easyjet	www.easyjet.com	0843 104 5000
Flybe	www.flybe.com	0871 700 2000*
Jet2.com	www.jet2.com	0871 226 1737*
Manx2	www.manx2.com	0871 200 0440*
Ryanair	www.ryanair.com	0871 246 0000
Skybus (Isles of Scilly)	www.islesofscilly-travel.co.uk	0845 710 5555
Thomsonfly	www.thomsonfly.com	0871 231 4787

Train

National Rail Enquiries	www.nationalrail.co.uk	0845 748 4950
The Trainline	www.trainline.co.uk	0871 244 1545
UK train operating companies	www.rail.co.uk	
Arriva Trains	www.arriva.co.uk	0191 520 4000
c2c	www.c2c-online.co.uk	0845 601 4873
Chiltern Railways	www.chilternrailways.co.uk	0845 600 5165
CrossCountry	www.crosscountrytrains.co.uk	0844 811 0124
East Midlands Trains	www.eastmidlandstrains.co.uk	0845 712 5678
Eurostar	www.eurostar.com	08432 186 186*
First Capital Connect	www.firstcapitalconnect.co.uk	0845 026 4700
First Great Western	www.firstgreatwestern.co.uk	0845 700 0125
Gatwick Express	www.gatwickexpress.com	0845 850 1530
Heathrow Connect	www.heathrowconnect.com	0845 678 6975
Heathrow Express	www.heathrowexpress.com	0845 600 1515
Hull Trains	www.hulltrains.co.uk	0845 071 0222
Island Line	www.islandlinetrains.co.uk	0845 600 0650
London Midlands	www.londonmidland.com	0121 634 2040
Merseyrail	www.merseyrail.org	0151 702 2071
National Express East Anglia	www.nationalexpresseastanglia.com	0845 600 7245
National Express East Coast	www.nationalexpresseastcoast.com	0845 722 5333
Northern Rail	www.northernrail.org	0845 000 0125
ScotRail	www.scotrail.co.uk	0845 601 5929
South Eastern Trains	www.southeasternrailway.co.uk	0845 000 2222
South West Trains	www.southwesttrains.co.uk	0845 600 0650
Southern	www.southernrailway.com	0845 127 2920
Stansted Express	www.stanstedexpress.com	0845 600 7245
Translink	www.translink.co.uk	(028) 9066 6630
Transpennine Express	www.tpexpress.co.uk	0845 600 1671
Virgin Trains	www.virgintrains.co.uk	08450 008 000*

Ferry

Ferry Information	www.discoverferries.com	0207 436 2449
Condor Ferries	www.condorferries.co.uk	0845 609 1024*
Steam Packet Company	www.steam-packet.com	08722 992 992*
Isles of Scilly Travel	www.islesofscilly-travel.co.uk	0845 710 5555
Red Funnel	www.redfunnel.co.uk	0844 844 9988
Wight Link	www.wightlink.co.uk	0871 376 1000

Phone numbers listed are for general enquiries unless otherwise stated.
* Booking line only

David Bellamy
Conservation Award

2012/13 BRONZE

2012/13 SILVER

2012/13 GOLD

Parks wishing to enter for a David Bellamy Conservation Award must complete a detailed questionnaire covering different aspects of their environmental policies, and describe what positive conservation steps they have taken. The park must also undergo an independent audit from a local wildlife or conservation body which is familiar with the area. Final assessments and the appropriate level of any award are then made personally by Professor Bellamy.

Parks with a current 2012/13 Bellamy Award offer a variety of accommodation from pitches for touring caravans, motor homes and tents, to caravan holiday homes, holiday lodges and cottages for rent or to buy. Holiday parks with these awards are not just those in quiet corners of the countryside. Amongst the winners are much larger centres in popular holiday areas that offer a wide range of entertainments and attractions.

The parks listed on the following pages all have a detailed entry in this guide and have received a Gold, Silver or Bronze David Bellamy Conservation Award. Use the Index by Property Name starting on page 283 to find the page number.

For a free brochure featuring a full list of award-winning parks please contact: BH&HPA, 6 Pullman Court, Great Western Road, Gloucester, GL1 3ND
t (01452) 526911
e enquiries@bhhpa.org.uk
w bellamyparks.co.uk or ukparks.com

Andrewshayes Holiday Park	Gold	Axminster	South West
Highlands End Holiday Park	Gold	Bridport	South West
Wooda Farm Holiday Park	Gold	Bude	South West
Ladram Bay Holiday Park	Gold	Budleigh Salterton	South West
Cofton Country Holidays	Gold	Dawlish	South West
Lady's Mile Holiday Park	Gold	Dawlish	South West
Halse Farm Caravan & Tent Park	Gold	Exmoor	South West
Atlantic Coast Holiday Park	Gold	Hayle	South West
Silver Sands Holiday Park	Gold	Helston	South West
Hele Valley Holiday Park	Gold	Ilfracombe	South West
Whitemead Forest Park	Gold	Lydney	South West
Porlock Caravan Park	Gold	Minehead	South West
Trethiggey Touring Park	Gold	Newquay	South West
Ross Park	Gold	Newton Abbot	South West

Tehidy Holiday Park	Gold	Redruth	South West
Seaview International Holiday Park	Gold	St. Austell	South West
Harford Bridge Holiday Park	Gold	Tavistock	South West
Trethem Mill Touring Park	Gold	Truro	South West
Juliots Well Holiday Park	Silver	Camelford	South West
Meadowbank Holidays	Silver	Christchurch	South West
Oakcliff Holiday Park	Silver	Dawlish Warren	South West
Watergate Bay Touring Park	Silver	Newquay	South West
Langstone Manor Holiday Park	Silver	Tavistock	South West
Dulhorn Farm Holiday Park	Bronze	Weston Super Mare	South West
Hill Cottage Farm Camping and Caravan Park	Gold	Fordingbridge	South East
Hurley Riverside Park	Gold	Maidenhead	South East
Appuldurcombe Gardens Holiday Park	Gold	Nr Ventnor	South East
Whitefield Forest Touring Park	Gold	Ryde	South East
Hardwick Parks	Gold	Witney	South East
Fen Farm Camping and Caravan Site	Gold	Colchester	East of England
Waldegraves Holiday Park	Gold	Colchester	East of England
Searles Leisure Resort	Gold	Hunstanton	East of England
Pakefield Caravan Park	Gold	Lowestoft	East of England
Sandy Gulls Caravan Park	Gold	Mundesley	East of England
Weybourne Forest Lodges	Gold	Weybourne	East of England
Vauxhall Holiday Park	Silver	Great Yarmouth	East of England
Wyton Lakes Holiday Park	Silver	Huntingdon	East of England
Grasmere Caravan Park	Bronze	Great Yarmouth	East of England
Rivendale Caravan & Leisure Park	Gold	Ashbourne	East Midlands
Beech Croft Farm Caravan & Camping Park	Gold	Nr Buxton	East Midlands
Skegness Water Leisure Park	Gold	Skegness	East Midlands
Ranch Caravan Park	Gold	Evesham	Heart of England
Island Meadow Caravan Park	Gold	Henley in Arden	Heart of England
Silver Trees Holiday Park - Static Vans	Gold	Rugeley	Heart of England
Upwood Holiday Park	Gold	Haworth	Yorkshire
Holme Valley Camping and Caravan Park	Gold	Holmfirth	Yorkshire
Otterington Park	Gold	Northallerton	Yorkshire
Cayton Village Caravan Park Ltd	Gold	Scarborough	Yorkshire
Crowtrees Park	Gold	Skipton	Yorkshire
Middlewood Farm Holiday Park	Gold	Whitby	Yorkshire
Northcliffe & Seaview Holiday Parks	Gold	Whitby	Yorkshire
Whitby Holiday Park	Gold	Whitby	Yorkshire
North Bay Leisure Park	Bronze	Bridlington	Yorkshire
Wild Rose Park	Gold	Appleby in Westmorland	North West
Todber Holiday Park	Gold	Clitheroe	North West
Castlerigg Hall Caravan & Camping Park	Gold	Keswick	North West
Woodclose Park	Gold	Kirkby Lonsdale	North West
Flusco Wood	Gold	Penrith	North West
Waterfoot Caravan Park	Gold	Penrith	North West
Willowbank Holiday Home and Touring Park	Gold	Southport	North West
Fallbarrow Park	Gold	Windermere	North West
Hill Of Oaks Park	Gold	Windermere	North West
Limefitt Park	Gold	Windermere	North West
White Cross Bay Holiday Park and Marina	Gold	Windermere	North West
Ocean Edge Leisure Park, Heysham	Silver	Morecambe	North West
Regent Leisure Park	Silver	Morecambe	North West
Waren Caravan and Camping Park	Gold	Bamburgh	North East
Seafield Caravan Park	Gold	Seahouses	North East
Belhaven Bay Caravan and Camping Park	Gold	Dunbar	Scotland
Linwater Caravan Park	Gold	East Calder	Scotland
Mortonhall Caravan and Camping Park	Gold	Edinburgh	Scotland
Glen Nevis Caravan and Camping Park	Gold	Fort William	Scotland
Linnhe Lochside Holidays	Gold	Fort William	Scotland
Tantallon Caravan and Camping Park	Bronze	North Berwick	Scotland
Garreg Goch Caravan Park	Gold	Porthmadog	Wales

National Accessible Scheme index

Establishments with a detailed entry in this guide who participate in the National Accessible Scheme are listed below. At the front of the guide you can find information about the scheme. Establishments are listed alphabetically by place name.

Mobility level 1

Lowestoft East of England	**Pakefield Caravan Park ★ ★ ★ ★**	127
Whitby Yorkshire	**Whitby Holiday Park ★ ★ ★ ★**	188

Mobility level 2

Ainsdale North West	**Willowbank Holiday Home and Touring Park ★ ★ ★ ★ ★**	215

Hearing impairment level 1

Lowestoft East of England	**Pakefield Caravan Park ★ ★ ★ ★**	127
Whitby Yorkshire	**Whitby Holiday Park ★ ★ ★ ★**	188

Visual impairment level 1

Lowestoft East of England	**Pakefield Caravan Park ★ ★ ★ ★**	127
Ainsdale North West	**Willowbank Holiday Home and Touring Park ★ ★ ★ ★ ★**	215

Walkers Welcome & Cyclists Welcome

Establishments participating in the Walkers Welcome and Cyclists Welcome schemes provide special facilities and actively encourage these recreations. Accommodation with a detailed entry in this guide is listed below. Place names are listed alphabetically.

Walkers Welcome & Cyclists Welcome

Dawlish South West	**Lady's Mile Touring and Camping Park ★ ★ ★ ★**	46
Dawlish South West	**Oakcliff Holiday Park ★ ★ ★ ★**	46
Tavistock South West	**Harford Bridge Holiday Park ★ ★ ★ ★**	50
Tavistock South West	**Langstone Manor Holiday Park ★ ★ ★ ★ ★**	51

VisitWales Walkers Welcome & Cyclists Welcome

Fishguard Wales	**Fishguard Bay Caravan & Camping Park ★ ★ ★ ★**	271
St Davids Wales	**Caerfai Bay Caravan & Tent Park ★ ★ ★ ★**	272

Families and Pets Welcome

Establishments participating in the Families Welcome or Welcome Pets! schemes provide special facilities and actively encourage families or guests with pets. Accommodation with a detailed entry in this guide is listed below. Place names are listed alphabetically.

Families and Pets Welcome

Dawlish South West	Lady's Mile Touring and Camping Park ★ ★ ★ ★	46
Holmfirth Yorkshire	Holme Valley Camping and Caravan Park ★ ★ ★	189

Families Welcome

Blackpool North West	Newton Hall Holiday Park ★ ★ ★ ★	212
Bouth North West	Black Beck Caravan Park ★ ★ ★ ★ ★	207
Dawlish South West	Oakcliff Holiday Park ★ ★ ★ ★	46
Otterton South West	Ladram Bay Holiday Park ★ ★ ★ ★	49
Slingsby Yorkshire	Robin Hood Caravan Park ★ ★ ★ ★ ★	185

Pets Welcome

Bamburgh North East	Waren Caravan and Camping Park ★ ★ ★ ★	230
Ipplepen South West	Ross Park ★ ★ ★ ★ ★ GOLD	47
Seahouses North East	Seafield Caravan Park ★ ★ ★ ★ ★ GOLD	231
Skegness East Midlands	Skegness Water Leisure Park ★ ★ ★	146

Swimming Pools index

If you're looking for accommodation with swimming facilities use this index to see at a glance detailed accommodation entries that match your requirement. Establishments are listed alphabetically by place name.

🛱 Indoor pool

Axminster South West	**Andrewshayes Caravan Park ★★★★**	44
Blackpool North West	**Newton Hall Holiday Park ★★★★**	212
Blackpool North West	**Windy Harbour Holiday Park ★★★★**	212
Bridport South West	**Highlands End Holiday Park ★★★★★**	53
Bridport South West	**Manor Farm Holiday Centre ★★★**	53
Crediton South West	**Yeatheridge Farm Caravan Park ★★★★**	45
Dawlish South West	**Cofton Country Holidays ★★★★**	45
Dawlish South West	**Lady's Mile Touring and Camping Park ★★★★**	46
Dunbar Scotland	**Thurston Manor Leisure Park ★★★★**	249
Filey Yorkshire	**Orchard Farm Holiday Village ★★★★★**	182
Fleetwood North West	**Broadwater Caravan Park ★★★**	213
Great Yarmouth East of England	**Seacroft Holiday Village ★★**	121
Great Yarmouth East of England	**Summerfields Holiday Park ★★★★**	122
Great Yarmouth East of England	**Vauxhall Holiday Park ★★★★★**	122
Hayle South West	**St Ives Bay Holiday Park ★★★**	39
Hemsby East of England	**Hemsby Beach Holiday Park ★★★**	123
Heysham North West	**Ocean Edge Leisure Park, Heysham ★★★★**	214
Hunstanton East of England	**Searles Leisure Resort ★★★★★**	123
Kingsdown South East	**Kingsdown Park Holiday Village ★★★★★**	82
Looe South West	**Tencreek Holiday Park ★★★★**	40
Lydney South West	**Whitemead Forest Park ★★★★**	56
Manorbier Wales	**Manorbier Country Park ★★★★★**	271
Morecambe North West	**Regent Leisure Park ★★★★**	214
Morecambe North West	**Venture Caravan Park ★★★**	214
Mundesley East of England	**Mundesley Holiday Village ★★**	125
Otterton South West	**Ladram Bay Holiday Park ★★★★**	49
Penzance South West	**Praa Sands Holiday Village ★★★★**	41
Rugeley Heart of England	**Silver Trees Holiday Park - Static Vans ★★★★★**	164
Scarborough Yorkshire	**Crows Nest Caravan Park ★★★★**	183
Scarborough Yorkshire	**Flower of May Holiday Parks ★★★★★**	184
Seahouses North East	**Seafield Caravan Park ★★★★★ GOLD**	231
Selsey South East	**Green Lawns Holiday Park ★★★★★**	85
Selsey South East	**Warner Farm Camping & Touring Park ★★★★★**	85

Selsey South East	**West Sands Holiday Park ★ ★ ★ ★**	85
Selsey South East	**White Horse Holiday Park ★ ★ ★ ★**	85
Shaldon South West	**Coast View Holiday Park ★ ★ ★**	50
Sheringham East of England	**Weybourne Forest Lodges ★ ★ ★ ★**	126
Skipton Yorkshire	**Crowtrees Park ★ ★ ★ ★**	185
Tunstall Yorkshire	**Sand le Mere Holiday Village ★ ★ ★ ★ ★**	182
Watergate Bay Newquay South West	**Watergate Bay Touring Park ★ ★ ★ ★**	43
Windermere North West	**White Cross Bay Holiday Park and Marina ★ ★ ★**	210
Witney South East	**Lincoln Farm Park Oxfordshire ★ ★ ★ ★ ★**	83

🏊 Outdoor pool

Amroth Wales	**Amroth Bay Holidays ★ ★ ★ ★ ★**	271
Appleby-in-Westmorland North West	**Wild Rose Park ★ ★ ★ ★ ★**	206
Bamburgh North East	**Waren Caravan and Camping Park ★ ★ ★ ★**	230
Bracklesham Bay South East	**South Downs Holiday Village ★ ★ ★**	83
Bridport South West	**Manor Farm Holiday Centre ★ ★ ★**	53
Bude South West	**Budemeadows Touring Park ★ ★ ★ ★ ★**	36
Camelford South West	**Juliots Well Holiday Park ★ ★ ★ ★**	37
Colchester East of England	**Waldegraves Holiday Park ★ ★ ★ ★**	119
Combe Martin South West	**Manleigh Holiday Park ★ ★ ★ ★**	44
Crowcombe South West	**Quantock Orchard Caravan Park ★ ★ ★ ★ ★**	57
Dawlish South West	**Cofton Country Holidays ★ ★ ★ ★**	45
Dawlish South West	**Lady's Mile Touring and Camping Park ★ ★ ★ ★**	46
Dawlish South West	**Oakcliff Holiday Park ★ ★ ★ ★**	46
Evesham Heart of England	**Ranch Caravan Park ★ ★ ★ ★ ★**	165
Great Yarmouth East of England	**Seacroft Holiday Village ★ ★**	121
Harrogate Yorkshire	**Rudding Holiday Park ★ ★ ★ ★ ★**	182
Hayle South West	**Beachside Holiday Park ★ ★ ★ ★**	38
Hunstanton East of England	**Searles Leisure Resort ★ ★ ★ ★ ★**	123
Lowestoft East of England	**Pakefield Caravan Park ★ ★ ★ ★**	127
Mevagissey South West	**Seaview International Holiday Park ★ ★ ★ ★**	40
Newton Abbot South West	**Twelve Oaks Farm Caravan Park ★ ★ ★**	48
Selsey South East	**Green Lawns Holiday Park ★ ★ ★ ★ ★**	85
Selsey South East	**Warner Farm Camping & Touring Park ★ ★ ★ ★ ★**	85
Selsey South East	**West Sands Holiday Park ★ ★ ★ ★**	85
Selsey South East	**White Horse Holiday Park ★ ★ ★ ★**	85
Watergate Bay Newquay South West	**Watergate Bay Touring Park ★ ★ ★ ★**	43
Weston-super-Mare South West	**Country View Holiday Park ★ ★ ★ ★**	58
Wroxall South East	**Appuldurcombe Gardens Holiday Park ★ ★ ★ ★ ★**	81

Index by property name

Accommodation with a detailed entry in this guide is listed below.

316

Index by place name

The following places all have detailed accommodation entries in this guide. If the place where you wish to stay is not shown the location maps (starting on page 274) will help you to find somewhere to stay in the area.

HUDSON'S MEDIA LIMITED

Published by: Hudson's Media Ltd
35 Thorpe Road, Peterborough, PE3 6AG
Tel: 01733 296910 Fax: 01733 209292

On behalf of: VisitBritain, Sanctuary Buildings, 20 Great Smith Street, London SW1P 3BT

Publisher: Lisa Barreno
Editorial: Neil Pope
Production team: Deborah Coulter, Rebecca Owen-Fisher, Rhiannon McCluskey, Sarah Phillips & Gemma Wall

Creative team: Jamieson Eley & Nicola Bennett
Advertising team: Ben Piper, Matthew Pinfold, Sumita Ghosh & Claire Hotson
Email: VEguides@hudsons-media.co.uk Tel: 01733 296913
Production: NVG – leaders in Tourism Technology. www.nvg.net
Printer: Stephens & George, Merthyr Tydfil
Retail Sales: Compass – Tel: 020 8996 5764

Photography credits: © VisitEngland: VisitEssex, Visit Peak District/Sarah Wyatt, Linda Bussey, Visit Dorset, jameskerr.co.uk, VisitWiltshire/Chris Lock, Pawel Libera, Jeremy Cangialosi, Andrew Marshall. VisitKent/Jean-Luc Benard. Hampshire, Go Ape, VisitBrighton, Destination Milton Keynes, VisitKent, Oxfordshire, VisitSurrey, Weymouth and Portland Borough Council, Visit Dorset, English Riviera, Alex Hare, Weymouth and Portland Borough Council/Cycle West – Tim Pestridge, Visit Wiltshire/Charlie Ross, BathTourismPlus/Colin Hawkins, Diana Jarvis, English Heritage/Iain Lewis, BathTourismPlus, VisitKent/benedictjohnson.com, Rod Edwards, VisitEssex/Daniel Bosworth, Woburn Safari Park, Visit EastLincolnshire, Experience Nottinghamshire, Yorkshire.com, MarketingBirmingham, Craig Fast, NewcastleGateshead Initiative, VisitYork, Marketing Cheshire, Marketing Manchester, VisitBlackpool, Visit County Durham, Visit Cumbria/Dave Willis, Beamish Museum, New Forest District Council, Cotswolds. com/Nick Turner, Sudeley Castle/Jo Ward, Owen Benson, Simon Kreitem, Heart of Devon, Paul Close.

© VisitBritain Images: Daniel Bosworth, Joanna Henderson, James McCormick, Pawel Libera, Britain on View, Simon Winnall, Martin Brent, Liz Gander, Grant Pritchard, Damir Fabijanc, Andrew Orchard, Eric Nathan, David Angel, Ingrid Rasmussen, Simon Kreitem, Ian Shaw, Adrian Houston, Rod Edwards, Steve Bardens, County Durham Tourism Partnership, Angus Bremner, Joe Cornish, Lee Beel, Andy Sewell, Dennis Hardley, Gary Latham, Olivier Roques- Rogery, Gareth Easton, John Coutts, David Shepherd.

Brecon Jazz Festival: Tim Dickeson, Discovery Museum © Tyne and Wear Museums & Dragon Boat Festival photograph courtesy Infinite Images.

Front cover: © Getty Images: Kaatya, pijama61, maomage.

© British Tourist Authority (trading as VisitBritain) 2014
ISBN 978-0-85101-526-2
A VisitBritain guide